The Essential Manager

IEEE PRESS

IEEE
Φ computer
society

The Essential Manager

How to Thrive in the Global Information Jungle

James W. Cortada

IEEE PRESS

Published by John Wiley & Sons, Inc., Hoboken, New Jersey.
Published simultaneously in Canada.

For general information on our other products and services or for technical support, please contact our
Customer Care Department within the United States at (800) 762-2974, outside the United States at
(317) 572-3993 or fax (317) 572-4002.

Wiley also publishes its books in a variety of electronic formats. Some content that appears in print may not be
available in electronic formats. For more information about Wiley products, visit our web site at www.wiley.com.

Library of Congress Cataloging-in-Publication Data:

Cortada, James W.
  The essential manager : how to thrive in the global information jungle / James W. Cortada.
    pages   cm
  Includes bibliographical references and index.
    ISBN 978-1-119-00277-2 (pbk.)
1. Management.   2. Information technology–Management.   3. Executive ability.   I. Title.
  HD31.C644749 2015
  658–dc23

                                                                    2014025846

Printed in the United States of America.

Contents

Preface   vii

1. Emergence of a New Managerial Style   1

2. When Management Confronts Information
   Ecosystems   40

3. How Technologies Affect the Work
   of Industries   85

4. New Organizations: What Changes,
   What Does Not   124

5. Emerging Economic and Business Realities   167

6. The Way Forward   200

For Further Reading   231

Index   236

Preface

The work of managers worldwide has been undergoing significant transformation over the past three decades, in fact, changing more rapidly today than in earlier years. Their activities are being shaped by the influences of intensified, yet also localizing, global trade, use of ever-tightly integrated international supply chains, and even more by their extensive reliance on information technologies (IT) in myriad activities. The combination of evolving economic globalization and the cumulative effects of so much infusion of digital technologies and telecommunications into their enterprises has led to so many substantive changes in how managers work that today we can speak of a new *style* of managerial practices. That new style is also being influenced by human behavior and various values of societies and businesses from one part of the world to another. The recognition of this new style of management separates this book from the thousands of published declarations that everything is or has changed. It is also a rough jungle because so many players in so many countries and cultures are involved in the game.

Let's be blunt about the matter. Many managers, if not most, are poorly equipped to succeed in the years to come because their knowledge base is too narrow and the environment they must operate is becoming too complex. They are fed insights and facts on ever-narrower topics at work, through business publications, and often at school and university. I argue that their world is becoming so complex and so serious that they need to broaden their appreciation for how business is evolving in ways that are not normally considered. How they should come to better understand the world around them and how to succeed in it is the reason for this book. Put more formally, the primary objective of this book is to make readers—primarily managers—aware of the critical features of the evolving workplace in which they must succeed. A second objective is to define many of the behavioral attributes managers need to thrive in the evolving environment described in this book. Get ready to explore a great many topics normally not pulled together within the covers of a single book. But, don't expect detailed case studies or massive quantities of data, this book's purpose is to point out the obvious issues you will need to wrestle with over time. Get ready also to have to constantly relearn and reboot your knowledge base. How?

This book achieves its objectives by addressing the accumulation of changes that have been underway for some time, and that are continuing to emerge, as part of a larger fundamental process of shaping modern management. Relying on history and observations of current trends, it describes the context in which we work and both obvious and some not-so obvious implications, making recommendations on how management should function. It also defines many elements of management that have not changed, despite the hype. Activities are occurring, despite cycles of prosperity and recession that simultaneously affect the global economy today. It offers you ways to think about your role as manager so that you can optimize your effectiveness in what many consider to be rather turbulent and uncertain changes in the profession of management.

In addition to describing the evolving nature of management, it makes recommendations in each chapter on what to do as a result of those events. If you are impatient for answers, go to Chapter 6, which summarizes them, but then go back and read the other chapters so you understand why. This book was intended to be brief in order to quickly understand my point. If you pay attention, you will dig deeper on those topics that resonate with you right now and, hopefully, you will continue to do that for the rest of your career.

KEY IDEAS OF THE BOOK

The transformations—what I am calling changes in managerial style—are characterized by such features as the extensive use of massive quantities of numerical data to inform decisions, modeling of options from such mundane things as budget options with a spreadsheet tool on a PC, use of social media, to deploying super computers to conduct R&D and model market performance. Their organizations have spread around the world, integrating enterprises together of various sizes and roles, creating what today we call extended supply chains, while flattening the hierarchical structures of ever-larger corporations and smaller ones competing globally. All of these events occurred, and continue to occur slowly and incrementally around the world, not just in those national economies known for their early or extensive use of computing, for example, or in the richest national economies.

I have elected to discuss those current realities in which management operates that are the most important in affecting the success of management today and in the next several decades. I use this method of describing emerging features and implications of their new style of work. I use the word "emerging" because that process is still unfolding. Neither you nor I have the time to consume a far larger book that is more comprehensive. As managers have to do, we need to practice cognitive triage because there is too much information and managerial advice "out there" for anyone to absorb. And that is one of the lessons for management today: acquire the skill to select what needs to be understood right now and at what level of detail. Let this book be an example of that practice at work.

My intention is not to write a history or a full description of the evolution of managerial practices, although many observations are set in historical context, because understanding what has happened so far is absolutely crucial for understanding changes underway today. So bear with me as I offer more history than you might want—I use history because too many managers do not have historical perspective for context. The work performed by management is becoming more cerebral and success more dependent on understanding the context in which they work that goes beyond the normal fare of economics, prices, competition, and business practices and that must now also include history, sociological issues, culture, and, of course, the ever-changing and expanding role of IT. Understanding the context of your reality must extend across economic, technological, and business realities at a minimum, and ideally if you can absorb it, the social values of your environment at home and abroad, inside and outside your company, and appreciate the behaviors that are the results of those dynamics. My approach is particularly essential for those who have to deal directly with the consequences of economic globalization, governmental and regulatory globalization, and, of course, with the fact that today many of their firms spend between 7 and 15% of their budgets on information processing technologies and telecommunications, which themselves have become embedded in every facet of their business and who have to train their managers (and their workforces at large) in new ways of working.

We also have to deal with the fundamental problem that corporations are not doing as well as portrayed in their annual reports. Cheap money, inflated stock values, and the mess whole industries created for themselves and others in 2007–2009 through their inability to deal with complex issues, such as real estate derivatives, all hint that managers have a serious set of problems facing them for years to come. In the United States, the banking world has had to pay penalties in excess of US$100 billion, in Europe managers are going to jail, in China corrupt corporate leaders have been executed, and so on. Dealing with complexity and hidden realities is serious business.

I argue that the transformation currently underway in how managers do their work has not, however, fundamentally altered their mission, the *raison d'être* for why we have managers in the first place. Scholars such as Peter Drucker, Alfred D. Chandler, Jr., Gerald Greenwald, Adam Brandenburger, Barry J. Nalebuff, and Rita Gunther McGrath spent their professional lives describing those missions; I have no reason to displace their good work. Rather, mine builds humbly on their efforts, and upon that of such others who have followed them, such as Don Tapscott and Laurence Prusak all conditioned by historical perspective, solid observations, always paying close attention to broader social and economic contexts, and not just traditional managerial practices. So this book links the information-influenced work of managers to fundamental changes in the economy, in which the further integration of global industries, markets, and national economies are themselves influencing the work of managers, the "visible hand" in an economy that Professor Chandler described so well.

THE AUDIENCE FOR THIS BOOK

Bluntly put, it is today's managers and those who aspire to be one. I speak directly to these communities, although with a tip of the hat to the academics and journalists who are helping to equip management with insights about running enterprises. This book is by and for managers about how our craft is evolving into a more structured profession at a time of enormous transition in global economics, political constructs, and technological transformations that extend beyond computing and telecommunications into many other fields. In short, they are working in a period of increased appreciation of the role of chaos in science and understanding of how people and societies function, and when businesses are entering a world potentially as different as the rise of the modern corporation itself in the late nineteenth century.

A diligent business school professor should recognize much that is in this book and, to a large extent, a competent MBA student should too, because so many had to have worked for several years before going to business graduate school. I need to remind both communities, however, that they make up only a tiny portion of the population of the world's business managers. I look to the academics to provide elegant and useful paradigms and the detailed case studies that we managers find so valuable. But as a manager, my worldview looks up from the trenches in which even small mistakes harshly cost managers their jobs, where 50–60 hour weeks are all too normal, where job pressures change personalities and behaviors, and where customers expect so much.

THE MEGA TRENDS AFFECTING MANAGEMENT

This book explores mega trends and activities that I believe are changing the substance of managerial work:

1. Business practices/environments continue to evolve—they have not stabilized as some would argue—due in large part to all manner of information and telecommunications technologies that continue to enter economic/business life, various human values, and behaviors.

2. Managers are actually facing greater changes in the organization of their businesses than in the past and consequently are challenged to find new ways of managing their enterprises. Opportunities for novel sources of revenue and new sources of threats present themselves that cannot be ignored.

3. It is more than the story about the Internet—the Internet's influence on business structures and opportunities are just barely beginning to be felt; everything so far has been minor in comparison to other effects of earlier uses of IT. We now face additional yet fundamental structural changes in industries and economies, not just firms.

4. The style of how management is conducted has moved sufficiently to new forms such that we can speak of evolving ways with which their daily work is done today when compared to how it was done even as recently as 20 years ago.

5. IT has become pervasive, much like process management became ubiquitous in the 1990s. But there is also a broad band of differences between corporate IT and consumer IT; both are often intermixed and confused by the press and observers. Each requires its own descriptions, strategies and, often, managerial practices. Selling or using iPods, iPads, LinkedIn, and Facebook is not the same as running a process driven by Enterprise Resource Management in manufacturing; the latter industry (manufacturing) still makes up roughly 27% of the World's GDP.

This book identifies key inconsistencies in practice versus beliefs, such as the notion that knowing about the future direction of an industry causes managers to take different actions today; in fact, they do not until forced to by immediate circumstances.

Today over 60% of all major commercial deployments of IT are initiated and managed by non-IT management. In fact, there is hardly a CEO who has not led an IT project sometime in their recent career, such as an implementation of an SAP software package or some other large system. Because so many non-technical managers are now involved in IT managerial issues, the insights and experiences of chief information officers (CIOs) need to extend into line management. Many experts on business management have already published on how the insights and knowledge of line management have to be part of the CIO's kit bag; this book takes the dialogue in the opposite direction, because of the pervasiveness of IT in the work of line management.

Because management as a body of practices is evolving into forms more suitable to an age in which networked firms and extensive use of IT pervades, a new style of management results across three dimensions: its causes, features, and resulting behavior. I use the term *digital style* in order to help move us away from a more manufacturing-centric (Fordist) model of earlier decades. I argue that we are already in a period of significant institutional (read business model, extended enterprise, etc.) transformation and deployment of IT that is extending beyond the deployment of the Internet, one moving toward a global technological and economic balance-of-power similar to that experienced generally by the world prior to modern times. I describe the way such a growing convergence of standards and economies of scale, among others, affect managerial behavior. This book is about today's general management.

"Only" a third of the world's human population uses the Internet today, so the lion's share of the story is about other forms of IT and their effects on the work of managers, and so that "other" part of IT will receive the bulk of my attention. Another reality is that today more devices than people use the Internet. The Internet will not, however, be ignored since it is a crucial component of the connected world that is emerging, and that will engage at least twice as many people in the next decade than today. I emphasize the notion of *entering* because the real effects of the Internet thus still lie in the future, when compared to the effects of earlier waves of IT on enterprises and governments.

The title of this book is intended to call attention to a frame of reference I want to use throughout this book and that I encourage you to adopt as you go about the work of managing for the rest of your career. It is the notion that we work in an information ecosystem—call it a jungle if you wish—but nonetheless an environment that like a biological ecosystem has a lot going on that affects whatever else is occurring in the same place. It is an old idea that has occurred to earlier business writers but was premature and not so relevant until the Internet and other forms of IT made most industries and vast land masses accessible and manageable at scales impossible to achieve as recently as 20 years ago. Like a forest (or jungle), there are big animals (corporations and governments) and little ones (small companies and towns), big plants (a large national economy such as that of the United States), and others dependent on the shade of the larger ones (members of a large corporation's supply chain). This ecosystem is one filled with information—data and insights—to such an extent that if we continue our ecosystem analogy, we can think of information as the animals and vegetation in the jungle. Just as natives in a jungle understand how to thrive there, so too, must management in its info-jungle. The analogy should not be carried too far, but it helps us to understand the nature of global economics, role of IT (especially the Internet and mobile computing), and the expanding cerebral nature of management and its appetite for analytics, modeling, and experimentation (sometimes mistakenly called entrepreneurialism).

Boiled down to two words, thriving in this ecosystem is all about *contexts* and *connections*. It is the ability of people around the world, and within a firm or industry, to be so closely connected to one another that people can interact as they normally would if in close proximity to one another, but in a global setting. That is a remarkable change for the entire world that only recently became a reality. That transformation ranks high on any list of human technological innovations that so profoundly affected the way humans went about their affairs, and is associated with such other important breakthroughs as the use of fire, invention of firearms, flight, and the birth control pill. It is the essential by-product of nearly a century of innovation in information handling but also in how the world works. Reliance on communications, for example, does not mean the world is flat, because various cultures and local practices have not homogenized as fully as some would have us believe. Rather, diverse industries, practices, and places are more connected, and therefore more able to collaborate and trade without necessarily giving up their individuality, collaborating with a growing set of common practices, which today we think of as today's way of managing and working.

HOW THIS BOOK IS ORGANIZED

This book consists of six short essays, that's it. Each one can be read independently of each other, because I assume you will not have time to read the whole book cover to cover the way all authors want you to do. Each is short for the same reason, you will want the key messages quickly, and I know that if something resonates with you, that you will probe more deeply and to help with that I include a short Library for Management to get you started. Each chapter deals with an issue that is, however, related to all the other issues discussed across the book, so ultimately you really should read the whole book. First I describe the key elements of the emerging management style, much of it already in operation, so you should find some of the material familiar. It is my hope that this is the case so that you will feel comfortable accepting other ideas still for you to encounter. I then head straight into a discussion about information ecosystems because those will drive your activities for the rest of your career. Chapter 3 gets the technology issue on the table since no business management book can ignore that, and as I demonstrate, it is tied to the information ecosystem conversation. We then move on to the most perplexing set of issues facing senior managers, and increasingly all levels of management, how businesses are organized and the issues they are facing. Ultimately for many business professors and senior management, the conversation is largely about organizational issues. But as Chapters 4–6 make clear, that is too facile a view of managerial life. Chapter 5 provides a global "big picture" view of the world, its economic realities, and how businesses are responding. Logically, we could have started the book with this chapter; in fact, I originally did that but decided many readers would prefer to understand those issues coming at them from the perspective of their own personal circumstances, which are the topics covered in Chapters 1–4. The final chapter (Chapter 6) is as brief synopsis of what, hopefully, by the time you read it, are obvious and relevant and so more of a checklist of things not to forget.

The ultimate compliment you could pay me is to read the book, and then come back and reread it 5 years from now. Then you and I would know that we focused on the right issues.

WRITING, LIKE MANAGEMENT, IS A TEAM SPORT

Because it is usually easier to appreciate what an author is doing if the reader knows the writer, a few words are in order about me. I was trained as an historian, then spent the next four decades in various positions at IBM in sales, consulting, and management. I sold computers in the 1970s and 20 years later was still trying to help management figure out what to do with them in various industries. Perched at IBM, I was able to observe at close range the massive adoption of IT across the world as they unfolded and how the work of management evolved. I have walked their paths. In the process, I surveyed, interviewed, or worked with several thousand managers and executives around the world just in the past decade alone; their experiences are the core ingredients of this book. For 8 years, I worked with colleagues at IBM's management research center, the Institute for Business Value (IBV), and now at the Charles Babbage Institute at the University of Minnesota, two excellent environments for absorbing what is happening and writing about it in a productive way. If you want to continue the conversation, reach me at jcortada@umn.edu. Teach me about your realities and I'll share them with others in future publications.

The views expressed in this book are my own. Failings and errors that exist in this book are of my own doing, not of IBM Corporation, University of Minnesota, or the publisher. Because the topic at hand is still undergoing transformation, I expect that some observations and recommendations will be superseded in the years to come. In the meantime, I intend this book to serve as a dispassionate, organized conversation about the emerging realities of modern management in business and government.

I want to thank two anonymous reviewers who made many suggestions for improving this book. Publishing a book is not a solo act. The editorial and production staff at John Wiley & Sons were efficient in moving this book through production. I also want to thank the editorial board of the IEEE Press in supporting my work.

James W. Cortada

CHAPTER 1

Emergence of a New Managerial Style

> . . . a time of turbulence is also one of great opportunity for those who can understand, accept, and exploit the new realities. It is above all a time for leadership.
>
> Peter F. Drucker[1]

Mexican cement manufacturer CEMEX and European toy manufacturer LEGO use social media tools to invite product and service innovations from employees, of course, but also from customers. In the case of LEGO, management pays royalties to ideas turned into products. IBM managers have employees who report directly to them scattered across the world, no longer down the hall, and so expect their workers to take charge of their own time and get things done without constant managerial intervention. Traffic managers in London, Singapore, and Stockholm use massive quantities of data that are collected automatically by sensors to model optimized ways to improve traffic flows, in some instances, several times a day. Marketing managers at Ford Motor Company, Canadian retail bank, TD Bank, and now many insurance companies host online communities of customers

The Essential Manager: How to Thrive in the Global Information Jungle, First Edition.
James W. Cortada.
© 2015 the IEEE Computer Society. Published 2015 by John Wiley & Sons, Inc.

who tell them how products and services are performing, even how to make a better hamburger (Red Robin Restaurants), and expect employees to train and mentor each other. Increasingly, the power and work of "management" has diffused further to employees and especially to customers far beyond what had begun as a trend in the 1990s. When looked at as a whole, we see that a new style of management has emerged.

Something strange has been going on quietly, unseen, hardly recognized. Stand on a busy street in any city in the world—and I really mean *any* city—and one can notice that almost everyone over the age of 12 and under the age of 35 or so, and many clearly over that age, are either plugged into some device (such as an Apple iPod) or radio, are carrying in one hand a mobile phone, or are texting on their "smart" phone. Look for the phenomenon; it is there. Go back in time just 10–15 years and you would have seen a few people with headsets listening to music. Walk into a conference room at any major corporation—and I really mean *any* large or mid-sized company or government agency—and you will notice the same behavior of people clutching mobile phones if they are under the age of 35 and doing a quick check for messages or peeking at Facebook. Other colleagues walk into the room with iPads that they skim during the meeting, rarely devoting 100% of their attention to what is happening, while those over the age of 50–55 will drag in their ancient laptops or one of those thin ones from Apple and quickly sit down and start working on e-mail. Only the host of the meeting will drop her two or three pieces of hardware on the table and quickly move to a Powerpoint presentation that will provide structure to the meeting. Fifteen years earlier, similar type of meeting would have been conducted with Powerpoint, and everyone might have had a laptop open, doing e-mail of course, but probably without access to wireless Internet, and the manager chairing the meeting would undoubtedly have been a man.

Incrementally, the signs of change were all around us—from the physical appearance of mobile phones and tablet computers to women attaining senior positions. All these changes in work practices happened incrementally, one tiny step at a time slowly over time, so almost hidden. These are tips of icebergs, however, because far more changed in the practice of management. Success in a managerial profession has long depended on understanding the craft of leadership and management, mastering the technical skills and knowledge of such work, and for the most successful, the art of success. This book is about how these three things are followed today, suggesting how they will be done during the professional lives of all those individuals clutching mobile phones, routinely dividing their attention between the Powerpoint presentations and the wealth of interesting contents pouring into their digital devices off of social media sites. In fact, many of these individuals work for organizations that are becoming social media sites themselves; these include municipalities that provide services online to consumers in every major city of the world, and in future to consumers in most towns and villages too, and companies that sell digital content, transfer information from organizations to people for free or fee, or operate almost virtually.

A personal story. In the 1980s, when I first entered the ranks of management at IBM, a secretary worked for me, I had an office, and had access to e-mail on a heavy terminal on my desk. After several promotions, gone was the secretary (I then shared an "administrative assistant" who was a man), gone too was my physical office (although I could borrow an empty one anywhere in the world), while I had a laptop connected to IBM's e-mail system, the Internet on a dialup line, and increasingly to large databases of business records and consulting materials. Fast forward to the early 2000s, and yet through two more promotions (defined as fancier titles, stock options, and bigger salaries), my manager lived in Amsterdam, I in Madison, Wisconsin; gone was the administrative assistant, although I could lean on one to help me if needed who worked in Boston, Massachusetts, while her backup was in Amsterdam; and my staff was scattered all over the world. In the 1980s,

I physically saw my manager every day; in the 1990s probably once in a month; while in the 2000s once in a year and only because we felt we should, but did not know really why anymore. I moved from being told how to do my job, and getting appraised on both the way I worked and the results obtained, to results obtained. Over a period of years, I incrementally had to evolve from a person able to operate in a hierarchical organization taking and giving orders for the most mundane activities to weaving networks of alliances and teams that functioned on their own as self-directed individuals and clusters of people willing to collaborate as long as it made sense to them. No managerial revolution was there at IBM—IBM was far too conservative for that—rather we underwent a continuous process of many evolutions, just as our customers did in all industries around the world, often at roughly the same time and pace.

While evolutions are often nearly invisible, if they are continuous, they ultimately accumulate into enough changes that will seem revolutionary in hindsight. The revolutions are obvious to see unfold, such as the introduction of the smart phone or a change in a government regulation, but the evolutions come at us quietly, slowly, incrementally, and so are not so evident. This book describes some of these evolutions, demonstrates how to spot them, and suggests answers to the most basic question, "So, now what do I do?"

HOW THIS BOOK AND CHAPTERS ARE ORGANIZED AND WHY

The fundamental purpose of this book is to help you to know the happenings around you as a manager, or as an aspiring one. The reason to do this comes from the fact that managers are today not as broadly aware of their circumstances as they need to be. Their education is often too narrow, they normally know just what they need to in order to perform their current jobs, and they remain too ill-equipped to transform into agile, entrepreneurial leaders, which is what the world of business is demonstrating is required more today than in previous decades. The need for agility and innovation is being forced on managers because the global economy is continuing to integrate, which means you will have more competitors with different business models to contend with and more technological and scientific advances and changes that will force you to work in different ways. You have no choice but to respond to those realities. The help you get is often inadequate or simply wrong. The books that managers read are too often focused on a single issue presented as the next "silver bullet" that will solve all their problems, from long tails to analytics, from "bings" to emulating nineteenth-century generals. So many commentators take an article they published in a business journal and develop it into a book that adds more case studies but not more insight.

Much of that behavior has to be seen for what it normally is: close to near nonsense and it has to stop. Management is a serious business that affects the life and lives of billions of people, the environment of the earth, even perhaps the survival of our species. Management is not an ad hoc or amateur activity. This book respects the growing professionalization of managerial practices, its complexity, and the seriousness with which all workers need to devote to it.

An operating assumption here is that everyone working today has some managerial responsibilities, regardless of title, because that is the way work is routinely done. Like the observer on the sidewalk, things change around us. First, those people clutching their mobile phones are not just embracing technologies—that is not so important—what they are doing is living in a more intensely connected world from which they willingly do not escape as their parents could, and in which they must devote ever less time to any one issue or problem as multiple people crash into their mental spaces. Second, armed with perspectives on what is happening, and all through this book, suggestions are made about how to deal with these changes. But, this is not a cookbook or a highly prescriptive list of "to dos." There is too much going on for that to work; rather, we have to be agile intellectually and physically able to work in different places, time zones, cultures, and business environments. These forms of flexibility are of considerable value, indeed for many decades. So understanding these and making such capabilities a way of life becomes an important objective. But, much will be offered in the way of telling lessons and actions to build on. We are talking about a style of working in today's and, more importantly, tomorrow's business world.

This style of working is not hubris and hype, but this is a serious business because your competitors are coming at you literally from countries you did not think about half a dozen years ago and from industries that did not exist a decade earlier. For example, many competitors to American companies in consumer goods in the 1960s and 1970s operated out of Japan; in the 1980s and 1990s, increasingly out of China and Eastern Europe; and in the early 2000s from the Philippines and Thailand. In case of software business, competitors were from India and China. But today, Vietnam and Indonesia have become the major contributors of consumer goods. That coming and going of international competitors will continue, forcing us to understand who they are and their values. In turn, then, we will need to craft new ways of doing business and of finding customers even in those countries.

To succeed, managers need to be aware of more issues and changes that are underway. They need to think more creatively, not just look at more data (but they need to do that too). They will need to experiment more with business models, terms and conditions, new technologies, and different products and services delivered in innovative ways. They will need to engage with new types of organizations too. The good news is, however, that there is much help on the way, from computer software for modeling situations and options with mountains of data and information, and a large body of managerial practices which business school professors have now spent several generations codifying in convenient ways. The bad news is we are now applying these assistive tools and insights in the ongoing development of our managers insufficiently. But let us be realistic.

A manager still needs the core skills that have evolved into the set of practices widely deployed over the past half century: process management expertise, strong project management practices, reliance on data and spreadsheets, being facile with mobile computing, and an ability to network within their organizations and with clients and industry colleagues in rather fluid circumstances. Their MBA degree would have taught them the basic "facts" of their profession—a good start to be sure—but it was only a start in their education on teaming, corporate politics, use of social media in marketing and product development, life in a supply chain, managing personnel without violating laws or "best practices," and so forth. Add in the evolutions discussed in this book, and we can see there is much yet to be done, a great deal to learn, and to keep doing constantly.

The strategy for accomplishing the purpose of this book is straight-forward. In the six chapters provided, you will be exposed to those issues that, to be blunt about it, in my opinion, are affecting your success the most. That opinion is based on the decades of my work experience at IBM and across over a dozen industries and countries, in mentoring start-up companies, and the research done on these critical issues. I have handled these issues the same way as important management gurus have, such as Peter Drucker and Alfred D. Chandler, Jr. If you have heard of Peter Drucker, and more importantly, read his work on the craft of management, then you know I am going to expose you to the context—most specifically historical context—and also to the profound role of various technologies on work, management, and society. We cannot ignore the power of information technologies, including but not limited to the Internet, social media, or our smart phones. The use of information technologies is as important to our lives as the deployment of electricity in the workplace was to a generation of managers over a century ago. Both are infrastructures that fundamentally changed how people worked and played. Welcome to your world. This chapter discusses some, but not all, of the new ways of management, quickly "netting out" the "big picture."

Chapter 2 addresses the ever thickening information ecosystem that physically and practically surrounds us and defines our work. Chapter 3 expands the conversation from an individual to the larger world of global industries because industries are large worlds of their own. Each industry affects our work in many ways today. If this book had been written in the 1980s or early 1990s, this chapter would only have been relevant to senior executives, but with global supply chains and competition from everywhere, its content is crucial to most employees and entrepreneurs. Chapter 4 defines who you work for, what that kind of organization looks like, and tones down the rhetoric to remind us of what is not changing yet. Your success is measured by how successful you are in that organizational environment, so understanding some emerging basics is as essential as eating and breathing. Chapter 5, similar to Chapter 3, takes us into a broader landscape of the global economy as it evolves because your work, industry, and company thrive or fail in large part by actions out of your control. The business jungle is growing new plants and new animals are thriving on these. Finally, Chapter 6 pulls together the various insights and recommendations made throughout this book.

This book is short on purpose because most readers do not have the time or the willingness to cover a large topic in detail. We live in a world where the "elevator pitch" is essential, required, and when presented properly, actually useful. To write a short book meant picking topics that seemed important and spending fewer or more pages again based on what seemed relevant. For example, this chapter may strike the reader as too long on history and some points dragging on beyond what is needed; trust me, it is shorter than the subject deserves. But, the reader does not need to take my word for it; there is a short list of important publications at the back of the book that can be read, which fills the gaps of interest to you and that can serve as a correction to my emphasizing one point more than another.

Chapter 1 more specifically focuses on those views, tools, and practices of management that are most influential in shaping the activities and prospects of current and future management. The fundamental idea is that the way a manager works has been and continues to transform into substantive ways. To describe that fundamental transformation, several features of those changes are discussed. Key conversations include the following: thinking in terms of systems and processes because that is the way work flows in an organization are structured today; the roles of simulations, models, and the attraction of numeric data are introduced for similar reasons and these are discussed again in future chapters in more detail; migratory habits of the modern manager since very few will ever spend their entire careers working in one or two enterprises, so there are important implications for individuals on how best to work; how the new style of management is applied at work; and a conclusion with a recap of key implications and suggestions.

My text will appear quite simple to those who want depth, detailed case studies, and intriguing ways of doing work. But there is danger with complexity, of course, and we have too much around us as it is. Clarity of thinking often calls for simpler statements. There is an old U.S. Navy advice to seamen and officers, which has proven of enormous use for decades, "Keep it simple, stupid." Had bankers crafting complex derivative real estate products in the early 2000s followed that admonition, the Great Recession probably would not have occurred. Complex mathematics in this instance confused even CEOs of large American banks. In the 1990s, Enron operated like a bank instead as an energy firm, which had a century of experience in its industry and called for more command-and-control managerial practices that relied heavily on well-defined processes. The rollout of the U.S. government's health-care enrollment system in late 2013 proved to be an unmitigated disaster to say the least, probably because the implementers failed to focus on getting right the three or four critical requirements that over two generations of software developers had learned were essential: adequate testing, rollout of pieces of the application and not everything at once, having adequate amounts of computing power to handle the volumes, and single focal point for all decisions regarding what functions and policies to implement. Instead, as in the other cases, management became victim to complexity. Complexity remains a continuing threat to the success of managers, as it has been for generations. As these recent cases remind us, there are basic managerial behaviors that the business school professors and historians remind us to be important, but too often these behaviors are forgotten by senior executives or are simply not learned by new managers. So, your first lesson is do not assume management even knows the basics of sound practices and fear complexity, yet remain open to changes that can be understood and explained simply.

A DOSE OF HISTORICAL PERSPECTIVE

When Peter Drucker published *Management* in 1974, no woman was the CEO of a *Fortune* 100 company. In the first year of the twenty-first century, several and 11% of all senior executives in these companies were women. By 2013, women served as the CEOs of some of the world's iconic companies: IBM, Yahoo!, HP, and Xerox to mention a few. Glass ceilings had been quietly shattered over the past two decades as women worked their way up corporate ladders and along the way changed the gender and ethnic demographics of management in the industrialized economies. Other transformations had slowly occurred. For example, on average, senior executives had been to school longer, more graduated with MBA degrees compared to earlier period, and were younger. They were reaching senior ranks (e.g., CEO, COO, Sr. VP, VP) in their early 50s, 4 years faster, than the earlier generation.[2] Professors and consultants documented the expanded professionalization of this younger set of management over the past quarter century, while other observers were complaining that not enough "evidence based" managerial practices had permeated the managerial caste.[3] To add to the churn and change, surveys as recently as 2012 still called out the global concern of senior management that their organizations found it difficult to develop rapidly enough skills within their firms needed with which to thrive, because employee skills were not aligned sufficiently with the needs of a corporation.[4] But Drucker found similar issues as well, most specifically the lament of management at the lack of sufficient skills among employees and managers, in general, echoing the concerns of the 1960s and 1970s.

Other things were changing at the same time as corporations went global and the economic fortunes of nations were in transition. As transformations were underway in global economic realities, management's work too evolved, extending a process that had started over a century ago with the creation of the modern corporation so aptly described by historian Alfred D. Chandler, Jr., as run by a new "mandarin class" of managers.[5] In a nutshell, what occurred over the past 30 years has been nothing less than the evolution of myriad managerial practices that emerged into a new *style* of management's work, as yet unnamed, but because of the profound role of computers in that transformation, it is sufficient for one to begin to view it as possibly a digital, networked, or connected age to label this style of work. But today's experts shy away from naming their views as digital. At 2013's Global Peter Drucker Forum, different concepts dominated. Georg Kapsch criticized the ineffectiveness of line organizations, while Don Tapscott wanted the audience to think about new organizational models. Charles Handy did too. The need for innovation remains, so driving fear out and constraining exuberant cost cutting are needed, replacing them with actions that encourage "creative confidence," to use the words of Tim Brown, CEO of IDEO. Managers have to stop being "zombies" (Umair Haque, Director, Havas Media Labs).[6] While self-organizing workplaces require IT and competing around the world does too, these and so many other management experts have got it right: it was never about computing alone, it was about organizing to address opportunities and squelch problems.

The process of shaping a modern manager has been impressively pervasive, extending beyond the confines of *Fortune* 100 or 1000 firms to include many who moved from those companies to other enterprises and government agencies, graduates of MBA programs around the world, book and magazine writers, and participants in professional associations, all of whom embraced most of the concepts described in the following discussion. Their process of transformation led to new practices created in complete awareness of the work of each other. Book and magazine writers who discussed new managerial techniques came from corporations where they practiced these skills or possibly acquired some of them during their MBA programs. Business school professors learned managerial techniques from their managers and students. Corporate management assimilated insights and lessons from their associations and from the literature they read on modern management methods. Associations too learned from managers, consultants, and professors. If the emerging style of management can be described as virtuous, then the roles of these sources of diffusion constitute such a circle.

An early observation to keep in mind is that managerial practices of the early twenty-first century are being shaped by a set of attitudes (call them beliefs if you will) and a predilection for using tools (software and practices in particular) that were not convenient or even available a generation ago. This book will discuss some of the most important of these with an eye to addressing complexity and the continuing need for innovation.

In several ways, how contemporary managers and executives think and work are the basis for arguing that a new form of managerial style has arrived which is now shaping the features of the manager belonging to the twenty-first century. First, they think tactically in terms of "systems" and "processes." Second, they rely extensively on data to inform their decisions, and especially on numerically rich results of modeling and simulations, today fashionably called Big Data. They measure the increasing amounts of activities and ideas drawn from sensors on machinery to leading indicators of economic trends. Third, they develop core skills that they take from one firm to another, as they change jobs more frequently than prior generations of managers. Executives and managers often think of their work as international and themselves as members of a transnational class of workers, reaffirming Richard Florida's idea of the "creative class" or as global business leaders. Fourth, they are comfortable working in flattened organizations with fewer levels of management than in the past, weaving networks of contacts and team members to accomplish goals. These four trends have been unfolding for over two decades, so the young manager can turn into more experienced ones for "war stories" and insights relevant to their immediate jobs to understand how best to leverage these as context must remain one of the most sought-after bodies of knowledge by all managers and executives.

THINKING IN TERMS OF SYSTEMS AND PROCESSES

As far back as the 1940s, army and navy officers in North America, Western Europe, and the Soviet Union had thought of battlefield tactics and military and economic strategies increasingly as integrated sets of activities. As technologies in communications, computing, and weapons systems became more integrated during the Cold War period in the subsequent three decades following the end of World War II in 1945, the notion of systems increasingly provided an international view for officers and their staffs. By the 1960s, they had already created software to simulate war fighting practices and strategies. Historians of the evolution toward a systems approach to warfare talked about a "closed world" view of fighting in which a battlefield or national war fighting strategy appeared almost as if a self-contained view of even an alternative reality, much like we experience with interactive video games.[7] The same occurred with national economic development when, for example, Japan and South Korea developed economies that contained within them all the elements of success they needed, exporting to the West their products and not relying on other countries to do their work.[8] That notion of a "closed world" has extended to the present; the mindset now is often called Network Centric Operations (NCO) or Network Centric Warfare (NCW), in warfare, but it applies also to scientific research, global and national economic development, and to much corporate strategy work.[9] It is a collective attitude that the world can be viewed as a collection of identifiable systems and processes, all of which can increasingly be shaped, managed, and indeed controlled.

That systems approach to planning and managing many complex events spilled over into the practices of private sector management. Initially called operations research, later the work attracted the language of the world of computer experts, *systems* being one of them. To a technologist, a system consists of all the various machines, wires, and software needed to make all the devices do the work assigned to them. Beginning in the 1950s and extending through the 1980s, many of the *components* of a *system* had to be *configured* together into compatible *systems* or *applications*. Today, the functions of various independent units are often *housed*, that is to say, installed in or *under the covers*[10] of a single machine, such as those elements necessary to make a laptop connect to a network; 30 years ago, those elements—known as modems—were in the size of small copiers. The italicized words above began as phrases used by computer experts, programmers, and *systems analysts,* but, by the 1980s, were seeping silently into mainstream language and thinking, the basis of a nescient, if primitive, world view of management.[11] Today, they are common vocabulary and a way of seeing how one does work.

Looking at work as a collection of organized steps dates back to the dawn of the twentieth century, often seen as part of the Taylorism in management thinking of that time, when the activities of individuals were linked to that of machines and the order of tasks that needed to be done repeatedly, such as the work of people on an automobile assembly line. Afterward, J. Edwards Deming, Joseph Juran, and other like-minded thinkers in the 1950s and later argued that work should be seen as collections of related processes. They introduced myriad statistical methods that could be used to measure the performance of a process and to identify mathematically and numerically what could be improved. By the late 1970s, Japanese managers had demonstrated the power of viewing work through process lenses, continuous improvement (*kaizen*), and peer populated work teams that did planning, strategy development, and execution (*hoshin kanri*). Their concepts spread rapidly through the Western world. Therein was born the "quality movement" of the 1980s, which management around the world embraced so thoroughly and quickly that, like systems thinking, people forgot were new ways of doing work.[12]

By the early 1990s, a more radical form of process management emerged in the West known as "process reengineering."[13] This thinking advocated replacement of incremental improvements of processes—the original strategy advocated for decades by J. Edwards Deming and Joseph Juran, among others—with radical redesign of how work flowed in an enterprise. In exchange for such an approach, one could eliminate budgetary and other forms of administrative or work in an organization, reduce the number of employees needed, delete unnecessary tasks, and so forth. In fact, such reengineering often led to the elimination of between 10 and 30% of the cost of people and other assets, but also contributed to the erosion of employee loyalty to a firm and to sharp declines in their morale.[14] Reengineering came as close as any managerial activity to sparking a "revolution" in business as one could find in recent decades.

One by-product of taking a process-centric view of work was that managers changed fundamentally the way they viewed activities. They looked methodically at the role of people, information, tools, and IT, and how they interacted with each other. Managers began thinking in terms of linked steps, left to right so to speak on a chart, extending these in formal and well-defined ways beyond their corporate boundaries into the operations of suppliers and business partners at one end of the spectrum and at the other end, into those of distributors, sales, services, and even customers. Into such processes, they embedded many of the statistical practices of Total Quality Movement, originally espoused by Deming and Juran. Often, data collection and analysis involved the use of digital and analogue sensing devices, and then software to do the mathematics and presentation of results. The language of process management, which originated in the quality management world as with systems, seeped into the mainstream of managerial lexicon and thinking. Today, such process terms as *attribute, base line, cycle time, benchmarking, change management, decision point, fishbone diagrams,* and *six sigma* (to mention a few) are commonly used by managers and their employees.[15] One rarely finds anyone who does not think of his or her work as parts of systems and processes. Much managerial training is, thus, tied to providing them with the tools used to implement those two notions. This approach includes reinforcing initiatives designed to sustain that way of thinking, especially by corporate education centers and, increasingly, even in academic business administration courses.[16]

Applying these useful ways of working requires managers to do three things well. First, they must learn the formal language, ideas, and tasks of what one does for a living. Those normally have been consolidated into structured, documented, and published descriptions. It is a body of knowledge that must be mastered, just as one must learn accounting, for example. For the most part, this body of knowledge is what one is exposed to in business school and industry training seminars.

Second, recognize that these bodies of knowledge and practices have their passionate devotees in every organization who promote their use too much, or not enough, and for various reasons; management needs to recognize the motives and consequences of such behaviors and their intents. Examples abound. There are those who advocate too much automation of decision-making (the artificial intelligence devotees), or of pushing customers to websites to get their problems fixed when what they really want is a conversation with a human (telephone company "help" desks), or those who want to cut budgets to make their profit targets to such an extent that they weaken the firm's ability to innovate or grow (as some IT vendors are doing). I liken this second task as almost understanding a new form of corporate politics, but also as the basis for much of today's managerial ideology, one that has evolved from being fads to accepted sound business practices.

Third, these practices have built into them an assumption that managers must continue to base their decisions more on measureable data and facts (think context and business realities) than just on experience or "gut feel" (more elegantly called tacit knowledge) because prior experience may be outdated, no longer a reflection of today's circumstances, particularly if they have been changing slowly and invisibly as I argue throughout this book. Steve Jobs of Apple Computer famously would argue that he paid less attention to what customer feedback sessions generated or the comments of marketing experts and instead went with his gut feel of what consumers wanted. In the process, he developed iTunes, iPods, iPhones, and iPads, making his company one of the largest in the world in less than one decade. Was he an exception? Google and eBay were created on the basis of tacit knowledge too; instinctively we know that was recently the case with Facebook and Twitter.[17]

SIMULATIONS, MODELING, AND THE ATTRACTION OF NUMERIC DATA

All of this thinking about systems and processes lead us to the issues of information, facts, data, as supporting infrastructure for these two notions, and to their role in the work of managers. The most popular uses (*applications* in the nomenclature of computing) of PCs in the first decade of their availability (1970s–1980s) were spreadsheet software products. As many as three thousand software *packages* of this class appeared. Managers began using these tools to create models of cash flows, to track and model changes in the performance of processes, and to ask the ultimate simulation question, "What if?" by altering numerical variables. By the late 1980s, word processors rivaled spreadsheets in popularity. Not until the 1990s was e-mail, a contender for most popular use of these small systems. Given the mindset of management that had developed before the arrival of PCs—largely thinking in terms of systems and closed worlds—use of spreadsheet software was a natural evolution in the deployment of IT. By the end of the 1990s, it had become very difficult to imagine a manager not using spreadsheet software to plan budgets, sales revenues, profit margins, to bid on consulting work, or to track progress of a project. There probably has not been a single

MBA student graduated from any university in the world since the start of the 1990s not familiar with spreadsheet software. Indeed, in many MBA programs in North America since the late 1980s, owning a PC or laptop was a formal requirement for participating in a curriculum. As managers integrated these tools into their daily work, they increasingly relied on numerical calculations with which to make basic managerial decisions regarding budgets, proposals, allocation of resources, and scheduling of work—all activities of management prior to the arrival of the PC were either done manually, and thus often sparingly, or with a less data-intensive technique of on the "back of a napkin."

Numbers have never been more popular with managers earlier than they are today. No compelling case for an action seems possible without quantifying the case for or against an initiative. Use of adjectives is diminishing in the language of business managers. The hunt is on for greater precision and the authority that seems to come only from numbers, not words. Only advertising and media relations people remain enthusiastic users of adjectives; but then ask a media expert about what is newsworthy and they will tell you data, survey results, numbers. A lawyer–author even wrote a book about thinking in numbers, calling it "the new way to be smart."[18] Analytics became the new buzz term in the early 2000s. The widely read consultant Tom Davenport defines it as "the extensive use of data, statistical and quantitative analysis, explanatory and predicting models, and fact-based management to drive decisions and actions."[19] To be sure, to sell books he has to announce it as "new," but we know that the process of relying on numerical data as being more "precise" or "scientific" or "unbiased" had its history in process management and, before that, operations research, accounting, and finance dating back to the nineteenth century.[20]

The most extreme case of the use of numbers close to the world of management involves economists who began embracing econometric methods following World War I, although not fully applying the notion of numerically, statistically, and mathematically intensive work until the 1960s. By the end of the century, it had sadly become nearly impossible to read much of their literature without a good grasp of calculus and statistics. Yet their work is important to managers, particularly for those who want to understand how their industry is structured and works or for those who want to learn about how a national economy functions, particularly if they are thinking of outsourcing work to firms in another country or to sell goods and services outside one's own nation.[21]

Many reasons led to so many people becoming so reliant on numeric data, but clearly on any short list of causes has to be computers, which made it easy to collect, analyze, and present numerical information in many ways. When use of computers was combined with new knowledge regarding mathematics and statistics in general, IT made it nearly impossible to ignore such classes of information as statistics and numbers in general. Analytical software continues to evolve. Data storage in computers to house vast quantities of data is continuing to expand, while simultaneously dropping in cost. More software tools keep appearing that can make decisions on the behalf of managers based on large volumes of facts (read, numbers). Such software tools also alert managers to situations in which they have to intervene to make a decision. Enormous progress has—and continues—to be made in the development and use of software to predict new circumstances (again modeling, reliance on statistics, and probability), ensuring, in particular, that those managers who were risk-averse will continue to use such tools. In short, they no longer are the preserve of brokers, bankers, and insurance companies.[22]

While the power of analytics and simulations will continue to attract even further use as software tools appear tailored to many industries and managerial areas of concern, there are cautions to keep in mind. First, an aspiring manager must come to understand specifically what simulation tools exist for their area of responsibility and become facile in their use, or in the commissioning of their use. The tools are practical, they work, and provide insight. But, second, do not kill the adjective in the process. Circumstances exist that cannot be quantified, such as political realities affecting the ability of a company to function in China, for example, or in Russia. This is all about the power of understanding context, actually seeking it out when it is not presented in the normal course of conversation about a decision or an issue. Asking what are the situations affecting a proposed action, why these are important, and how to deal with them to take leverage a circumstance or avoid a threat, have to be asked. Regional cultures remain important because the world is just not as flat as we are told so often. A manager can observe when these steps are not taken: the American firm Google runs into problems in China but not in the United States, the Italian automotive manufacturer Fiat runs into problems when it tries to merge with a competitor in another country (as it tried to in the United States), and so on. Context and culture are not described in numerical terms, so Americans are frustrated with Indian bureaucracy, German managers with French and Spanish labor laws, and the list goes on.

Balancing numbers and adjectives requires diversity of workers, or at least people who show up in conference rooms. This is not an issue of having men versus women, old and young, white and black managers. This is about diversity of opinions, education, and experiences. It is increasingly obvious that there had better be people in the room who have lived or grown up in other cultures; do not let everyone in the conference room be either an engineer or an MBA; include "numbers people" but also folks with a humanities education, yes even an English major on occasion. Include in a conference call assessing a situation or proposing an action, a variety of people, to be sure, but also remember that culture plays a role even in the way the meetings are held. I have personally found, for example, that Americans are generally not shy in talking on a conference call to a group of strangers, but Asians often play a quieter role, while too many Europeans will wait for the senior person on the call to lead the dialogue. I admit these are generalizations, but I make them to point out that managers need to form opinions about how people behave in a diverse workforce so that they can insure actions are taken to force participation and extraction of information from them relevant to the discussion at hand.

To continue the horrible generalizations, the problem exists everywhere. So, for a specific but often existing example, if I participate in a meeting in South Korea, where I am the only American, and I have white hair, invariably the most senior Korean in the room and I will have a two-way dialogue while everyone else will remain silent, even though they represent the next tier of management or experts working in the same department as the senior Korean. That manager, I contend, is not leveraging the knowledge of his staff, even though they have provided him with numbers and even biographical data about my company and I. Nor can I benefit from the perspectives and knowledge of his staff. Moral of the story is do not just rely on simulations and spreadsheets, as good as they are.

MIGRATORY HABITS OF THE MODERN MANAGER

From meetings in conference rooms in other countries to jobs in different cities and industries represent additional realities of today's managers. Workers in their 20s are not the only gypsies in the world, nor are they the only people looking for the ideal job. By the early 1980s, it had become evident in the United States, and later in Europe, that turnover of managers in large corporations was beginning to pick up; small enterprises had long experienced this loss of people as almost the norm.[23] By the 1990s, economists and business school professors were looking at the trend more closely than before, not just because it was taking place in the United States, which had one of the most fluid labor markets in the world, but also in other large corporations managed out of Europe and parts of East Asia. One of the first experts to study the phenomenon in modern times was Peter Cappelli and his colleagues. They concluded that workforces were undergoing fundamental transformations in their relationships with their employers. As corporations began to downsize and outsource work, they destroyed the implied compact between management and labor that essentially had promised lifetime employment in exchange for absolute loyalty and dedication to the interests of the firm. The primary reason for the change was obvious: pressure on management to improve productivity, that is to say, to protect and enhance sources of revenue and profit. The added perception that firms should be flexible in what products and services they offered also motivated this fundamental change in worker–manager relations.[24] It may have largely started in the United States, but with the near meltdown of Japan's economy in the 1990s, even the Japanese began breaking their long-standing compact of full employment and lifelong commitment to one firm, as happened recently at Sony, among others.

Managers, of course, were not immune to this new gale of change. All through the 1990s and early 2000s, companies hollowed out their middle manager ranks, forcing many individuals to find employment elsewhere, or not. That process destroyed management's lifelong sense of loyalty to the firm that had hired them right out of school. A decade later (early 2000s), Cappelli was still looking at the labor issue, only this time more specifically at management. He documented the increasingly global flattening of organizations, a story told by many observers; but in Cappelli's case, he also observed that there had been about a 25% decline in the amount of time a senior executive spent in his or her current firm in the early 2000s when compared to 1980. Turnover in smaller companies continued as well. In *Fortune* 100 companies, he found that only 45% of senior executives had spent their entire careers in their firms, as compared to 53% in 1980. Younger companies had even more turnover of management at all levels. Wholesale trade and financial industries experienced some of the greatest organizational (structural), technological, and marketing churn, and so had the greatest amount of turnover as managers moved from one company to another in their climbing up the ever-shorter corporate ladder. Conversely, industries with the least of these three kinds of changes provided the fewest opportunities for advancement, although stagnant economic performance led to outsourcing and layoffs among managers. The most relatively stagnant industries included computers, retail, manufacturing, automotive, and paper manufacturing.

The consequences of such macro changes in industries could have been predicted. First, managers were willing to move from one firm to another, taking with them their experience, knowledge, and internal information to a potential competitor, or simply for the purpose of getting a better job. Second, such migratory behavior reinforced stockholders' impatience with long-term business strategies, favoring instead short-term results and, in the case of managers, more immediate rewards for their shorter term performance. As Cappelli's data demonstrates, managers were spending less time in a particular job before either being promoted or filling an opening or that they took themselves by simply going to work at another firm when they felt ready to take on a different responsibility. Career paths increasingly varied too. For example, an executive with profit and loss (P&L) responsibility at a US$10 million firm could take the same job at a similar, but larger, company of US$100 million and make more money. Also acquiring skills needed by one industry from another became another common practice. In the 1980s, as utility companies became more customer focused, they hired call center managers from telephone companies. In the early 2000s, firms eager to establish a presence in China or India recruited managers from other firms and industries with necessary experiences or they hired very young Indian or Chinese managers and promoted them rapidly to general managers. Today, this practice involves experts in social media practices.

In addition to the structural conditions that had dramatically reduced loyalty to one's firm was the growing skill base of managers. By the end of the century, most managers had at least an undergraduate education, while higher percentages of middle and senior management in advanced economies (i.e., large and multinational firms) also had formal training in business, usually MBA degrees, despite the continuing flow of complaints about the lack of practical skills not being taught by business schools.[25] Additional skills were acquired "on the job." Right into the new century, some of the fastest career paths were financial, which required more of the formal training one received in an academic setting than in the workplace.

Sociologist Richard Florida has documented the migratory practices of many classes of highly skilled workers, such as programmers, movie animators, and creators of video games, but also of management. Simply put, workers move quickly from one industry to another and most noticeably from one country to another, facilitated by globalized networks of contacts, telecommunications that permitted movement of digitally-based creations, and the attraction of physical locations, like New Zealand or warm climates.[26] Research on migrations of workers puts additional hard data to the matter with the result that one can say with reasonable confidence that over 200 million workers around the world are routinely employed in countries other than those of their nationality. Furthermore, in interviews with public officials responsible for providing these individuals with services, pensions, and healthcare, they expected these numbers to increase over the foreseeable future.[27] In short, managers were moving around the world with a great number of other workers. It was not uncommon for these managers to feel quite international: bilingual or more in many cases, normally with a good command of the English language, and often with an advanced degree in business administration or in a technical subject, such as engineering or software design. There is no plausible reason to believe that this trend will diminish since the global economy continues to grow, expanding even in previously less developed areas such as Sub-Saharan Africa, parts of Latin America, and Central and Eastern Europe.

What are we to make of this migratory behavior since it cannot be stopped, and one can easily argue that it provides new blood into many enterprises? If one is a senior executive, the firm needs to decide whether to implement policies and practices that retain managers, recruitment processes that can replace them, or that encourage some rate of turnover, channeled to control costs and to enhance the managerial horsepower of specific divisions or lines of business. Strategy and values intermix. If costs need to drop sharply, loyalty to employees suffers as work is moved about or people replaced with less expensive ones. If tacit knowledge is less valued in the workforce then the strategy has possibilities. On the other hand, if deep knowledge and skills are required, then loyalty to employees is imperative, as is needed, for example, with researchers in highly complex industries, but less so in retail firms where specific bodies of knowledge can be rented from advertising and marketing agencies and shop floor workers employed quickly when needed.

Companies change their values as their business circumstances evolve. IBM as late as the 1980s strongly held to the notion that employees were to be hired for life and periodically retrained to deal with new realities. After a disastrous period from the late 1980s to the mid-1990s, the firm did a 180-degree and now hired and fired to meet short-term needs. Regardless of how a reader may feel about this change, it was arrived at rationally, made by IBM's new CEO, Louis Gerstner, and while historians have yet to weigh in on that decision, the turnaround that he managed proved to be a resounding success. In 2013, GE and a number of other large American corporations fundamentally changed the nature of employee health plans, essentially reducing the amount of coverage, getting out of the business of providing such coverage, and forcing employees and their retirees to find their own insurance using health exchanges. Employees perceived this change as significant as the elimination of pensions. The point is, changes occur, and managers make (or implement) them. So, changes encourage, or motivate, people to come and go.

For the individual manager, if eager to move on, it is about beefing up their resumes with relevant work experiences and skills so that they can sell themselves to the next organization. But, I would argue that the same strategy of beefing up one's resume is needed just to stay in the current organization, even in the same job. Either approach requires managers to also become students of career management by focusing on the strong and weak areas of others, discuss career options inside and outside their current firm on a regular basis, and if confident, to test the waters by applying for other jobs. The core issue to resolve is what does an individual want to be good at, what do they want to be known for, and what do they want professionally. Answering these questions is essential as opposed to the more traditional approach of accepting the career ladder conventional in their current firm or believed in their industry. Whatever is done, it will occur in an environment where moving around within and outside a firm, and within and outside one's industry or home company is now considered normal, even competitive.

What is absolutely new since the mid-2000s is the requirement for managers to create their personal brand. We will discuss this further later in this book, but for the time being the lesson to pull out of the last several pages is that you have to decide what you want to be good at, create the expertise, gain the experience, and make sure everyone knows what it is. That is nearly a full time job since daily work feeds hard evidence into that brand.

HOW THE NEW STYLE IS APPLIED AT WORK

There are some broad general patterns observable which give us a view into the future of managerial practices. We can begin with the ever-growing use of information to illustrate the process at work, because some characteristics of data continue to change in ways that encourage greater use of facts in the daily work of management and their employees. Simply stated, it continues to become ever cheaper to collect data about the world that managers can use. This is caused by automation of data collection (e.g., use of scanners and measuring instrumentation), better software to transport information to computers and then to process and analyze the data, and cheaper digital storage devices. The nature of data is also changing, from the tables of ordered numbers of old to more heterogeneous collections of current information presented in graphical and other visual formats. The ugly side of this trend, however, is that as the volume and scale of digitally stored information expand so too does the difficulty in extracting meaning from it. In turn, that situation leads to further use of software tools to simulate, analyze, and present results.

Computer scientists conducting research on database management tools and techniques understand perfectly well the continuing need to have new ways of identifying significant changes, exposing patterns, and discovering relationships. For trends, managers want to understand what is changing from what they knew before; for pattern analysis, it is to describe realities against some template or worldview; and for the discovery of relationships that make clearer combinations of parts and wholes, much as is occurring in the study of informatics and biology. In all three instances, management and their employees have to use structured and unstructured data.

It seems that to make things more complex, data also has to be more verbose. The amount of useful information available over the Internet, for example, is almost beyond reasonable comprehension. This circumstance means managers must spend more time finding, organizing, and studying data, then putting it in forms useful to them and their staffs by doing "data measurement," what MIT economist Erik Brynjolfsson once called "the modern equivalent of the microscope."[28] It is why so many computer scientists at places such as IBM or at the School of Informatics at Indiana University, to mention just two, are developing or conducting research on text mining and database management tools to aid people in their hunt for trends, patterns, and relationships. It has been a process of organizing data underway since the 1950s and which shows no signs of slowing. It would be hard to find another research topic that has been as consistently active as this one; it is also one of the least publicized of all.[29]

Even the way management looks increasingly at the process by which technology or information is gathered and used has come under the umbrella of formal, structural schema. Figure 1.1 is an example drawn from the work of a group of computer scientists which displays a model of a technology landscape. This figure documents the development of specific technologies over a year-long period, and attempts to define a trajectory for the development of other technologies, in this case within the rapidly transforming world of biotechnology and pharmaceuticals. We do not need to go into a detailed analysis of the model, simply to call out the fact that modeling, even of the tools management uses, is now part of the new style of how managers think of their world, closed or open.

Any manager familiar with process reengineering and the techniques of Deming or Juran rely on fishbone diagrams, which they often use to describe the relationships of one data or factor to others. In the days before the use of Powerpoint slides and rigorous engineering-style techniques, a manager might have done a similar analysis of causal effects as an *ad hoc* exercise of applying George Herbert's old poem, "for want of a nail the shoe is lost, for want of a shoe the horse is lost, for want of a horse the rider is lost."

Business professor Andrew McAfee argued correctly that a feature of the modern manager is that he or she has to have the skills with which to control and use information technology in the effective support of their organization's capabilities. He, like so many others, called out the fact that management spends more on IT today per employee than in earlier times. Although thinking largely of the United States, his findings hold true for companies all over the world. There are more IT things one can acquire, for example, making the shopping experience more complex: "It's hard for executives to figure out what all those

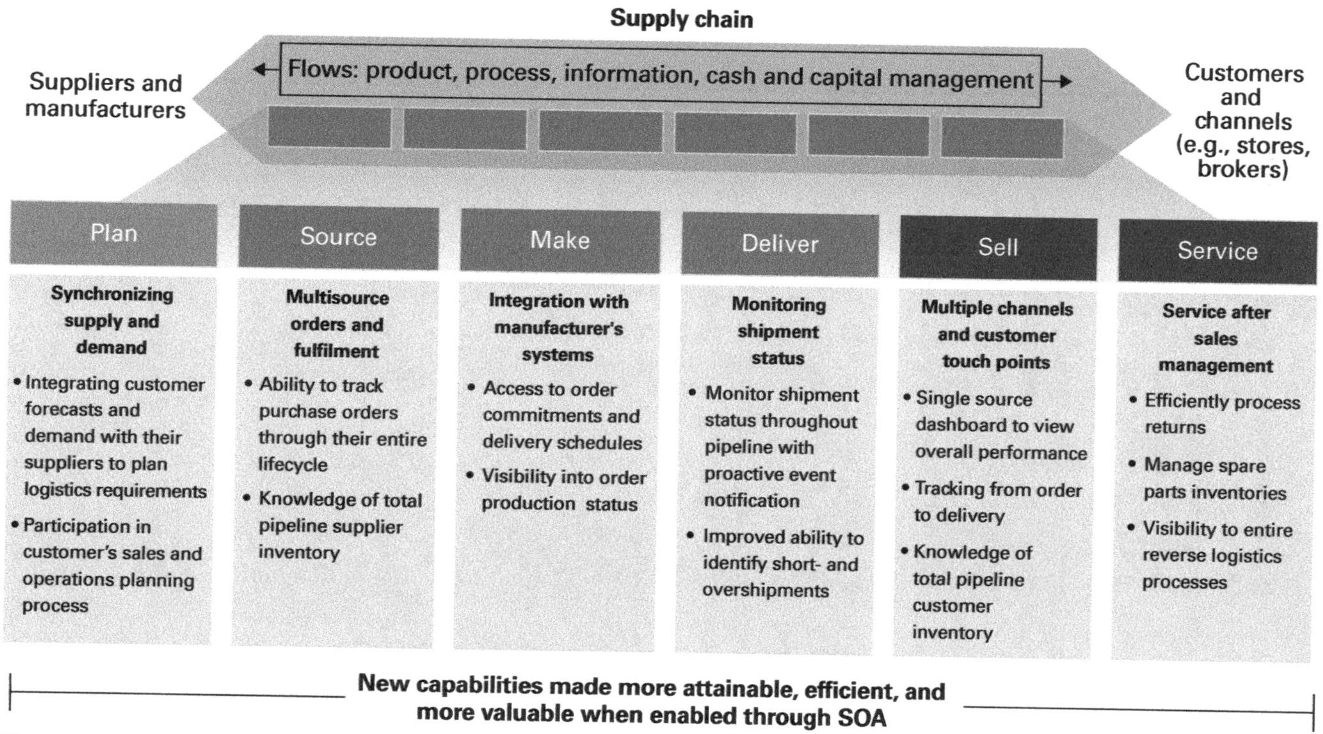

Supply chain

Suppliers and manufacturers

Customers and channels (e.g., stores, brokers)

Flows: product, process, information, cash and capital management

Plan	Source	Make	Deliver	Sell	Service
Synchronizing supply and demand	**Multisource orders and fulfillment**	**Integration with manufacturer's systems**	**Monitoring shipment status**	**Multiple channels and customer touch points**	**Service after sales management**
• Integrating customer forecasts and demand with their suppliers to plan logistics requirements	• Ability to track purchase orders through their entire lifecycle	• Access to order commitments and delivery schedules	• Monitor shipment status throughout pipeline with proactive event notification	• Single source dashboard to view overall performance	• Efficiently process returns
• Participation in customer's sales and operations planning process	• Knowledge of total pipeline supplier inventory	• Visibility into order production status	• Improved ability to identify short- and overshipments	• Tracking from order to delivery	• Manage spare parts inventories
				• Knowledge of total pipeline customer inventory	• Visibility to entire reverse logistics processes

New capabilities made more attainable, efficient, and more valuable when enabled through SOA

Figure 1.1   Model of a supply chain.

systems, applications, and acronyms do, let alone decide which ones they should purchase and how to successfully adopt them."[30] It is a complaint heard since the birth of the computer over a half century ago. But, then it was voiced at conferences and in offices, rarely in print, but now it is discussed as a measure of the increasing importance of the issue.

Now McAfee could publish about the issue in the prestigious *Harvard Business Review*. So, one could not dismiss the lament as some peevish carping. He urged management to look at the installation of IT as part of the process of changing organizations, because of the extensive use of IT, a message relatively new and an admonition relevant to the modern manager. To close out his discussion, McAfee advocates looking at IT as one of the following three types:

- IT executes more efficiently a task than it was possible before (e.g., using word processors, spreadsheets, computer-aided design software, simulation tools).
- It enhances communications among people and organizations (e.g., e-mail, instant messaging, blogs) as these improve collaboration and team work—clearly a cultural and organizational issue involving the style by which management wants to work.
- "Enterprise IT" is used to support and is part of an enterprise's key process (e.g., supply chain management, cloud computing, customer relationship management, EDI).[31]

Observe the managerial style and values at work. He explores the role and importance of simulations, insights, teaming, collaborations, the hunt for value, and not just simply efficiencies—all hallmarks of today's managerial ethos, the contemporary interest in effective (some call best) practices.

Not all is necessarily well, or constant, in this view of managerial practices. The most influential commentators on the role of business opining in the last several decades were strongly in agreement that management was, and is, a profession. From Chandler to Drucker on the academic side, or from Alfred P. Sloan to Jack Welch in management, all spoke about the profession. But, at the same time, there has been an undercurrent of a different sort that aspires to make business practices and management more scientific. Professors in business schools are accused of sacrificing the teaching of practical ways of management in favor of rigorous arcane scientific research on irrelevant issues,[32] while others speak, for example, about "the new *science* of sales force productivity" (my italicization).[33] In the latter case, the rising popularity of data handling tools encourages this thinking: "the data, tools, and analytics that companies are increasingly using to improve their sales forces will not only help top performers shine, but they will also help drive sales force laggards to the middle of the curve."[34] For any reader who has managed a sales force, the message is only partly true as the greater skills needed are the ones recognized decades earlier: leadership, vision, personal communications, sense of urgency, and decision-making with imperfect data. Yet science is fashionable, when in fact, much of what has been described in this chapter is the adoption by management of tools more similar to those of the engineer than to the scientist.[35] The truth is we have much to learn about human behavior and business before we can characterize management as a science.

Yet, increasingly, both sets of practices—engineering and scientific—are directed toward personal and enterprise-wide skills essential to the successful operation of a modern firm; specifically, toward the increased ability of a company to be agile in a variety of ways. Managerial and institutional agility calls for the capability to come up with new products, services, and contractual terms and conditions that meet various market requirements, and to push back competition. Speed in developing and deploying these represent yet other forms of personal and institutional agility.[36] Changing or upgrading internal organizational and personal skills, tools, and technologies is also another way of looking at the whole concept of agility. All of these manifest themselves in the daily work of managers who go about changing (improving) processes, developing new offerings and products, and acquiring, or disposing, of new customers and business partners. In recent years, surveys have suggested that in addition to these forms of agility are others emerging at least as important, such as the ability to redesign how organizations are created, or, how one shapes successful mergers and acquisitions.[37] We devote a whole chapter later to the issue of building today's effective organizations.

Research is increasingly being conducted on the skills needed by managers to operate in these more agile environments. For example, one group at the Sloan Management School identified a set of managerial practices that resonated with experienced managers to such an extent that they are worth summarizing. The ability to articulate a quantifiable business case for such forms of agility as changing organizations and IT, or to optimize core competencies and business modularity (plug-and-play structures), is essential and most closely resemble the skills others have identified over the past century. However, across all of these forms of agility, structured project management skills are essential. In fact, no other body of formal operational skills has become such an integral part of a manager's tool kit over the past 20 years as has project management.

One cannot imagine a manager today aspiring to be a leader with demonstrated results who does not use formal project management skills to one degree or another. These are normally learned in one of four ways: as part of formal education in business and engineering schools at universities, through professional training by employers or industry associations, being a business process consultant, or by implementing processes, normally in collaboration with a services consultancy expert in these techniques. My personal experience would suggest that the third one—on-the-job-training—is the most widely used.[38] So, if insufficiently experienced in the use of project management skills, move into either a job or a project where one picks those up or hire a consultancy to fix an existing process of yours and get involved in the effort.

Another set of skills needed relates to the realities that today's—and tomorrow's managers—need is the ability to be facile in their management of IT. Specifically across all manner of agility, knowing how to create IT architectures, run IT steering committees, integrate IT into processes, set goals and measures of performance relevant to IT, manage funding for such projects, and work comfortably in the establishment of institution-wide standards are now essential core skills, especially for those most responsible for implementing changes in an enterprise or government agency. These skills apply specifically to middle and senior management. This too is a large corpus of tactical skills and managerial practices that are actually even more complex and voluminous than project management. So, while explaining the "how to" details would consume many books, and thus we cannot discuss these here, understanding the context in which they are applied is the subject of Chapter 4 in this book. Again, the purpose is to make a manager aware of a large body of skills, knowledge, and experiences that they must acquire to be successful in the years to come.

After extensively interviewing management around the world, one highly respected business research team reiterated the importance of having well-executed managerial practices involving the creation and operation of processes, establishing guiding principles for enterprise architectures, and general oversight of daily operations. The newest component of the modern manager's skill set is that of enterprise architectures. Put in simple terms, these issues are about change management in an organization. As a rough rule of thumb, the larger the enterprise, the more important one needs such skills. It is an area of management that today is the subject of extensive research by business school professors, economists, business think tanks, consultants, and commentary by senior officials and executives. In the secular vernacular, it is one of "the hot topics" of the day and for good reason. What is new is the combination of creating new organizations within a company in response to changing circumstances using process and project management skills and that leverage new forms of IT, such as the use of social media, market intelligence, and global organizations (either within a company or conjoined to others, such as suppliers and customers).[39]

There is a related change in the way work is done which expands continuously as part of this emerging style of management. It involves the growth in collaboration at ever-lower levels of the enterprise, often called teaming. But it is more than peer workers being told to go solve a problem, work together, and be collectively held accountable for their results. That paradigm of teaming has now been around for several decades. Rather, the emerging changes involves increasing numbers of organizations participating in a teaming activity, increases in authority to bring about substantive changes, or to get the daily work done involving receiving something from another department or firm, performing an action, and then forwarding their *outputs* (another IT term in management's vocabulary) on to another group (team) of people inside or outside their organization. There is, as a result, a massive increase in the requirement for building consensus and implementing collaborative behaviors. At one time that might have been the responsibility of higher level managers negotiating protocols between departments or divisions, senior leaders in universities, or elected public officials, but now this occurs at all levels of management. Employees too are expected to exercise authority and influence, and that skill requires building relationships, presenting one's case well, being socially affable, and networking well across an enterprise. In short, at all levels of an enterprise, polished behavior and acceptance of a considerable amount of personal responsibility is required, even when authority is not formally granted to an individual.

Case studies might make for interesting reading but may not necessarily be useful on this point because each individual has a unique situation. Management success has always depended on a few people saying "I know how to fix this problem" and then they go ahead and form a group of friends, volunteers, or employees that go do something. And they stick with it until resolved, making sure they communicate up and down the organization to keep everyone happy and to increasingly get the resources they need. One example helps, however. At one point, Volkswagen decided to stop manufacturing Beetle that had been the iconic product of the firm for decades, largely because it was impossible to manufacture cost-effectively and they had to meet various regulatory requirements. So it was dropped from the product line. A group of VW engineers decided to secretly design a modern version of the car, eventually got a member of the board of the firm to find financial assistance for further work, and eventually brought the new design to senior leadership, with appropriate pre-selling of the ideas, of course, and got approval for the manufacture of what is now the current Beetle. It became a highly successful product! Success came from personal commitment, good design skills, excellent communication and political skills too, and a willingness to work nights and weekends on something important.[40] Most efforts are not so dramatic, but they share the same requirements of commitment, energy, and effective workmanship.

Weaving webs out of seemingly nothing in some instances is often a good analogy of what is called for in all manner of management. Even generals have a difficult time ordering people to do things. U.S. Secretary of Defense Donald H. Rumsfeld in the early 2000s faced stiff resistance at all levels of his department when he tried to implement (read, dictate, or force) fundamental reforms; even sergeants and junior officers fought fundamental cultural changes.[41] The CEO at even highly disciplined IBM has to persuade 450,000 employees to do her bidding, because many could consider ignoring her wishes largely because they live in such a large ecosystem (IBM) that she cannot arbitrarily command and control everyone. So, her effectiveness is highly dependent on how well she exercises leadership through the hierarchy, of course, but also by leveraging the corporation's culture, its style. This reality takes us back to a point made by Drucker, but which must be executed so extensively today all up and down any corporate organization. Ordering change is no longer the normally effective style of modern management. Indeed, it may take longer to get something done that way than to take the time to "sell" employees on an approach. While almost every recently published management book argues that young employees must be persuaded to do things and that Boomer employees remain loyal to organizations and work hard, the fact is most employees of any age want to be persuaded, want to understand why they are being asked to do something, and want more elbow room to get their work done than might have been the case for any age employee as recently as the mid-1990s.

Scholars and management experts have yet to explain adequately causes for today's renewal of leadership and collaboration as exercised, but one can be identified and that is the power of teams working within processes that may, or may not, be fully aligned with how enterprises are organized.[42] Essentially, all parts of an enterprise have undergone the process of the most important and expensive or labor intensive work of being systematized and put into defined processes. From product development through manufacturing and distribution, the notion of supply chains has become common fair. In fact, today, of all the collections of non-accounting/financial work, the supply chain is probably the most structured, organized, and process-centric. Figure 1.1 illustrates a high-level contemporary model of a supply chain. Similar models could be exhibited to illustrate that all departments within an enterprise have such views of their work. Note that in Figure 1.1, supply chains are routinely seen to extend outside a corporation's boundaries, a point made earlier in this chapter, but worth repeating because where a firm begins and ends has become increasingly fuzzy since the late 1980s. What is subtle, yet clear, is that once managers begin looking at their organizations to see work through this near-Newtonian lens (*machina*), that is to say, as if parts making up the greater whole (firm), it is not such a leap in logic to see them measuring the cost of doing the work of pieces of the chain themselves and comparing those expenses to what some other firm might be able to do. So the whole notion of "plug-and-play" logically next becomes a reasonable view to take of how to put together a business or to optimize current or desired work.[43]

As management began viewing work this way, it became more possible to expect that the tasks within a process could increasingly be standardized and, thus, be eligible for comparison to those of other firms. This examination, routinely called benchmarking by the 1980s, reinforced the notion of commoditization of many work tasks. Such thinking (and practices) was buttressed further by the growing availability of software in support of a supply chain that once created, caused a user to do things in a certain way, and that way being similar to those of many other firms that installed the same software. Financial and human resource planning tools, normally called ERP (Enterprise Resource Planning) became one of the most widely installed software tools in the 1990s that were not part of the Internet. Customer Resource Management (CRM) packages emerged as another similar cluster of software products that began standardization of this class of activity and led to some commoditization of sales work in the early 2000s. Marketing and strategy groups also used CRM packages. The same occurred in finance, accounting, tax administration, and human resource management. While media around the world has long focused on various "computer revolutions" that happen, medium- and large-sized companies were quietly going about disciplining great swaths of their work, using ERP, CRM, and other software. They spent billions of dollars to organize work so extensively that one has to go back to the 1910s–1930s to find a period of comparable structuring of tasks.[44] At that earlier time, it was to leverage the new thinking about mass production and Taylorist organization of firms, assets, work, and people.

The issues related to how the new style of management functions lead quickly to several key actions that senior management should foster in their organizations (both public and private), and that managers at all levels personally should embrace and learn to do. They essentially boil down to three criteria and are as follows:

- Understand the power of agility, learn to use how to implement it in all that you do, and then measure results.
- Treat all work as projects embedded in processes. That means formal planning, setting targets, measuring results, and doing post-project reviews to learn from these.
- Collaborate using more than just teaming and good social behavior, such as social media tools and processes (particularly crowd sourcing methods) and the enormous variety of analytical software tools now so convenient to use.

When you see managers work in these three ways, you know the emerging *style* of management is being practiced.

IMPLICATIONS FOR MANAGEMENT

If you are an executive or manager, or aspire to be one someday, recognize that the profession of management continues to evolve, to acquire new bodies of practices, and to be complicated by myriad issues of globalization, localization, and the rapid transformation of business conditions and evolving forms of public administration. Every profession in modern times has undergone periods of rapid transformation, and it appears management has entered one of those periods. Peter Drucker codified much of what was accepted as sound managerial practices, largely in the 1970s and 1980s, yet since then new findings and circumstances have, in effect, added to his collection. For managers that means more things to take into consideration, additional skills to acquire, new directions to take their departments, agencies, enterprises, governments, industries, and in the case of emerging economies, whole nations.

But, let us sum up a key point made in this chapter. The new style of management that the managers will live with in the next decade or more has already arrived. For those who seek new revelations, or revolutions, my apologies, but the main lines of development are apparent, and only individual events, shocks to a business routine practices if you will, are unpredictable and will have positive and negative effects. 9/11 and the Great Recession were shocks, but even such major events did not fundamentally alter the new style of management that began earlier. To be sure, they slowed or expanded trade, regulatory activities, for example, or have little or no effect on some practices, such as the use of mobile communications, cloud computing, and greater reliance on "big data" analytics. But, there are qualitative changes underway, so let us summarize the most obvious ones:

- More topics and situations to stay current about than even a decade ago
- Greater collaboration with customers, colleagues, and suppliers, which will become even more the case
- Important shifts in the use of computing with more analytics, cloud computing, ubiquitous sensors, and data collection
- Probably less work in large organizations and more work in smaller enterprises, leading to a more complex and diverse career than forecasters thought even a decade ago

- Greater need for personal brands, hence less personal ties to one enterprise's identity
- Massively larger markets to work with as over a billion new members of the middle class has started spending, and another billion babies will be born in the next decade
- Africa, all of Latin America, and today's poor half of Asia have started competing well against your company
- Evolutionary changes occur in how the new generation of political leaders run China and possibly continued dysfunction in Indian public administration in a nation that will have close to a half billion members of the middle class
- As much as one-third or more of Africa finally comes "online" as more than just a horribly mismanaged, dangerous, and poor part of the world that is only valuable for raw materials or as a chaotic market in which to sell energy and to be supplied with the world's charitable largesse.

So, while this book will read as if very little has changed, do not be fooled. As our list suggests, the evolutions as opposed to the revolutions, will continue, creating daily angst for many managers. But the trajectory of their profession is clearly visible. The key to one's success is tied closely to understanding as many of its characteristics as is possible to identify.

Because of this changing agenda, the rest of this book introduces managers to a number of issues that they should take into consideration for them to succeed at their work. It is why we turn next to address the fundamental role of information and its technologies—computing and communications—followed by a discussion about the enormous role of industries in combination with technologies. With those notions clearly present in one's thinking, we then turn our attention to the management of organizations—what most managers spend almost all their time on—set within this broader context of technologies and global industries. Then the reader is exposed to emerging economic and business realities in which their actions, the role of technologies, and the functions of whole industries can be better understood. While suggestions and questions to consider are raised in each chapter, a series of recommendations and implications are offered throughout and in Chapter 6.

Management is continuing to become more professional, more complex, fact-based, and subtle. It is being buffeted by the enormous churn of international economic development in the period of human history that is more *turbulent* (Peter Drucker's word) by the long-term political events following the end of the Cold War and more immediately by the consequences of the Great Recession and the transformation of Asian economies. As one becomes a more senior manager, the more they will need to understand and participate in the shaping of whole industries, national economies, and possibly the fate of the human race. That expanding set of duties exceeds what was required of them in earlier decades. The connected world is no longer a concept; it is a rapidly emerging reality. The rest of this book is aimed at identifying what management will need to know and do. So, the first piece of advice to management is "learn widely about what is going on in your industry and the world at large, and get in the habit of studying your profession in an organized and routine way."

Prior experiences are no longer adequate; in fact, they might mislead you. The features of changes already underway indicate that the future has already arrived to a certain extent, because trends unfold slower than specific events at different speeds from one industry to another, and from one nation to another. Individual events create the sense of chaos and uncertainty that leads managers to want forecasts, but broad trends provide a certain amount of certainty about what needs to be done. That is the power of sound appreciation of some history, embracing an historical perspective of what has happened and is unfolding, understanding the evolution and use of technologies, grounding in some basic economics, and equipped with a healthy supply of skepticism about the wisdom of business fads. This advise is complicated by the fact that the art of management continues to move toward the profession of management, a profession based more on sound principles of proven policies and tasks, informed by deeper insights about the minds of humans, use of myriad technologies (not just IT), and evolving economics and public administration that should be both understood and be taken seriously. Truth and insight lie all around us, the challenge is to separate it from fad and fantasy. Every reader will look back some day and be shocked at the amount of change they experienced, but a lesson to take away is that they will experience thousands of evolutions and possibly no revolutions.

Since managers operate in complex commercial ecosystems called enterprises that are not monolithic but more like cities with communities of interest, routinely made up of information worlds and, it is to that environment that we turn to in Chapter 2.

NOTES

1 Peter F. Drucker, *Managing in Turbulent Times* (New York: Harper & Row, 1980): 5.

2 Peter Cappelli and Monika Hamori, "The New Road to the Top," *Harvard Business Review* 83, no. 1 (January 2005): 25–32.

3 Jeffrey Pfeffer and Robert I. Sutton, *Hard Facts, Half-Truths and Total Nonsense: Profiting from Evidence-Based Management* (Boston, MA: Harvard Business School Press, 2006): 3–28.

4 Reconfirmed through a global survey in 2007 of over 400 organizations in 40 countries, IBM Global Business Services, *Unlocking the DNA of the Adaptable Workforce: The Global Human Capital Study 2008* (Somers, NY: IBM Corporation, 2007) and in nearly a half dozen subsequent surveys conducted over the next several years, all available at http://www-935.ibm.com/services/us/gbs/bus/html/2008ghcs. html (last accessed September 15, 2013).

5 Alfred D. Chandler, Jr., *The Visible Hand: The Managerial Revolution in American Business* (Cambridge, MA: Harvard University Press, 1977): 3, 8–9.

6 Steve Denning, "A New Center of Gravity for Management?," *Forbes*, November 18, 2013, available at http://www.forbes.com/sites/stevedenning/2013/11/18/a-new-center-of-gravity-for-management/ (last accessed December 15, 2013).

7 Described by Paul N. Edwards, *The Closed World: Computers and the Politics of Discourse in Cold War America* (Cambridge, MA: MIT Press, 1996).

8 As an example of continuing change, however, Japan and even China now are beginning to outsource fabrication and manufacturing work to other economies that have less expensive labor forces than even they do, most notably Vietnam, Philippines, and Indonesia.

9 The discussion is largely led by the U.S. military which, after China's, is the largest set of uniformed services in the world; David S. Alberts, John J. Garstka, and Frederick P. Stein, *Network Centric Warfare: Developing and Leveraging Information Superiority*, 2nd ed. (Washington, DC: U.S. Department of Defense, Command and Control Research Program, 2003).

10 The word covers refers to the metal shell of a computer within which are the components of the machine. Think of the cover as analogous to the metal outer body of an automobile.

11 The subject of language has been studied frequently regarding IT slang, but not the migration of such language into that of management in general. Management literature has largely ignored the issue, including those authors examining knowledge management and communities of practice.

12 Robert E. Cole, *Managing Quality Fads: How American Business Learned to Play the Quality Game* (New York: Oxford University Press, 1998); James W. Cortada, *21st Century Business: Managing and Working in the New Digital Economy* (Upper Saddle River, NJ: Financial Times/Prentice Hall, 2001): 51–134.

13 The phrase was created by James Champy and Michael Hammer, *Reengineering the Corporation: A Manifesto for Business* (New York: Harper, 1992).

14 Historians have yet to study the history of processes, reengineering, and the quality management movement, but for an early attempt at describing these, see Robert E.

Cole, *Managing Quality Fads: How American Business Learned to Play the Quality Game* (New York: Oxford University Press, 1999).

15 For a book-length description of these quality management terms, which have become so much part of modern management's vocabulary, James W. Cortada and John Woods, *McGraw-Hill Quality Terms and Concepts* (New York: McGraw-Hill, 1995).

16 There has long also existed disagreements about the nature of this training, Rakesh Khurana, *From Higher Aims to Hired Hands: The Social Transformation of American Business Schools and the Unfulfilled Promise of Management as a Profession* (Princeton, NJ: Princeton University Press, 2007).

17 On personal note, I belong to a group of about 100 experienced managers and entrepreneurs in Madison, Wisconsin, called the Merlin Group, which provides pro bono mentoring to startup entrepreneurs, most of whom are under the age of 40. The successful entrepreneurs invariably have arrived at what they want to do through tacit knowledge or "gut feel," both in terms of what they want to offer and the value proposition involved.

18 Ian Ayres, *Super Crunchers: Why Thinking-By-Numbers Is the New Way to Be Smart* (New York: Bantam, 2007).

19 Thomas H. Davenport and Jeanne G. Harris, *Competing on Analytics: The New Science of Winning* (Boston, MA: Harvard Business School Press, 2007): 7.

20 One of the earliest of the widely-used studies on process improvement and management was by Thomas H. Davenport, *Process Innovation: Reengineering Work through Information Technology* (Boston, MA: Harvard Business School Press, 1993).

21 In fact, there is now a growing backlash within the world of economics by some who argue they have all gone too far in the use of mathematics and elegant econometric models, drifting away from the reality of their field. For an example of the push back and the move to a more narrative view of economics, see Economics Nobel Laureate Douglas C. North, *Understanding the Process of Economic Change* (Princeton, NJ: Princeton University Press, 2005), especially pp. viii–x, 70–71.

22 Almost every industry has a trade association that publishes a magazine. These are often some of the best sources for new trends on the use of computing in one's industry, appearing as often as once a month. Another useful source is the IEEE Computer Society's flagship magazine, *Computer*, written by IT experts but accessible by non-computing managers.

23 Reasons vary, but usually larger firms could offer higher salaries, larger opportunities to increase income, medical and other benefits, and more job security.

24 Peter Cappelli et al., *Change at Work: How American Industry and Workers Are Coping with Corporate Restructuring and What Workers Must Do to Take Charge of Their Own Careers* (New York: Oxford University Press, 1997).

25 For a recent example of this kind of criticism, see Anne Fisher, "The Trouble With MBAs," *Fortune*, April 23, 2007, available at http://money.cnn.com/magazines/fortune/fortune_archive/2007/04/30/8405397/index.htm?cnn=yes (last accessed November 24, 2008).

26 Discussed in considerable detail in two books by Richard Florida, *The Rise of the Creative Class: And How It's Transforming Work, Leisure, Community and Everyday Life* (New York: Basic Books, 2002) and *The Flight of the Creative Class: The New Global Competition for Talent* (New York: Harper Business, 2005).

27 Brian Lee-Archer, Chris Brailey, Marc Le Noir, and Oliver Ziehm, *For the Sake of the Global Economy: Social Protection for the Migrant Worker* (Somers, NY: IBM Corporation, 2007), available at http://www-935.ibm.com/services/us/index.wss/ibvstudy/gbs/a1028559?cntxt=a1005266 (last accessed November 7, 2011).

28 Quoted by Sue Halpern, "Are We Puppets in a Wired World?" *New York Review of Books*, November 7, available at http://www.nybooks.com/articles/archives/2013/nov/07/are-we-puppets-wired-world/ (last accessed December 19, 2013).

29 Eric Siegel, *Predictive Analytics: The Power to Predict Who Will Click, Buy, Lie, or Die* (New York: John Wiley & Sons, 2013); Viktor Mayer-Schönberger and Kenneth Cukier, *Big Data: A Revolution That Will Transform How We Live, Work, and Think* (Boston, MA: Eamon Dolan/Houghton Mifflin Harcourt, 2013).

30 Andrew McAfee, "Mastering the Three Worlds of Information Technology," *Harvard Business Review* 84, no. 11 (November 2006): 141–142.

31 Ibid., 141–149.

32 For a recent criticism of training of business students and the narrowing of business professors' research agendas, see Rakesh Khurana, *From Higher Aims to Hired Hands: The Social Transformation of American Business Schools and the Unfulfilled Promise of Management as a Profession* (Princeton, NJ: Princeton University Press, 2007).

33 Dianne Ledingham, Marc Kovac, and Heidi Locke Simon, "The New Science of Sales Force Productivity," *Harvard Business Review* 84, no. 9 (September 2006): 124–133.

34 Ibid., 124.

35 Jeffrey Pfeffer and Robert I. Sutton, "Evidence-Based Management," *Harvard Business Review* 84, no. 1 (January 2006): 63–74.

36 The concept of business value derived from doing things more quickly has been understood since at least the 1980s. The classic practitioner's study on this theme, and that is as urgently relevant today as when published, is George Stalk, Jr. and Thomas M. Hout, *Competing Against Time* (New York: Free Press, 1990).

37 Ross, *Research Findings on IT and Business Agility*; IBM Global Business Services, *Expanding the Innovation Horizon: CEO Study 2006* (Somers, NY: IBM Corporation, 2006), available at http://www.ibm.com/services/us/gbs/bus/pdf/ceostudy.pdf (last accessed November 7, 2012).

38 I spent 20 years either participating in projects or applying formal project management methods inside of IBM and within several dozen organizations in various industries, as much teaching employees how to use such tools and methods as applying them to redesign and implement new business processes.

39 Ross, J. W., *Research Findings on IT and Business Agility*, unpublished white paper, circa 2006.

40 David Kiley, *Getting the Bugs Out: The Rise, Fall, and Comeback of the Volkswagen in America* (New York: John Wiley & Sons, 2001).

41 A problem shared by every one of his predecessors and so well described by the department's own senior historians, Roger R. Trask and Alfred Goldberg, *The Department of Defense 1947–1997: Organization and Leaders* (Washington, DC: U.S. Government Printing Office, 1997).

42 The issue has been with management for some time, Joseph L. Bower and Clark G. Gilbert, "How Managers' Everyday Decisions Create or Destroy Your Company's Strategy," *Harvard Business Review* 85, no. 2 (February 2007): 73–79.

43 Susanne Berger, *How We Compete: What Companies Around the World Are Doing to Make It in Today's Global Economy* (New York: Currency, 2005): 57–90.

44 One might think that the Y2K initiatives of the late 1990s would have been the driving force behind implementation of so many of these systems; however, installation of these began over a decade before Y2K remediation initiatives began in earnest. The earlier efforts had little to do with Y2K and were taken on because of the potential economic benefits they offered a firm.

CHAPTER 2

When Management Confronts Information Ecosystems

In guessing the direction of technology it is wise to ask who is in the best position to profit most.

Ben H. Bagdikian, 1971

The issue at hand is not about the whole industries that were built on IT, such as computer vendors in the United States, manufacturers of computer chips all over Asia, or software support services in Russia and India. The total population of managers at IBM, Microsoft, Google, and several thousand other IT firms around the world is small, roughly several percentages of the total workforces of these firms. The real issue is about you and the tens of millions of managers who use their products—users—who have so much computing that, like electricity and air conditioning, makes IT ubiquitous. It is everywhere and in everything. As a manager you must know a great deal about IT, not just about your industry or your company's use of the technology. Today's manager must understand several things and keep updating that understanding:

The Essential Manager: How to Thrive in the Global Information Jungle, First Edition. James W. Cortada.

- How technology changes and what the consequences are of those changes. That does not mean being a computer scientist, but when *Wired* magazine points out a step change, they have to pay attention, as occurred when copper in computer chips made clunky mobile phones of the late 1980s instantly shrink to pocket-sized devices that could hold data.

- How your industry as a whole uses IT because it is all aimed at both making a profit and devastating your company. Industry standards are important to appreciate, changing telecommunications regulations and how governments are supporting their favorite local industries with IT support.

- How computing can help support your company's fundamental business strategy, your value add, and your go-to-market tactics. Do your sales come from phone banks (now Internet-based), from B2B face-to-face sales, or retail operations? Each requires very different uses of IT, and each of these collections of IT need to be understood as they are all constantly changing.

- How IT affects your corporate culture—the way people act and what they do—because technology can speed up or retard innovation and innovation remains one of the most important sources of new products revenues and competitive advantages in a period of churn such as we are living in today.

In short, IT is a secret sauce that spices up performance or that over-salts everything. So, to repeat advice from Chapter 1, watch for the patterns, understand the context (usually history and current economic conditions), and then the features of an IT will make a great deal more sense than the flash and buzz of a new device. So, let us begin with a bit more history for context.

In the early 1950s, the transformation to the emerging business climate described in this book began when General Electric installed the first computer to do commercial work, that is to say, the work of a profit-driven company, in this case a manufacturing plant's accounting, inventory, and manufacturing planning. Until then all computers had been experimental and were used by government agencies, scientists, and universities. Management worldwide took notice; the *Harvard Business Review* and other journals covered the event. It was supposed to have been the Nuclear Age, thanks to dropping atomic bombs at the end of World War II just 5 years earlier, but now, maybe not; maybe it was going to be the Computer Age. The event had a clear WOW effect, very impressive. Up to then there were barely several dozen systems in the world. Managers in the private sector acquired them now to automate accounting and clerical functions and incrementally to help with inventory control. By the end of the 1970s, every large corporation in the world used computers, so too most mid-sized firms, or rented time on one at a service bureau. Applications of this technology spread rapidly from accounting and inventory control to production management in manufacturing, marketing, and order processing in the distribution sector; case and policy management in insurance to some fairly expanded account management; and order processing in the brokerage business. Systems went online in the 1970s; PCs came rapidly into the corporate world in the 1980s to such an extent that their combined computing power often exceeded that of large company data centers by the end of this decade. It seemed everyone had a network and the nature of work was visibly changing; it was obvious to management at all levels.

In the early 1990s, the Internet next spread rapidly and by the end of 1998—the year by which much new software had appeared that could protect files and financial transactions from hackers routinely usurping data—it seemed everyone had a presence on the Web. Over half the corporations in the United States and an estimated 25–35% in Western Europe did too. The experience of using the Internet at work is within the living memory of almost 65% of all workers and managers in the advanced economies of the West, North America, and some parts of Asia and Latin America.[1] In short, one would be hard pressed to find any class of technology that spread so quickly across so many firms and economies as did digital technologies and their accompanying telecommunications. Adoption grew dramatically, beginning in the 1970s, as managers began merging together computing and telecommunications. One consequence was that by the end of the 1980s, hardly any function in any moderate or large-sized company functioned without some reliance on computers. By the end of that decade, major chunks of work (and even some minor decision-making) were now done increasingly with computers. "Intelligent" robots in the 1990s and 2000s defused bombs and explored accidents in mines, while other software programs interacted with people in automated telephone systems. Another Cold War development, GPS, made available to the public in the 1990s and is now being applied in business. Amazon announced in December 2013, for example, that it planned to use drones in the future to deliver packages; that would be impossible without the existence of GPS, nor could you drive conveniently in a strange city without it barking out instructions. IT changes in work practices was becoming significantly more radical in affecting the roles of management.

So, today's managers work in an environment so densely filled with IT that they must deal with all manner of technologies as a regular part of their work. Knowing more about how that happened—indeed, still happens—helps them appreciate the features of their work environment that in turn assists them to shape the work they do for the purposes they intend.

To help managers with this ongoing unfolding of changes affected by IT is the role of this chapter. To do that we look at how IT changes, then quickly move to an overview of causes the work of managers to change. It is important to understand why, so we immediately plunge into a short "So What" conversation before moving to the more substantive discussion about opportunities and competitive practices involving IT. If you are in middle management or higher, you have to deal with the roles of knowledge management (KM), innovation, and corporate culture, so we discuss those. But, everyone has to pay attention to industries as they have a profound influence on how you deal with computing—a recurring issue we come back to several times in this book—then we examine what economists and academics are learning about the best uses of IT, since they largely come at the topic from both an enterprise or industry perspective.

After a heavy dose of context, I discuss several IT developments to watch out for in the next few years on the assumption that they will affect your work as a manager, such as the greater use of drones, robots, and wearable computing. How to look at new technologies is a critical skill to have. As with all our chapters, this one ends with a short wrap up and discussion of implications for management in general.

HOW INFORMATION TECHNOLOGY CHANGES CAME ABOUT

These trends crept up incrementally, almost stealth-like. Managers normally made small, frequent decisions on how to use computers to solve a problem here and another there, to automate some activity and then link incrementally an automated task to another, thereby creating a system, such as in accounting, finance, or in order processing. Over time, these systems grew in scope. But each time an incremental use came into being, how work was done changed, if ever so slightly. The next decision about a change was based on the fact that a computer was now doing something it had not done earlier, resulting in the consequence of the next decision proving cumulative. Reaching a third sequential decision, a manager based that one on the circumstances created by the implementation of the second decision. Rather quickly consequences accumulated, making it impossible to retreat back to a prior way of doing business. Just as it was impossible to abandon electricity and motors in a mass production factory for a return to steam-driven belts and expensive craft skills, so too managers incrementally, yet irreversibly, changed the world they worked in and how they interacted with computers and all manner of activities. This is essentially the notion of path dependency in practice today. It is the constant incremental changes always underway that shape the nature of managerial work. That is both how IT affects our world and why paying attention to new IT is so important, and yet so difficult to do.

This situation is made even more difficult by the fact that subtle forms of change show no signs of slowing; rather, they appear to be increasing, during good and bad economic times. We know this because the volume of installations of software and hardware continues to accelerate as new systems are invented and deployed by ever increasing numbers of organizations. We also are increasingly coming to understand this transformation because surveys done in the 1990s–2010s tracking increasing percent of management's budgets going to IT, while the cost of hardware and software products kept declining, in fact, have for over 60 years.[2] No manager does this without the expectation of real returns, such as lower operating costs, improved quality of products and services, introduction of new products and services, increased market share, and so forth. While economists debated the "productivity paradox" in the late 1990s and early 2000s,[3] managers caused the IT industry to grow to over $2 trillion in sales per year. There was no revolution, rather a massive number of rapid evolutions.[4]

With so much hardware and software installed, and with over a half century of this pattern well documented, managers and observers of IT are beginning to learn more deeply how technology affects operations of departments and divisions within firms, and the work of management and senior executives. Several trends critical to the successful performance of firms evident today are by-products of prior cumulative consequences of IT implementations.

An escalating trend most evident within the largest firms worldwide has been the shift from conducting business largely within one national market to an environment involving transactions in multiple countries. Think of this shift as having been made from closed business ecosystems to open networked business ecosystems, facilitated by a variety of factors. Firms went from vertically highly integrated enterprises of the 1970s and 1980s, in which they often made all their own products and serviced them, to what came to be fashionably called "multi-firm value nets," which essentially means that management held internally core competencies but relied increasingly on business partners and others to make, deliver, sell, and service their offerings in multiple countries.[5] Their MO (*modus operandi*) shifted from classical "plan and push" programs in highly hierarchical organizations to collaborative models of behavior characterized more by "pull" strategies in which demand drove activities. In such changed circumstances, organizations flatten in structure as responsibilities for decisions drifts lower and outward in an enterprise toward those able to create demand. This also means employees, divisions of firms, and their business partners moved increasingly to self-organized forms of structures and, of course, diffused around the world.[6] There are no signs that such forms of organizational behavior are going away; IT has facilitated these kinds of structural ways of organizing and doing work. Let us now dig a bit deeper.

HOW MANAGERS USE COMPUTING TO CHANGE THEIR WORK

What happens to the daily work of managers and employees, that is to say, within work processes? There had been enormous emphasis by management since the 1980s to integrate more intimately all manner of activities within a firm, in effect, hardwiring many functions into tightly redesigned work processes that may or may not have included business partners. The most obvious example was the tight integration of supply chains during the last two decades of the twentieth century. At the same time, however, a new trend emerged in which management began to view various parts of their enterprises as components—think of children's building blocks—that they could put together with those of other firms to create new supply chains or value nets. This view exhibits two characteristics: they are reasonably modular, hence reconfigurable at speeds not possible as recently as the 1990s, and one could hunt for appropriately skilled labor around the world to populate these increasingly modular value nets. In short, firms could move away from being highly dependent on labor pools in a few countries to larger sources of workers around the world. Whereas that global capability was limited to 20 or more countries as recently as 2000, now one can speak about applying that modular approach to over 150 countries and, as a quite recent development, to all continents, most notably now to big chunks of Africa.

Acquiring employees could happen quickly. For example, in 2002, IBM had only 3,000 employees in India. By early 2007, there were over 53,000 and nearly double that number a few years later, making India the largest home of employees of the firm. These Indian employees included PhDs in computer science, business and IT consultants, software programmers, call center workers, and sales personnel. IBM also had Indian general manager–level executives responsible for activities extending around the world.[7] The same pattern of using Indian workers was evident in many other firms, such as Google and Microsoft, which had increased their presence in the region as well.

The information technology profile of this trend shifted as well over time and, indeed, nothing described in the previous paragraph could have been possible without changes in how IT functioned. Specifically, in the 1960s through the 1980s, most IT systems reflected the construct of the closed highly integrated business in that systems were proprietary, supported individual divisions (often called silos then and now), and hardly extended outside of the enterprise. When they did, it was often as a function that gave a supplier access to an existing internal system, such as what American automobile manufacturers gave to their suppliers of components. They made available to suppliers views of data on the design of new vehicles and production schedules and plans at the factory level so that these vendors could design and deliver parts and sub-assemblies on time to the right plant.[8] By the end of the 1990s there began to appear the early inklings of a new way of using IT, one based on open standards, interoperable software tools, and that could be installed and integrated into those of other corporations. Those tools made links between suppliers and manufacturers more interdependent and closer, blurring corporate boundaries while continuing the longer term historical shift of managerial responsibilities toward a model in which the work of managers was shared and dispersed across a group of companies now dependent on each other for success.[9]

With the use of social media tools today, customers and employees get in on the act. At Ford Motor Company and at American Express, for example, customers play an active online role in articulating their needs and desires, in effect "voting" on decisions. By assessing performance, more activities can be taken seriously by management. Movie directors occasionally do the same by selecting from alternative endings posted to their websites for viewers to judge; in some instances, viewers propose their own. Eli Lilly, the pharmaceutical company, posts to the Internet research problems, soliciting the help of anyone interested in proposing solutions. Open systems and social media are now being extensively used by city governments around the world to engage citizens in local decisions, deliver services, and promote voluntarism. Such tools and methods are extending the scope of management's role in coordinating the activities of many in highly connected ways.

SO WHAT?

This wonderfully obnoxious question draws our attention to the value of such behavior on the part of managers. A student of historic trends of various technologies over the past several centuries, Carlota Perez, argued convincingly that the period in which management now works is one where existing IT is being deployed to fill in the use of computing into all kinds of daily operations of businesses. So what? She contends that several clearly discernable behaviors are emerging.[10] First, managers are experimenting with myriad novel business models. The most obvious to all are the Internet only–based companies of the 1990s and early 2000s, such as E-Bay or Google, and today the 300,000 plus "app" providers creating services accessible through our smart phones. The integrated enterprise about which we have more to say throughout this book represents a second trend recognizable today. Perez and others demonstrated that use of IT and innovative corporate structures began a long period of sustained growth and creation of real value in the 1990s, a point made by many economists.[11] One head of the U.S. Federal Reserve Board, Alan Greenspan, opined in 2007 that between globalization, which gave firms access to inexpensive labor, and the use of technologies in general more intensively, inflation could be expected to dampen for the foreseeable future, a trend reinforced by the Great Recession which suppressed salaries and demand for goods and services.[12] We now know that this trend began a decade earlier in the 1990s.[13] In a seemingly contradictory trend, when implementing technology to fill out whole industries, a shift is occurring in the use of production capital as managers continued their search for cost efficiencies simultaneously with their hunt for new sources of profit.

A long accepted notion is that one cannot overemphasize the importance of profit, as it is the most basic of incentives for any form of capitalist economic business activity. It is more precious than revenue. It continues to affect the value of stocks (along with growth in revenue), hence rewards management and investors can expect from a firm. But the wisdom of this idea gets challenged from time to time. During the late 1990s, for example, it was widely believed that startup Dot-com companies needed market share more than profits, so as to insure a flow of profits at some future date; many went out of business before they could reach that future state. Firms and consultants hype the prospects of profits, but how real are they? For example, since 2008, the infusion of money at low interest rates into national economies by governments fueled a great deal of profits, including the increase in the paper value of our personal stock portfolios. Financial engineering is one result of this activity, puffing up balance sheets to reflect increasing profits while top line revenue growth or the increase in transactions (think sales) did not grow in proportion. The financial meltdown that began in 2008 caused by complex financial derivatives is one example of the problem of profit puffery.

In Deloitte's *Shift Industry* report of 2013, researchers attempted to strip away much of this financial engineering woven into corporate financial reports to identify the return on assets of American firms, the most aggressive users of financial engineering methods. The result was not pretty: the rates of return are only a quarter of what they were in the mid-1960s; in other words, managers have increasingly done a worse job in capturing profits (economic benefits) as time went by.[14] Discussions about passion for one's work and innovation as crucial to future profitability, thus, degenerate into hype if you cannot turn these into tangible results. Given that awful performance, yet continued celebration of paper profits, increases in the value of stocks, and the payout of salaries and bonuses, what is profit? How valuable is it? Where is it? So, even the conventional wisdom that profit is precious, indeed essential, in a capitalist economy has to be questioned, because it appears that one could run a business for a very long time without real profits, before events catch up with management. For today's management, the notion of profits really requires some serious head scratching and a deeper understanding of what is really driving the performance of their firms.

Improving productivity of operations (the process reengineering that began in the 1980s and shows no signs of slowing with extensive use of IT) when combined with controlling costs of labor (an early motivator for outsourcing work to multiple nations, such as to China and India from North America) has increased the possibility of profits, however, across many industries.[15] But for most firms, the hard benefit was lowered operating costs, something that had to occur before one could attempt to measure real or presumed profits. Perhaps that is a reason why lowering costs as a major initiative, and for some firms their primary activity, has proven so popular for the past two decades. Lowered costs are easier to measure than profits.

From an IT perspective, we now live in a time when managers are continuing to deploy technology to make possible such things as global value chains, use of relatively less expensive labor, new sources of workers, and so forth, regardless of wars and economic recessions. They are only constrained in the speed with which this process unfolds, and even then constraints exist normally only in the supply of credit needed and temporarily diminished market demands, and even the latter largely is limited to the mature economies of North America and Western Europe. Use of open standards and organizing parts of firms almost as components (complete with their own modularized use of IT) are being implemented around the world. Focus shifted from acquiring hardware and software often by first-time users in many firms in the 1970s–1990s to leveraging what they had and replacing incrementally older hardware and software with newer versions more capable of supporting current work practices. The most notable example was the Internet, which most medium to large firms around the world spent the majority of the period since the late 1990s integrating into existing operations and through which they channeled ever larger volumes of work, sales, and customer interactions.[16]

Today that task has essentially been completed. Corporations and many government agencies are now busily at work in making the use of mobile communications integral to their work and in how they interact with customers. It is only just now that many managers are realizing the strategic significance of "apps," the primary software delivery mechanism for getting your work and products in front of employees and customers via a cell phone or tablet. The other IT development that managers are now spending an enormous amount of time on is the application of social media tools in the work of their organizations and in interacting with customers. It is easy to see that both technological developments—mobile communications and social media—are connected and that today they are so profound, that conversations about the Internet itself are almost antiquated, like talking about the power of electricity. If history of IT adoptions teaches anything, it is that the full exploitation of these two technologies will take another 10 years or so before they are "business as usual." At the same time, over a billion more people will come online who will use these two technologies. Learning how to use these as business tools will be the central IT "to do" for all levels of management for the next decade. Failure to do this well pretty much insures business failure. Given that most employees under the age of 35 are already quite familiar with the use of these technologies, one could reasonably expect that they will get the job done, just as their same age cohorts did with the Internet back in the mid- to late 1990s.

CHANGING OPPORTUNITIES AND THREATS

These and other information technologies are having various other effects on firms and industries around the world. Most obvious is in lowering barriers to entry to both new firms and customers into markets, something that became very apparent by the end of the 1990s, thanks to the availability of the Internet. By giving people access to massive amounts of information, a great deal of it through the Internet for fee or free, coupled to the growing and inexpensive communications infrastructure made possible by the Internet and already installed in companies and in the communications and computing individuals use, people can participate more readily in any market they want to today than they could as recently as the early 2000s. A side effect is that new scientific discoveries also enable customization of products and services, as is increasingly becoming evident too in biotechnologies and with medicines.[17] These changes are manifesting themselves in various other ways in many industries too. In communications it is the rising popularity of user-created content (such as blogs, Twitter, Facebook) and the move toward open systems to distribute these; in media and entertainment it is ongoing technological innovation that continues to alter how consumers want their products (e.g., iTunes has led to people buying single songs not whole CDs), and to shortened consumer attention spans as options for entertainment increase; and in radio and television it is about broadcasting with content delivery becoming increasingly independent of the delivery network, in effect platform-agnostic. Put another way, everyone and any enterprise can become a producer or programmer given where the technology is today, increasingly shifting control to consumers over their viewing experiences. In retail, traditional markets are fragmenting partly because consumers are taking greater control over how they interact with businesses, forcing retailers to become more flexible in how they do business, while expanding the number of partners with whom they work.

In a global study conducted by the IBM Institute for Business Value, interviewing over 23,000 executives, the message was loud and clear, customers were influencing company agendas far more than even a decade ago, making dialogue between customers and suppliers very intense, forcing expanded collaboration between the two across more parts of the business than ever before.[18] While this may sound obvious, it is the intensity of that dialogue that is new. Customers demand it, young employees expect it. Managers must, therefore, find ways to open up to customer influences in increasing ways, probably incrementally, while continuing to adopt the mobile/social media IT paradigm as essential to their infrastructure, all the while crafting offerings attractive to customers but that somehow are also profitable to the firm. The first two tasks are relatively new, while the third is "business as usual."

Even conservative firms in less changing industries are not immune to the transformations at hand. For example, in the insurance industry in the United States, informed consumers are increasingly working with nontraditional operators, such as automotive insurance companies over the Internet, while in retail banking, both mega banks and niche players operate, with technology improving inexorably in making new offerings possible, giving consumers the ability to switch vendors more conveniently than was even possible as recently as the early 2000s.

In the most advanced economies all over the world, healthcare is increasingly being equipped with more expensive technologies with which to provide medical diagnostics and treatment. Patients are accessing more information about a particular ailment than their own doctors have time to keep up with and, increasingly, of course, are going around the world to get their treatment (for instance, major procedures in India and plastic surgery in Brazil or Central America). In short, consumerism has arrived in healthcare. The list could be expanded to account for manufacturing, government and, increasingly, higher education. But the implications for management are clear here too. In the health industry, providers and payers, in addition to doctors and clinics/hospitals, are going to have to acquire the kinds of skills widely deployed in the retail industries. More broadly, managers in one industry will increasingly need the core skills available normally in another. Routinely trolling for necessary skills is now a critical task of managers.[19]

But, the story for management is not about ever-more useful computing. Brakes are in use all over the place that managers have to decide individually whether they are good or not. For example, the types of IT devices that could be used to monitor patients remotely are increasing but not their adoption. Why? Doctors in many cases do not understand the technology, hospitals and insurance companies have yet to accept the economic value to them of using such devices, or, as is the case in the United States, the insurance reimbursement culture will pay for treatments more quickly than for wellness practices, although that is now changing. Regulators have yet to step in and approve such devices, a process complicated by the fact that many are involved, such as those regulating communications, or medical devices, or medical practices. Hovering over all of this is the element of risk to patient and medical provider should such technologies as remote heart and blood pressure monitors not perform as expected. Data security and privacy issues vary in form and intensity from one country to another, and with millions of travelers the issues go international very quickly. We write books about the glories of IT, but managers have to deal with the realities of complexity, of which only a few are technological.

If much of what has been discussed in the past several pages sound vaguely familiar, especially to those who studied business administration in graduate school, it is. The amount of hype about the power of IT is so intense that it becomes easy to forget that all useful computing must be subservient to sound business practices: it has to be affordable, it must generate value, and it should support the current strategy of the firm. It really should contribute to profitability unless some other circumstance is at play, such as regulatory requirements or risk management and even then, the IT community and its technologies should be challenged to add value. Borrowing best practices from other industries can be most useful here, and a great deal of information about what to borrow can be found by reading the industry magazines of other industries and by discussing these issues with your business consultants who routinely watch trends in other industries and firms, and through trade shows showcasing IT (but be cautious of the hype). The technology remains complicated, despite enormous advances that occur, so incrementally adding new goods and services that are based on reliance on IT, especially the Internet, remains a prudent approach.

The use of complex, or not well-known technologies, routinely leads to discussions about "best practices." The concept is both a source of good ideas and is a comfort to management, but it can also be a dangerous, indeed complex, approach, often leading to false expectations. The concept behind it is simple enough: that there are sound and practical ways to do many things in business better than other ways and, hence, that the best of these should be adopted. For example, if your firm has a company suggestion process used only by 2% of your employees while a Japanese automotive company also has a suggestion process used by 70% of its workers, then that auto firm has a best practice, certainly better than yours. The logic then is to go copy that firm's suggestion process and plant it right into yours, normally with little to no modifications. The reason why the more intensively used suggestion process works so well—that is used by so many people—may have more to do with the operating culture of the firm than the process itself, so just downloading it into your company or department may not deliver results that you want. In the case of the 70%, you would want to understand the nature of those suggestions, what percent were adopted, their value to the firm, why employees participate, and so forth. You will invariably find that the answers to these questions will lead you to either conclude it is not a best practice for you, or, that what your company needs is a very different type of suggestion process.[20]

ROLE OF KNOWLEDGE MANAGEMENT, INNOVATION, AND CORPORATE CULTURE

KM, innovation, and corporate cultures have been evolving into IT-rich issues over the past 15 years. Over time, they have become increasingly integrated, with strategies and understanding of their issues connected into such IT issues as use of the Internet, security of mobile communications and, of course, role of social media. As far back as the 1980s, management began hearing a great deal about KM. It is the notion that information itself could have economic value and lead to services based on data, hence frequently on the use of IT in new ways. To be sure, academics had explored KM as an economic phenomenon in modern economies as early as the 1950s. By the 1990s, management was also hearing about how they could facilitate the managed use of tacit knowledge (such as experience, unquantified insights) of their employees scattered around the world, thereby eliminating problems of physical distance. A petroleum company with a crisis at an oil drilling operation in the North Sea could tap into the wisdom of other oil drillers working off the coast of Vietnam or in the Gulf of Mexico to help resolve the problem in the North Sea. Bringing together the right experts in a timely cost-effective way is an example of KM at work. To be sure, these kinds of KM had been around since the 1950s.[21] But what now had come to the fore was the idea that tacit knowledge—not just information/data/facts—could be harnessed in some scientific or engineering manner using IT in the process. In fact, this became so rooted in the work of management that when we discuss how managers function in the rest of this book, we must return to this notion. However, for discussion here, it is important to point out that increasing activities within firms, industries, and economies that rely on the use of information and KM principles incrementally shifted from just improving the efficiencies of processes (1980s–1990s) to also leveraging the creativity of workers (tacit knowledge) and promoting innovation in the creation and delivery of new goods and services (2000s–2010s). Technology connected dispersed employees in a way that made them perform nearly as effectively as if in the same room.

By the early 2000s, discussions about innovation had again become fashionable in managerial circles and as noisy as process reengineering had been in the 1990s.[22] But, it made sense because today the technology and the data it offers, when coupled to convenient forms of telecommunications, make it more possible to implement open, collaborative, and multi disciplined approaches to the resolution of operational problems and to the creation of potential new sources of revenue.[23] Some firms now rising in importance are based on information, mixing in traditional growth strategies with new offerings. Thus, for example, Infosys, Tata, and Wipro—Indian IT and consulting firms—increased their revenues, rates of profit, and markets by leveraging low-cost labor-based work with information. Meanwhile, more traditional information services providers in the West increased their revenues per full-time employee, such as ADP, IBM, CSC, EDS, and Accenture. At the far extreme of creating new intellectual assets that could be sold and delivered at a premium— hence a part of the information market requiring much tacit knowledge and innovation—are other familiar names: Dunn & Bradstreet, Equifax, and First Data. But cases of KM at work as a fundamental building block of modern management could be drawn from almost any industry.

To be sure, IT has not been the dominant miracle ingredient in all of this. Traditional issues remain, affecting use of technology, KM, and global supply chains as concerns. But that observation is also a trend. External to the firm, management still wrestles with governmental and other legal and regulatory constraints and issues, such as over trade and property protections and most recently, availability of credit, and monetary and banking stability as a result of the Great Recession. Economic uncertainty remains virulent and dangerous and will be for the rest of the working careers of every living manager.[24] The complaint that enabling technologies are never sufficiently available as management keeps finding new ways of using what they have continues to exist; so too the chronic lament that they have insufficient information and data, a problem of growing concern as managers become more dependent on these with which to make decisions.

Finally, myriad workforce issues around the world remain, involving skills, cost of labor, lack of flexibility in hiring and firing, salary and benefits management, working conditions, political and economic disturbances, corruption, and inadequate transport for these.[25] Those are historic external obstacles and problems that have been with managers since the First Industrial Revolution of the eighteenth century.[26] But as the potential workforce one can draw upon increases around the world, so too do the variations of these issues.

Within their own enterprises, managers know that their corporate cultures tend to lag—read, resist—changes brought about by various causes as always the single most important brake on change and innovation. There also never seem to be large enough budgets to invest in new ways of doing work, and one's own workers can present obstacles to change, such as by not having the right skills, technical, or otherwise. Less chronic, but, nonetheless, evident as firms morph into new forms of business models can be the immaturity of existing work processes and, from an IT perspective, inflexible old software systems.[27] Add in the transformations just starting to affect corporations and whole industries brought about by scientific findings, most notably in biology and medicine, and one begins to understand why managers cannot ignore or discount these non-IT issues that continue to affect their role. But from a KM perspective, as with IT, the question always before management is: How can we best harness these to create value for our customers, value which translates into revenue?

To put a fine point on the observation that IT itself is only one of many factors affecting management's performance, look at the extreme case of the financial sector, made up of banks, insurance companies, and brokerage firms, all of which have long been extensive users of all manner of computing and telecommunications and whose product is really monetary data. Global returns on equity have fallen over time as myriad circumstances affected competition and appetite for their products and services, leading to the obvious conclusion that managers will need to continue finding new ways to generate revenue and profits in the decades to come. In the case of large banks, illegal or bad practices in the early 2000s led to the global recession that began in 2007 and that in addition to declines in normal business transactions led regulators to impose nearly US$200 billion in fines so far, with criminal charges starting to be imposed as this book went to press. But problems exist in many industries. IBM's surveys confirm these trends and concerns. The biggest drivers of change over a decade or longer ranked by the degree of influence, however, speaks to the role of IT: expanded electrification of financial instruments and information availability, which empowers customers and that speed transactions and ability to respond rapidly enough to changing market conditions, remains on the top of the list. Immediate concerns as recently as in 2008–2013 proved more traditional and low tech: regulatory issues, organizational structures that impeded the ability of a firm to grow or change, speed of both commoditization of offerings and upgrading needed skills by employees, speed of competition taking market share, and poor or selfish parochial managerial decisions and practices.[28]

Therefore, speed and agility can almost be seen as flip sides to the same coin. Jeanne W. Ross at the MIT Sloan School of Management looked at the issue of agility, paying particular attention to the role of IT and its effects on businesses. Ross discovered that factors driving the need for agility were the same ones discussed above. Equally so, agility surfaced as elsewhere, involving process improvement and changes, product development, and the ability to acquire new firms and capabilities, including partnerships. This study presented impressive evidence in support of the notion that IT standardization directly effects the ability of firms to improve efficiencies, changes in the structure of a firm, development of new products, and the capability to expand organizational boundaries (such as to include partner firms).[29] This finding is consistent with the historical record of what standardization of IT systems and tools did over the past quarter century. For standardization, Ross also had a traditional time-honored definition: how data in machine-readable forms are organized and are used by customers, suppliers, and with products. Many of the same benefits appeared that process standardization brought in the 1980s and 1990s to R&D, marketing, operations, customer service, logistics, IT, purchasing, human resource management, and, of course, to financial and accounting practices. The lesson is obviously that there are some ways of using and dealing with IT that over time has continued to make sense and so should be appreciated by managers.

When it comes to how best to invest in IT standardization to improve agility of all types, the best places to spend on technology are on those functions that improve IT efficiency, optimize core functions of the firm, and promote sharing of IT infrastructures. For improving business modularity—the idea mentioned earlier of organizing around components of business organization, assets, and IT and the notion that organizations are never permanent as markets change—standardizing how data is managed and made available increases sharing of information, a critical capability essential to a firm.[30]

IBM's own studies dealing with the economic value of senior management paying close attention to creating enterprise architectures as essential direct influences on how agile a firm confirms this insight.[31] In a different study conducted by Professor Ross, we see that for the foreseeable future for businesses that need modularity, these would have to invest in "plug-and-play" business modules facilitated by IT. For those that need to optimize core skills and offerings, prior experience indicates managers should invest in IT systems that are enterprise-wide that support some hardwired processes or databases, such as for personnel and accounting practices. For those still standardizing their use of IT, a central task remains to develop shared technical platforms across the enterprise.[32]

One final thought and suggestion to help management: since these issues, like so many others cut across an enterprise, find ways to break out of their niches, silos, departments, divisions, and organizations. There are several ways to do this so that (i) employees and customers can share information, (ii) discussion can occur about how to leverage an initiative across the organization to optimize something and to reduce risks of harm and negative unintended circumstances, and (iii) that encourages collaboration to execute well a new project. Increasingly, companies and government agencies are forming cross-functional committees and boards (if they want them to last for a considerable period) or task forces (for limited time) to either make recommendations on behalf of the entire enterprise or who also are asked to implement and then improve what they do. Granting authority to implement (also to be held accountable) with budget and appropriate other resources (such as staff) is proving effective across big and small firms and government agencies, and across industries, nations, and regional cultures. A second emerging strategy is for such governance boards to rely extensively on social media approaches to engage the rest of the enterprise in their efforts in a structured and manageable way.

These suggestions may seem incredibly obvious, and they are; less obvious is the fact that they are not always applied, particularly in the lower levels of management. Individual managers and executives can initiate these in almost any culture, from an informal coffee clutch to a formal pronouncement and kickoff by the chief executive officer. Use of such *ad hoc* organizations is, however, increasingly becoming fashionable. This represents one type of managerial behavior where transparency is actually quite effective in reducing the risks of failures and embarrassments on the negative side, but also as a way of getting ideas, supporters, and involvement from multiple levels of an enterprise. CEOs report regularly now that these organizational structures are stimulating innovations, the mother's milk for growth and success, however measured: customer satisfaction, market share, revenue, profits, reputation.

WHY INDUSTRIES ARE STILL SO IMPORTANT TO FIRMS AND MANAGERS

While I devote a whole chapter to this crucial issue later, a few key ideas need to be understood in the context of our discussion of management and their reliance on information technologies. Companies have long identified with those communities that they rely upon for ideas, expertise, employees, parts and supplies, and customers, and to pay attention to the activities of their competitors. Managerial practices and the use to which firms put IT are shaped by shared world views and activities of a manager's industry. That was as true in 1913 as in 2013, but also with a few differences.

Throughout the twentieth century, industries became more organized as entities within national economies than they had been in the nineteenth century, and nowhere more so than in North America and to nearly a similar extent in Western Europe. By the late 1900s, industries had long-standing features, the most important of which included industry-wide associations to which all manner of rivals and ancillary organizations and enterprises belonged in every key industry; industry magazines and newspapers that told the news of an industry, but also became a vocal and visual sounding board reflecting issues and interests of its constituents; lobbying groups that worked on behalf of an industry's members to shape law, regulations, and taxation policies of local, state/provincial, and national governments, and those of such international organizations as the European Union (EU), United Nations (UN), and World Trade Organization (WTO). They hold conventions and training sessions for themselves; they share information about widely embraced practices; form alliances and partnerships; and members borrow, trade, and cajole employees away from each other. But, perhaps most important, industries help shape the values and purposes of individuals and firms within their orbit. Those are attributes managers within any industry would argue is why an industry exists as an identity and more generally across an economy as a series of physical and intellectual meeting grounds.

When a new concept or technology comes into existence, it normally is an industry association (or task force) that will provide the initial broad-based rationale for investigating or adopting a new way of doing things, not some consultant or academic presenting new findings or proposals for changes. For example, the American Banking Association (ABA) routinely brings to American bankers both news about new forms of IT and reports on how best to apply a new technology to the world of banking. It was usually LOMA that ran seminars for decades to teach all levels of management in the life insurance industry about effective uses of IT. *Best's* published thousands of pages in its journals aimed at all kinds of insurance firms around the world about trends in IT, yet, also regarding those involving every other conceivable business issue that impinged upon an insurance manager's working ecosystem. No industry or major line of work was exempt. School teachers have their associations and industry meetings; so too law enforcement officers, professors, bed and breakfast inn operators, owners of restaurants, computer manufacturers, and so forth; the list is endless. Each of these industries has shared information about IT with its members. Indeed, modern management is very tribal and looks to its industry's information ecosystems for knowledge about new things that can be done advantageously within their firms. These organizations are not merely for connections.

Yet, industries are both very social and peer influencing. Managers often act as schools of fish, turning in one direction or another based on what others in their industry are doing, and for the same reasons.[33] While that behavior is not always the smartest to undertake, they do need to understand what their competitors are doing, and industries are a major source of such intelligence, presented to its constituents in extremely useful forms. New and effective managerial practices are often first disseminated widely not by academics in business schools, nor by consultants and book authors, rather by industry associations, which, in effect, give new ideas its blessings. One can trace the acceptance of such recent managerial practices as KM, supply chain management, process reengineering, distributed IT, use of the Internet, social media, and so forth, to this process of dissemination. It is through industries that group decisions are often made essential to the functioning of an industry's members. For example, in banking, it is essential that all members embrace a set of agreed-to technical standards so that funds, and information about funds, can be transferred as part of their daily work. Thanks to industry-wide standards, for example, checks, credit cards, electronic/digital cash transfers, and debit cards look very similar around the world, while ATMs seem almost universally able to access one's bank account in nearly 200 countries. Often decisions about what technology to embrace come out of recommendations of an industry-supported task force, as occurred when the American grocery industry hosted a consortium of firms that led to the adoption of the modern bar code and its positive implementation by grocers and food suppliers in short order, and the vast majority of consumer goods manufacturers and retailers in large swaths of the world.[34]

Industries do things that clubs and private associations do, but at a national or international level. As the amount of interaction among firms and across industries increased in the world of IT during the last three decades of the twentieth century, the more essential it became to establish and work with technical standards. There are only three ways for a technical standard to be introduced. The first is for a vendor of a particular form of IT who so dominates the market that their way (standards and products) is the only acceptable approach, as happened with Microsoft's PC operating system and office products and with IBM and large mainframes. The second is if a technical standards body specializing in some technology proposes, promotes, and persuades everyone to embrace it. Electricity comes to mind, but that would too narrow the myriad of standards promoted by the International Organization for Standardization (ISO), International Electrotechnical Commission (IEC), and International Telecommunication Union (ITU), for example. A third approach is in evidence when an industry association speaking on behalf of the needs of its members and after being satisfied with a standard imposes it, in effect, on its members, enjoining government regulators also to embrace and support the process. Sometimes, it is the regulators who play that dominant role, as happened, for instance with the U.S. Federal Reserve System as early as World War I setting in place a series of standards for the electronic transmission of monetary data. Today it is the EU in establishing environmental protection practices in Europe.

Four generations of managers have now become used to working within the ecosystem of "their" industry. Hardly a day passes without an industry sponsored conference somewhere in North America, and the same is almost as true in Europe and increasingly in East Asia.

Industries also have their limits. While we discuss these in Chapter 3, keep in mind that innovative business models may find regulatory and industry resistance as both value in practice the status quo, regardless of their declarations about the glories of innovation. Managers need to understand that tension, particularly as they engage in selling goods and services into other industries. Also, industries are not the same world-wide. For example, banking regulations vary from one region or nation to another, which is why people could "hide" accounts for so long in Switzerland (not so much anymore) or in the Caymin Islands (still very much so) and absolutely not in the United States and Great Britain. A lesson for young managers in particular: as your work causes you to pay attention to the culture and activities within your industry, seek out information about how these vary from one country to another. It is amazing how little this is done, particularly by individuals who have not traveled much in other nations!

WHAT ECONOMISTS AND OTHER ACADEMICS ARE DISCOVERING

Economists and business school professors also pay attention to indus-tries because they have known for decades that industries influence profoundly the actions of firms and their employees to a far greater extent than most managers ever realized. Economists more so have long used the concept of industries to collect data about the magnitude of a particular type of economic activity, such as the volume of sales of automobiles in a country, or the number of telephones and the associ-ated expenditures of customers on them. Government economists routinely organize their national economic reporting schema around industries as well. Business school professors wax and wane in their enthusiasm for industry constructs, not always appreciating how really important they are to modern management and their staffs.[35] As man-agers become more information dependent to do their work, so too does their reliance increase on the data gathering and teachings of an industry. Academic researchers have long studied the patterns of economic, man-agerial, and social behavior of industries and of the firms within them. Today, industries are in fashion, particularly with business school professors.[36] This renewed interest is actually quite important because firms have a long history of paying attention to industry-wide patterns of behavior and practices, and many strategy consulting firms have built their entire business around industry-centric expertise.[37] Invariably, a time-honored assignment for such firms is to explain to a management team of middle managers or senior executives what was going in the world of IT within a particular industry.[38]

Ultimately, however, we should also ask: How the injection of so much IT into industries affects their role and, equally important, what is the influence of globalization on them? Conversely, what are the effects on the furtherance of globalized trade and work? Over a period of several decades, management in many countries incrementally deployed IT and telecommunications in ways often quite consistent with existing and evolving operational practices evident within their own industries. For example, American automotive manufacturers tend to have more, or less, the same kinds of product development practices as their rivals and to implement them more at roughly the same time. Technology makes it possible to spread the work of an industry around the world and no more obvious case of this exists than the globalization of supply chains to such an extent that there really is no American or Japanese car anymore, for example; its parts are made all over the world and then assembled in various countries. To say otherwise is a misnomer. Instances of the globalization of such basic sets of tasks as those of supply chains can be found across all industries, some intensely so, as in manufacturing, and in others more loosely, as in media industries. All the major manufacturers of computer chips design in their home countries, sometimes in others, then manufacture in "fabs" located in low-wage countries. Books may be written in Europe, be published in the United States, but distributed electronically through servers located in Asia; physical printing of copies is routinely dispersed into several countries. I have written all my books in the United States and were acquired by American editors, mostly working in the New York and Boston areas, but were typeset in the United States, Europe, and India, and physically manufactured in Ireland, the United States, and India, and that is just for the English editions of those books! They have also been distributed electronically through computers (servers) located in Vietnam, Ireland, North Carolina, Brazil, and I suspect in China, and for sure out of South Korea. In short, desegregation within supply chains is alive and well, because it drives down costs, improves productivity, and a great number of people know how to do this.

In general, management works today in industries that have an increasingly common "look-and-feel" to them around the world. Back to our automotive example: a car or truck assembly plant today is laid out roughly the same way in Germany as in Japan or in the United States. An individual familiar with the industry can spot such a plant from a distance while driving past it by its physical appearance, because they look the same around the world. Within these compounds, work is more similar than not. In the automotive industry, they even have a name for it used around the world, the Toyota Way.[39] Banks use ATMs in a similar fashion, while the pharmaceutical industry operates in a highly similar, extensively integrated manner with its research and testing partners, often with practices dictated to all by regulatory agencies, such as the American Food and Drug Administration, whose policies are often emulated by other nations. In short, national industries are now also increasingly international in scope, creating much larger ecosystems within which managers work and create their sense of identity and to which they peg their successes.

But technology cannot be seen as simply the tail wagging the dog, causing firms and industries to work the same around the world. Managers have always had choices on how best to use technology. The history of their decisions is littered with examples of various options taken or declined. So diversity of thinking remains a feature of the continued expansion and integration of activities within industries around the world. Yet, global conditions have conversely influenced the increased role and visibility of industries as well. As increasing numbers of national economies embraced market capitalism over the past half century, the greater the potential markets that opened up to firms. The collapse of the Soviet Union in 1991 exposed the fallacies of alternative models. Alan Greenspan, who witnessed the exposure and had to deal with it as a central banker, was quite clear about the effects on globalizing economic behavior.

The defining moment for the world's economies and global industries was the fall of the Berlin Wall in 1989, revealing a state of economic ruin behind the iron curtain far beyond the expectations of the most knowledgeable Western economists. Central planning was exposed as an unredeemable failure; it was dropped from the world's economic agenda.[40]

In the 1990s, whole industries rapidly expanded their markets. Indian officials dropped their neo-Soviet styled socialist economic policies and the world discovered how intrinsically entrepreneurial Indian managers, citizens, firms, and industries could be, even during the global economic recession that began in 2008. The world is still trying to make sense of what happened at the same time in China which, during the early years of the new century, year after year led the world in its rate of economic growth, making it the second largest economy in the world after that of the United States.

In short, two events complimented each other. The technologies needed to operate firms and whole industries globally became available and were already implemented by enterprises to such an extent that when market capitalism expanded, management could take advantage of the situation to seize the moment, so to speak, to reach out to new sources of components, labor, and customers. It is a massive process still unfolding and in its early stages. Barring some unforeseen natural disaster or global war, managers reading this book can expect to spend the rest of their careers seeing their industries expand around the world in much the same way their industries did within the confines of national or regional markets, the process lubricated by IT. It is such an important topic that the next chapter (Chapter 3) continues to explore the role of industries.

INFORMATION TECHNOLOGIES TO PAY ATTENTION TO RIGHT NOW

As one comes to understand how your firm works within its business ecosystem of industries, customers, regulators, and national economies, the importance of IT becomes intuitively obvious. But since IT keeps changing and affecting the performance of companies and government agencies, we have to keep watching what the technologists are up to. Every "expert" has her list, I have mine, and it changes every few years because of the evolution of IT. In the immediate past few years, readers have surely heard about analytics, big data, security systems, sensors, the Internet of course, social media, and mobile communications. All are important, each is still transforming, and none have played out their full effects on firms, work, or whole industries and economies. But you already know that and by this point in the book, know to keep watching developments in those spaces. But, now for a few that are on the horizons about which we hear very little outside of the technical communities, but will "go public" over the next 5 years in ways that possibly could disrupt some businesses, will deliver new niche opportunities for revenues and profits and that will change the nature of how and who does work. Each will take time to flower in the fullness of their capabilities and so should be ongoing stories for managers, consultants, academic researchers, and the media to discuss for at least two decades, which is about the amount of time it takes for a new technology to have widespread effects on organizations and people. But let us begin with one already now, but slowly, making its way into the world of management: cloud computing.

CLOUD COMPUTING

Cloud computing is the practice of storing information on computers usually outside of one's company or government agency that is managed as a service. It is accessed over the Internet. In theory and increasingly to a certain extent in reality, with cloud computing you do not need an in-house computer or IT staff nor do you need a personal computer. The promises of cloud computing—which means your data is up there in some cloud in the sky—include that you can rent only as much computing as you need, not a full system, so you only spend for what you need; you do not need a technical staff to maintain your system, so you reduce personnel costs and the issues of managing technical staff; you can rely on experts to maintain systems, data security, and so forth, which it is argued is not the core competence of most organizations; and you can take advantage of economies of scale to lower the costs of infrastructure while improving the quality of IT performance. That is the promise. The negatives include that your data is now outside of your control and thus potentially at risk of being accessed by a competitor willfully or not; that you are dependent on the quality of some other organization's staff to provide you with services at a level that you need; that there may be greater difficulties in getting applications changed (or not at all if you are buying a service); and that raises the question what happens to you if that service provider goes out of business? We call that last question business disruption and that is always a board of directors' issue, not where most managers want to have to discuss this issue.

That said, after many years of discussion, cloud computing has taken off. A week does not go by without major announcements. As this chapter was being written in 2013, in addition to many companies beginning to embrace cloud computing, the U.S. Central Intelligence

Agency (CIA) announced it was outsourcing some of its computing to Amazon.com. There are several remarkable points to be made here. First, the CIA management felt comfortable enough that the technology was stable and secure enough for it to outsource to a private company some of its data and that its personnel could get to it at the speed they needed in the event of some national urgency. That is a remarkable testimonial to the maturity of the technology. Second, that Amazon won the business, as it has been doing with a number of companies, as it enters the cloud computing market, suggests major shifts underway in the business opportunities for existing large data processors like Amazon, and conversely, the potential threats to such iconic providers of IT as IBM, HP, and Cisco to mention a few. Third, this is an example of industry boundaries in a mess, because Amazon was not in the IT industry, it has always been seen as in online retailing. Remember, books, now e-books, and Kindle? Now cloud computing? So, even who one would buy cloud computing from seems to be shifting around.

As recently as 2012, if a manager wanted to use cloud computing, he had to acquire the service much as a utility: one type of water, one type of electricity. There were few options, essentially just a standard one-size-fits-all set of offerings and if they were appropriate great, if not, conform to them or defer the decision to go to cloud computing. In 2013 industry-specific offerings began to appear, that is to say, services tailored to such functions and industries as B2B sales, retail, and banking industry. A survey of large enterprises in mid-2013 had a third reporting already using cloud computing, but more important to us, that this percentage would double in the next 3 years to some 72%.[41] Their forecast is probably accurate given the history of IT interview surveys of this type and so we can conclude that cloud computing is making its way into many organizations, regardless of whether or not in 3 years 72% are using it or not. A tipping point was reached in 2013 that suggests this may well be the start of a significant change in how business computing will occur.

Already, if one uses the Internet to get information or to place an order that goes outside of your organization, you are already participating in cloud computing. So the leap to more uses is smaller than we might think. Second, large organizations, like IBM and the CIA, or Amazon and others will undoubtedly practice three forms of computing: out-and-out cloud computing for a specific application, internally run cloud computers for multiple similar users or divisions, and old fashioned glass house computing. The first two will use the

Internet for telecommunications, and possibly the third hybrid, such as intranets, where all communications stays inside your firm's firewall. A manager's responsibility, therefore, is to start paying attention to cloud computing's role in their profession, line of work, and industry. Industry trade literature will provide most of the case studies and surveys they will need to get just enough information to stay informed until such time as they want or are ordered to move some or all activities to "the cloud."

WEARABLE COMPUTING

Think of a watch and you understand what wearable computing is. As computing shrinks in size, and also in cost, we can carry on our bodies' devices that can perform more functions than in the past. The hottest digital real estate market on our bodies is our wrist, of course, where we today have our watches, but increasingly as they become "smart," something already available, we can download data off the Internet, could use it as a telephone, or to access e-mail among obvious applications. It has several important characteristics that will affect usage. First, like a watch, it remains "on" connected to whatever system it is supposed to interact with, which means that someone using it will either be sending data continuously to a central database, such as sensors on such a device or will receive data and instructions as needed. Wearable medical devices are an early example of this technology just now becoming available. People already use this technology in more primitive forms, such as to measure the number of steps taken, speed and distance in running, listening to music (with headsets instead of wristworn devices), and as sensors to indicate temperature or levels of oxygen. Fibertronics/e-textiles—cloth with digital, hence smart threads—is another version of this, that can track body temperature and functions, and potentially be used to further insulate or reduce insulation as needed and like all wearable electronics do these things in real time, that means whenever needed immediately.

The newest wearable technology to receive wide attention around the world as recently as 2013 is the Google eyeglasses, which has a tiny camera/screen in the upper right hand corner of what looks like a normal pair of eye glasses. It can take photographs, transmit them, and allow the wearer to receive information and to issue verbal commands. That would allow one to read and respond to messages, place orders, receive work-related instructions or directions on how to go from one place to another. Google calls it a "wearable computer," yet another experiment exploring where to place computing on the human body.[42] Google's device is still experimental, and not yet commercially available, but it is only a matter of time before it becomes a product. How will you use it at work? That is a question that will probably be answered incrementally, as is happening with tablets. First consumers will try it, use it for applications now done with smart phones and tablets, and then new uses will suggest themselves. As a manager, you should participate in that experience as it unfolds so that when the cost and functionality come together in a way that is useful for your work, it will make sense. A couple of instantly useful applications might be for coaching of selling points to call out to a customer as one is proposing a sale, or explaining terms of a contract. I can imagine a conference call using the glasses while looking at Powerpoint texts or spread sheets as one is traveling or otherwise moving about. The point is, start paying attention to this technology.

AUTONOMOUS VEHICLES

This is a technology still in the experimental stage of development, like Google's eyewear, but unlike the glasses, which we can expect to come to market very soon, autonomous vehicles will take many years to make it to market. These are self-driving vehicles, often also called robotic cars or driverless vehicles. Already automation is extending to commercial vehicles using cameras and sensors to spot hidden objects behind a car or that causes alarms or automatic breaking to prevent a crash. Cars are now appearing that can self-parallel park. All major automotive and truck manufacturers in the Western world have experimental projects underway. At the heart of this technology are sensors connected to onboard computing that makes it possible to be aware of the vehicles situation and to take action that would increase safety (protection), suggest alternative activities, such as route to take (think onboard mapquest), efficient ways to expend energy (already done on most vehicles), and that can operate the vehicle without human involvement. They combine GPS, radar, cameras, sensors, and driving software. Several states in the United States and in Europe have passed laws permitting such functions to occur on roads, although again the technology is in experimental stages. The promises of such technology for society are obvious: avoidance of accidents, conformance to traffic laws, and improved environmental driving practices.

But for managers, there are additional potential possibilities. Like robots, these could be used in cold or bad weather, in environmentally dangerous conditions (as in a nuclear plant in trouble), without use of lights in a warehouse, and most intriguing of all, without human drivers. That alone would justify the massive use of such vehicles by management because it would save on the cost of personnel, the complexities and time needed to manage people, they could potentially work 24 hour a day, which is more than a person, and thus could optimize logistics, specifically use of vehicles. Inventory turns could be increased because merchandise to be delivered can be moved more quickly or simply sooner, while we sleep in our homes at night, the truck or aircraft or drone drives to a destination. However, a few cautions are in order. First, hype will precede the effectiveness of this technology long before it is ready for commercial use; in fact that has already started. Forecasts will show it being used sooner, and often by your competitors, long before in fact that occurs. You will need to avoid the temptation of being the first to use such a new technology. Second, because it involves air space, public roads, possibly railroad tracks, tunnels, and underway routes, government regulators will take their time in authorizing the use of such technologies largely out of a legitimate concern about safety. Nobody wants a robotic truck going down a major highway at 65 miles an hour that is not 110% safe. As a manager you will want to be concerned about liability and insurance, both of which will delay deployment of this technology for a considerable period of time. Software glitches will be inevitable; we can reasonably presume some will be serious, expensive, and fatal to people. Finally, there is always one problem that appears with every new technology: the reluctance to do it the new way, in this instance, for a driver to give up control of their vehicle. The problem goes away someday when drivers do not have to ride with the robotic vehicle. But as we have learned with commercial aircraft, which are largely operated robotically, and have for many years, airlines and regulators still put human pilots into cockpits with the capability of overriding the autonomous vehicle.

BIOTECH-INFORMATICS-INFORMATION TECHNOLOGY

It seems odd that a technology that will be used sooner than autonomous vehicles does not yet have a good clean name to it. But of any cluster of technologies, one could speak about that would most profoundly change the lives of managers, at least personally, these are it. In fact, these are so profound that it would be nearly impossible to chart out their implications because they may shape, if not define, the nature of human life in ways never seen before in the history of mankind. Heady stuff, but we must deal with it as managers. For well over a century, medications were based on combination of chemical compounds administered to us as pills, injections, liquids, and, most recently, patches attached to our skin. But that is all about to change because the fundamental basis of medicines is transforming from chemical-based medications to those based on living systems and organisms, think of programming cells in your body to fight cancer, or to grow a new organ. We hear a number of terms being used related to this subject: biotechnology, bioengineering, genomics, recombinant gene technologies, new forms of pharmacogenomics, and so the list continues. For a half-century, many of the scientific concepts underlying the use of living cells to transform other living structures have been worked out in agriculture and the breeding and care of livestock. Now those findings are beginning to work their way into human medicine. Medical knowledge and practice in this area is just starting to be known and felt and is analogous to how computers were just being used in the late 1940s. As with computers, the basic underlying science takes decades to understand before practical applications become possible.

What does this all mean for managers? For some, it truly is a game changer. The pharmaceutical industry built its knowledge base and products on chemical treatments; in the years to come that will be replaced with this new base of knowledge. Instead of making one medication applicable to millions of people, we will begin to see medications that are tailored to one person. That development alone will upturn supply chains, business models, make and destroy careers that depend on bodies of knowledge that will no longer have economic power. The industry has been measured in its transition, some might argue too slow, as it depends too much on block buster drugs coming off patent and not enough on developing these new classes of medications. So the industry is moving into crisis. Managers of hospitals and clinics will obviously see new procedures; doctors use the word protocols to mean the same. Since roughly one-third of all medical costs involves the expense of hospitalization, pressures to reform these institutions and challenges to existing business and cost models will intensify.

Managers outside of these two industries will encounter unknown consequences that we can only guess at. Early on, one can speculate that employer provided medical coverage and leaves of absence will probably require changes. In time, it is quite possible that people will live incrementally longer lives, with implications for how long healthy people will/should work. Will they then retire in their 70s, or 80s? Or, even later? Cleaning up water and new medications, such as antibiotics, increased life spans in the Western World in the 1900s by over 20 years. There is no inherent biological reason why that cannot be done again and as quickly as before—less than a half century—which is why there could be dramatic implications for how people work. At a personal level, this could mean that careers could be longer, that one would experience multiple full careers. Will CEOs of companies have to take longer (be older) before they assume that senior position? Today they tend to be younger, but that could reverse. Will laws governing mandatory retirement change, and what will constitute age discrimination from both a legal and practical perspective? We just simply do not know, but what we can expect is that many of these issues will land in the laps of middle to senior management certainly by the early 2030s, barely 10–15 years from now.

Finally, an undercurrent in all of these developments is the rapid merger of information technology and biotechnology. Medical informatics is already a defined discipline and many of the biggest "big data" projects in the world involve the hunt for either new medications or a deeper understanding of genomics. Computer scientists are beginning to speak about computers made out of living cells, while the thought of building computers as smart and with the capacity of a human brain is no longer a pipe dream. IBM's Watson computer, which has a primitive capability to learn from what it does, is acknowledged even by very cautious scientists and engineers as potentially transforming how computing is done in all fields. But the nuts-and-bolts of computer science pushing this machine's technological base forward is right now largely playing out in medical science. In other words, medical application in the use of this machine is already generating revenue for IBM. Watching what happens with Watson and medical informatics will give managers new ideas about how to use computing in the next 5–10 years in such areas as customer relations, marketing, risk management in finance and banking, and in strategy work. That is why biotechnology should not be seen as an abstract topic, but rather something managers should start getting comfortable with right now.

QUANTUM COMPUTING

Now we return to very small and very big data computing with a new class of devices still in their infancy but that hold out the promise of becoming quite useful during the life time of new and mid-career managers, so worth keeping an eye on. In horribly simple terms, quantum computing harnesses physical phenomenon, rather than digital data, to perform information collection and calculation. It is based on what we know about quantum theory, ideas that help to explain the nature and activities of energy and matter. What is involved here is the promise of increasing the volume of computations by a billion times over today's computing, along with many more permutations of calculations. There has been extensive research going on in both the public and private sectors on this technology since the 1980s. Quantum theory, by the way, says that energy exists in units, like pieces of a Lego set of blocks, not as waves. This new form of computing would be able, in theory, to track and analyze activity at the atomic level and take into account millions of prior computing activities associated with whatever is being analyzed at the atomic level.

An early practical application would be to search through unstructured databases, for example, using an algorithm that reduces the number of activities required to perform the search. The military is interested because such computing could break encryption keys by physically looking at all possibilities. The biotechnology folks look forward to performing DNA modeling, while other scientists want to analyze complex material science questions. The latter holds out the promise of new materials with which to make products, such as lighter aircraft that uses less energy. The problem right now is that this form of computing is either just a hand full of years away from starting to be used or many decades—there seems to be no agreement. However, given that companies like IBM, the American military, and research institutions like MIT are spending considerable resources on this subject, we cannot be too far away from early business applications. Perhaps we can expect some crossovers of what is happening with Watson-style computing and quantum computing. It is the sort of topic, however, that can be digested in pieces as it evolves through the popular science press, such as in *Wired* magazine, *National Geographic*, and even on rare occasions in such trade publications as the *Economist* or *Financial Times*.

PERSONAL ROBOTICS

The last set of information technologies that one should pay attention to over the next several years involves personal robotics. Industrial robotics has been in use since the early 1960s, in such applications as repeated activities in manufacturing (painting cars in automotive factories), by the military to diffuse bombs or to enter buildings to see if there were enemy combatants inside, by warehouse managers to store, track, and collect items to ship, such as is done by large retailers such as Amazon. com. Those applications of intelligent programmable robots continue to spread as a way of improving the quality of work done, to reduce the cost of employees, or to do things that are too unsafe for humans, as occurred in Japan with its nuclear plants when people needed to understand the levels of radiation in collapsed buildings. But personal robotics is different. These are devices that can be used by individuals, such as programmable home lawn mowers, devices to clean home or commercial swimming pools, and in a house, vacuum cleaners. Japanese manufacturers have also produced robotic toys and lead the world in the conversion of this technology into entertaining products.

Currently, the market for personal robotics is small but is expected to start growing with forecasts of nearly US$20 billion in global sales not out of the realm of possibility by about 2020. These devices build on what has already been learned from industrial robots, and leverages the continued miniaturization of electronics that has made, for example, or cell phones so small yet so rich in functions. Avatars, or even physical representatives of people at remote meetings (telepresence robots), could mean managers could spend less time traveling to meetings. For consumers, a closer to reality use would be to monitor elderly relatives who live in other homes or communities; the same for use by doctors monitoring the activities of patients, especially the elderly. Not too far in the future, the use of such robotic servants to clean house, bring someone a beer watching television, and possibly doing more advanced activities, such as cooking, become possible. Today vacuum cleaners and entertainment products are a reality, but not for much longer before some of these other uses become available.

The issues we face as managers concern how could such technologies convert into consumer, medical, and other business/industrial products? To what extent can the work of employees be replaced with less expensive-to-own-operate devices, such as clerks in stores? Put a PC-like capability in these devices and you can perform counting and mathematical work with a device that moves about, unlike our static PCs that sit on desks and still require extensive human intervention. As the "internet of things" communicating over the Internet continues to unfold, are there yet more tasks that can be assigned to such devices, including supervision of tasks assigned to humans (think digital foreman)? Economists are beginning to worry that computing is extending so fast into so many business functions that the industrialized world may experience significant job losses for humans in the next decade.[43] Managers will want to start thinking of possibilities and learning who are the vendors for such devices.

MANAGEMENT'S TAKEAWAYS

Consider several actions growing out of our discussion of the business environment comprising of firms, professions, industries, and a host of new technological possibilities. First, become a member of your industry's association; then get in the habit of reading its trade publications. Second, attend its annual conventions and training sessions from time-to-time to learn from others, network, and to come home with fresh ideas. Third, time permitting, get involved in its activities so that you can influence agendas and find help for the actions you wish to take back in your home company or agency. The issue of influencing agendas can be applied handsomely in causing the association to use its research and communications capabilities to introduce readers to emerging technologies before they are surprised by their use by competitors coming at them from other industries.

There are several other important "takeaways" for managers in all industries. By the early 1970s, Peter Drucker had spent many years explaining that management was a discipline, one with a codex of roles and practices. Managers were leaders and teachers—people who worked with other people—and they could be expected to perform and be held accountable for such things as the growth of their businesses, development of their employees, and the proper stewardship of their society, economy, and, increasingly, the environment. He already was quite sensitive to the global nature of management—the role proved similar regardless in which country someone was a manager—and certainly that universality of responsibilities and objectives of managers helped make it possible for firms, and their business partners and alliances, to work in a globalized economy: "a generic function which faces the same basic tasks in every country and, especially, in every society."[44] Those thoughts still resonate today. Managers trained in India and Japan, or in China and in Central Europe, hear similar messages and embrace many of the same concepts. The globalized economy is increasingly demonstrating that just as industries spread their values and *modus operandi* around the world, homogenizing many practices through the use of shared IT standards, integrated supply and value chains, occurred with familiar roles and responsibilities. If we consider management a profession, then it has more of a common "look-and-feel" to it today around the world than it has differences. To be sure, local social and cultural values still influence their behavior, but the general observation increasingly holds true.

Implications for Management

There are a number of implications for management from the story presented in this chapter. Perhaps the most obvious is that as managers around the world collaborate with others via their interdependencies brought about through outsourcing, transnational supply chains, and international rules of economic and regulated behavior. As a by-product, they are coming to know more about how their competitors think and work on a worldwide basis regardless of the size enterprise in which a manager works. That reality alone will further stoke the fires of competition. Information technologies will continue to speed up even further and make more convenient myriad types of information needed to make this observation true; indeed, it has already begun.

A second implication for management, and one pointed out by many observers concerned with the growing power of international firms, is the fact that managerial practices, and who does the work, has already

begun to internationalize to such an extent that at least in large corporations, it is becoming anachronistic to speak about American, Japanese,
or European managers, although they still retain some localized styles,
but increasingly share the ways of working too. As time passes, one can
hand off the work of most levels of managers to individuals in other
countries with growing expectations about what that means. Specifically,
a product development manager in South Korea can be expected today to
perform in ways similar to that of his or her counterpart working in
Silicon Valley in California or at the Philips Corporation in the
Netherlands. They have gone through similar education and training,
maybe even used the same textbooks. They have held the same kinds of
jobs over their careers. They are dependent on the work of managers,
firms, and industries around the world to accomplish their own work. In
the process, they and their firms have begun slowly to shed national
work identities as they move tasks around the world and, indeed, as they
serve out their careers in multiple countries. All the while they are leveraging various forms of IT and communications. They share values and
industry associations and networks to stay "plugged in" with colleagues
anywhere in the world.[45] Just as industries have internationalized in a
fairly dramatic fashion during the past quarter century, so too have small
and large firms and, consequently, many managers.

One can point to exceptions to this trend, because it is one whose
extent has yet to play out fully. But, there is no mistaking the trend
toward more internationalization of work, even when the gales of trade
protectionism blow periodically across one economy or another, as it
appears began happening again toward the end of the Great Recession.[46]
To be blunt about the point, the world's economy has returned to a
pattern of global trade similar to what existed intensely prior to the disruptions of the two world wars and the Cold War of the twentieth century.
But, they still speak Korean in the halls of Hyundai Motor Company,
German at BMW, and English at American Express, and all their cafete-
rias serve indigenous foods wherever they are located. Ultimately,
however, the work habits of their managers are more similar than not.

With the rapid diffusion of all manner of technologies, including IT,
the world is arriving at a technological balance-of-power in which most
national economies and markets have access to the same technologies
as any other part of the world, a status that should absolutely be reached
in the twenty-first century. Even in extremely underdeveloped economies, this is rapidly becoming so with, for instance, mobile telephones

in sub-Sahara African nations and access to the Internet across Latin America and Central Europe. We have not seen that evenness of deployment since roughly the 1500s when both the use of technologies of many kinds and even the standards of living of many societies were roughly comparable. To be sure, travel on the road to this emerging balance-of-power status has proven highly uneven so far, especially during the last four decades, with Africa and Latin America slower in adoption and change than evidenced in all of Europe, North America, and large swaths of Asia. The reasons for this slower pace need not detain us here; many others have explained the situation.[47] The diffusion of technologies of all types, coupled to the growing availability of capital for further investments and innovations, often brought about by the productivity improvements made possible by the use of technologies, simply made the world both richer and more dependent on various trading partners.

Between 1500 and 1820, world trade grew by just slightly less than 1% per year; between 1820 and 1870—a period of massive increases in technological innovations—world trade grew by over 4% annually, a rate that only dipped to 3.40% by the start of World War I. In the next period of massive innovations in all manner of technologies, including the introduction of computers, that is to say, from 1950 to 1973, world trade grew annually by 7.88%, and during the last three decades of the century, by 5.22%.[48] The lesson for management is quite clear: the world is in a historic period of steady growth in its internationalization of trade, much of it made possible as consequences of using various technologies, not the least of which is IT.

One other implication for management in addition to the expansion of trade is the internationalization of their work and practices, and thus the proverbial progression of technological evolution is not a zero sum game. Over the past 1000 years, during which most of humankind's technological innovations emerged, human population expanded 23-fold and per-capita income 14-fold. GDP grew by over 300-fold. To be sober about the data, increases in GDP went to support the massive growth in population that occurred in the same period, which in turn experienced continuous increases in the standard of living, even though advances in per capita income proved much slower. Over the last two centuries, household income grew ninefold, population sixfold, and per capita income by roughly 1.2% per year; in other words, it expanded 24 times as fast as during the period roughly from 1000 to 1820, all the while when the world's population was growing at about 1% annually.[49] One can site statistics like this for myriad issues, such as the lengthening of life spans, and so forth, but the point is clear: so long as populations continue to grow, managers can expect more customers who financially are increasingly able to acquire goods and services, who are more educated, and thanks to myriad forms of digital technologies, have access to more information and suppliers of goods and services than in prior times. These are processes at work that go far to explain why the work of management continues to evolve.

This is as lot of history to wade through but essential in order to arrive at the proper managerial conclusions. The opportunities to sell more goods and services around the world are clearly there and measurable. The chances of severe competition is too, with your rivals leveraging the large disparity in wage levels, the cost of physically transporting goods and people across the globe, and economies of scale. One could reasonably expect that the fight for profits—not revenues—will become far more severe in the next 40 years than in the previous four decades. That ultimately may be the greatest challenge management will face across all industries and the winners in that titanic struggle will be those who are the quickest and most effective in leveraging reasons and allies around the world, that is why IT and industries are so much more important today. They can facilitate success, but also the quick death of many firms.

As the arena in which management must work expands, so too does that occur with their firms. Don Tapscott frequently talks about the self-organizing learning that is increasingly occurring at the institutional level. The actions involved in this development are the tasks managers perform to create communities of people who learn and then apply what they learn into products, services, or more efficient ways to run an organization. John Hagel would go further and argue that organizations, hence their management, are coming to understand how to implement "scalable learning from scalable efficiency," as firms change in response to so many data inputs from complex and constantly changing markets. This is not blue sky thinking, it happens today. That calls for connecting a great number of smart people within your firm to a great number of equally smart people outside: experts, consultants, media people, customers, regulators, professors, and competitors. Even the public sector is not immune with some observers suggesting that after collecting massive quantities of social data, for example, that nuggets of creativity that is effective in social behavior and public administration be extracted and disseminated. What an interesting application that might be for a Watson computer or later, quantum computing. Getting to such new levels of thinking, let alone performance on a wide scale will call for industry leadership, and not simply the case studies of exceptions which business professors and consultants are so good at pointing out.

The issues described in this chapter suggest that going forward managers have some immediate practical questions to answer about how they will thrive. Theirs is a business environment with many moving parts, new risks to personal and firm prosperity, all set in delicately integrating, often fragile, economies generally migrating toward market-driven forms, but still with vigorous nationalist protectionism provided by their national governments bent on taking care of local businesses. Particularly for middle and senior managers in government and private industry, in both large enterprises and in smaller ones reliant on global supply chains for their business, there are crucial questions to answer. These include:

- How will we track emerging technological trends in the use of IT, for example, that we can either take advantage of, such as social media, or that we must defend against, such as competitors from other continents?
- What process do we have for identifying ways to project our offerings and services to ever-changing, larger communities of customers and citizens? How good is this process?
- How effectively do we inject technological considerations into our decision-making processes?
- What is our organization's social business strategy? Do we even have one?

Briefly summarized, the key things to remember from our discussion in this chapter are as follows:

- Managers need to understand that there is a set of global best practices and that products and services are delivered to global customers
- Managers need to track emerging technological trends in IT
- Managers need to build technological considerations into decision-making.

The issues discussed in this chapter are embedded in a large ecosystem—industries—that today are tightly connected communities both at the national level and increasingly globally. Technologies have played an important role in integrating industries and in making these ecosystems real, forceful, and important. So, for those reasons, we turn next to them in greater detail than we have so far, leaving forecasts of the future aside for the moment, spending more time on today's issues: improving coordination of activities, understanding what is happening in the world, doing work cost effectively, and growing one's business.

NOTES

1 A finding explored in more detail in James W. Cortada, *The Digital Flood: The Diffusion of Information Technology Across the U.S., Europe, and Asia* (New York: Oxford University Press, 2012).

2 I documented this in some 40 industries over many decades and reported results in *The Digital Hand*, 3 vols (New York: Oxford University Press, 2004–2008).

3 Summarized by Graham Tanaka, *Digital Deflation: The Productivity Revolution and How It Will Ignite The Economy* (New York: McGraw-Hill, 2004).

4 I summarized many of the findings behind this statement in "*The Digital Hand*: How Information Technology Changed the Way Industries Worked in the United States," *Business History Review* 80 (Winter 2006): 755–766.

5 Don Tapscott has written a series of books on this and related topics; see his most recent study, coauthored with Anthony D. Williams, *Wikinomics: How Mass Collaboration Changes Everything* (New York: Portfolio, 2006). Many of the conversations about innovation, networked, or extended value nets and supply chains also include discussion of open technical and managerial systems. For an excellent review of the issues, see Henry Chesbrough, *Open Business Models: How to Thrive in the New Innovation Landscape* (Boston, MA: Harvard Business School Press, 2006).

6 Don Tapscott, *Information Technology and Competitive Advantage* (Toronto: New Paradigm Learning Corporation, 2005).

7 "Big Blue Shift," *BusinessWeek*, June 5, 2006, available at http://www.businessweek.com/magazine/content/06_23/b3987093.htm (last accessed November 5, 2011).

8 For an early description of this process, see Rebecca Morales, *Flexible Production: Restructuring the International Automobile Industry* (Cambridge: Polity Press, 1994).

9 Steven Weber, *The Success of Open Source* (Cambridge, MA: Harvard University Press, 2004): 65–72; Josh Lerner and Jean Tirole, "Economic Perspectives on Open Source," in Joseph Feller, Brian Fitzgerald, Scott A. Hissam, and Karim R. Lakhani (eds.), *Perspectives on Free and Open Source Software* (Cambridge, MA: MIT Press, 2005): 47–78.

10 Of the hundreds of books published on the history of technology since the 1980s, her's has been the most influential on the thinking of senior business executives,

particularly in the world of IT, Carlota Perez, *Technological Revolutions and Financial Capital: The Dynamics of Bubbles and Golden Ages* (Cheltenham, UK: Edward Elgar, 2002): 3–8, 170.

11 Alan Greenspan, *The Age of Turbulence: Adventures in a New World* (New York: Penguin, 2006): 11–12.

12 Ibid., on IT, 172–174, about labor, 364.

13 Documented extensively in the first two volumes of Cortada, *The Digital Hand.*

14 http://www.deloitte.com/view/en_US/us/Industries/technology/center-for-edge-tech/ 26d62345e0032210VgnVCM200000bb42f00aRCRD.htm (last accessed December 12, 2013).

15 Robert Brenner, *The Economics of Global Turbulence: The Advanced Capitalist Economies from Long Boom to Long Downturn, 1945-2005* (London: Verso, 2006): 332–333; Tanaka, *Digital Deflation*: 84–90.

16 This was a pervasive discovery I made for each industry I looked at when conducting research for each of the three volumes of *The Digital Hand*. Every industry also embraced the Internet through the course of several stages of adoption at approximately the same time, proof to me that managers learned from within their industries and from sources in other industries about the evolution and appropriate uses of IT.

17 Described by a series of experts in Sean Ekins and Binghe Wang (eds.), *Computer Applications in Pharmaceutical Research and Development* (New York: John Wiley & Sons, 2006).

18 IBM Institute for Business Value, *The Customer-Activated Enterprise* (Somers, NY: IBM Corporation, 2013), available at http://www-935.ibm.com/services/us/en/c-suite/csuitestudy2013/ (last accessed December 15, 2013).

19 There is now a substantial body of research on these new forms of learning. For an introduction to this work, see Rob Cross and Sam Israelit (eds.), *Strategic Learning in a Knowledge Economy: Individual, Collective, and Organizational Learning Process* (Boston, MA: Butterworth-Heinemann, 2000).

20 As a process consultant in the 1990s and early 2000s, I designed a number of corporate suggestion processes, and other processes that too drew from what other firms were doing reputed to have best practices. In every successful case, the "best" offered some morsels of insights and wisdom, but the actual process had to be designed fundamentally different from one firm to another. Even the software tools were different since these applications (processes) had to integrate into preexisting ones in the firm. Twenty years of this experience made me highly suspicious of what were "best practices," although trade magazines, book authors, and consultants love the notion.

21 One of the first scholars to document the role of knowledge management was economist Fritz Machlup in a series of books published from the early 1960s into the 1980s. His initial seminal study was *The Production and Distribution of Knowledge in the United States* (Princeton, NJ: Princeton University Press, 1962), summarizing research conducted during the 1950s. For historical perspectives there is James W. Cortada (ed.), *Rise of the Knowledge Worker* (Boston, MA: Butterworth-Heinemann, 1998).

22 For most of the twentieth century, discussions about the economic value of innovation were left to the economists, often with Joseph Schumpeter leading the way, at

least in the first half of the century. However, management first became acutely aware of the role of innovation with the publication of Richard Foster, *Innovation: The Attacker's Advantage* (New York: Summit Books, 1986). For an example of how innovation plays out in high-tech industries, see Henry Kressel with Thomas V. Lento, *Competing for the Future: How Digital Innovations Are Changing the World* (Cambridge, UK: Cambridge University Press, 2007).

23 Dale Neef (ed.), *The Knowledge Economy* (Boston, MA: Butterworth-Heinemann, 1998); Dale Neef, G. Anthony Siesfeld, and Jacquelyn Cefola (eds.), *The Economic Impact of Knowledge* (Boston, MA: Butterworth-Heinemann, 1998); Dale Neef, *A Little Knowledge Is a Dangerous Thing: Understanding Our Global Knowledge Economy* (Boston, MA: Butterworth-Heinemann, 1999): 1–68; Dominique Foray, *The Economics of Knowledge* (Cambridge, MA: MIT Press, 2004): 21–48.

24 A recent analysis of this problem provides examples and an excellent discussion, "The Gated Globe," *The Economist*, October 12, 2013, "Special Report World Economy," 3–20.

25 IBM Institute for Business Value, *The Enterprise of the Future: Global CEO Study* (Somers, NY: IBM Corporation, 2008) and IBM Institute for Business Value, *Working Beyond Borders: Insights from the Global Chief Human Resource Officer Study* (Somers, NY: IBM Corporation, 2010).

26 A line of historical research attracting the attention of historians. For examples, see Joel Mokyr, *The Gifts of Athena: Historical Origins of the Knowledge Economy* (Princeton, NJ: Princeton University Press, 2002) and James Beniger, *The Control Revolution; Technological and Economic Origins of the Information Society* (Cambridge, MA: Harvard University Press, 1989).

27 Same as Lesser and CEO survey.

28 IBM's business research center, The IBM Institute for Business Value, continuously tracks these issues and publishes between 35 and 50 reports each year and also updates data on key earlier studies. To keep up with these reports, go to www.ibm.com/iibv.

29 Jeanne W. Ross, "Research Findings on IT and Business Agility," May 2, 2006, Center for Information Systems Research, MIT Sloan School of Management, available at http://mitsloan.mit.edu/cisr/ (last accessed November 7, 2011).

30 Ibid.

31 IBM Global Business Services, *Expanding the Innovation Horizon: The Global CEO Study 2006* (Somers, NY: IBM Corporation, 2006), available at http://www.ibm.com/ibm/ideasfromibm/us/enterprise/mar27/ceo_study.html (last accessed November 7, 2011).

32 Jeanne W. Ross, Peter Weill, David Robertson, *Architecture as Strategy: Creating a Foundation for Business Execution* (Boston, MA: Harvard Business School Press, 2006).

33 In each of the three volumes of *The Digital Hand*, passim.

34 James W. Cortada, *The Digital Hand*, vol. 1, *How Computers Changed the Work of American Manufacturing, Transportation, and Retail Industries* (New York: Oxford University Press, 2004): 318–322.

35 Some argue very effectively how industry-centered perspectives can damage the ability of a firm to grow its business, see for example, Rita Gunther McGrath, *The*

End of Competitive Advantage: How to Keep Your Strategy Moving as Fast as Your Business (Boston, MA: Harvard Business Review Press, 2013): 9–12.

36 One recent example illustrates the trend, Anita M. McCahan, *How Industries Evolve: Principles for Achieving and Sustaining Superior Performance* (Boston, MA: Harvard Business School Press, 2004). Most of the literature is specifically about one industry. I have cited many of these in the bibliographic essays included in each volume of *The Digital Hand*.

37 For a sorting by type of consulting, see Kennedy Publications, *The Directory of Management Consultants* (Fitzwilliam, NH: Kennedy Publications, annual).

38 The Charles Babbage Institute at the University of Minnesota has an extensive archive of such materials and well-developed finding aids. These can be found at http://www.cbi.umn.edu/collections/archmss.html (last accessed April 7, 2013).

39 Jeffrey Liker, *The Toyota Way* (New York: McGraw-Hill, 2003). It epitomized concepts of lean manufacturing. The notion was introduced to non-Japanese automotive manufacturers largely by Taiichi Ohno, *Toyota Production System* (Portland, OR: Productivity Press, 1988).

40 Greenspan, *The Age of Turbulence*, 12.

41 IBM Institute for Business Value, *The Customer-activated Enterprise.*

42 http://www.google.com/glass/start/what-it-does/ (last accessed December 15, 2013).

43 Benjamin M. Friedman, "Brave New Capitalists' Paradise: The Jobs?," *The New York Review of Books*, December 6, 2013, available at http://www.nybooks.com/articles/archives/2013/nov/07/brave-new-capitalists-paradise-jobs/ (last accessed December 6, 2013).

44 Peter F. Drucker, *Management: Tasks, Responsibilities, Practices* (New York: Harper & Row, 1974): 17.

45 A pattern of practice identified by many observers by the 1990s. See, for example, Peter Cappelli and his team of coauthors, *Change at Work* (New York: Oxford University Press, 1997).

46 "The Gated Globe," *The Economist*, October 12, 2013, "Special Report World Economy," 3–20.

47 Angus Maddison, *Growth and Interaction in the World Economy: The Roots of Modernity* (Washington, DC: American Enterprise Institute Press, 2005): 10–16. I have commented further as well in James W. Cortada, *Information and the Modern Corporation* (Cambridge, MA: MIT Press, 2011) and in *The Digital Flood: The Diffusion of Information Technology Across the U.S., Europe, and Asia* (New York: Oxford University Press, 2012).

48 Angus Maddison, *Growth and Interaction in the World Economy: The Roots of Modernity* (Washington, DC: Aei Press, 2005): 22.

49 Ibid., 5.

CHAPTER 3

How Technologies Affect the Work of Industries

> ...it is uncanny how often executives—even within the same firm—disagree over how they [industry] should be drawn.
>
> Anita M. McGahan[1]

Has anyone ever seen an industry? Is there a building one can walk into that has a sign out front announcing that this is the Automotive Industry or the Insurance Industry? And yet, industries are real, the ultimate virtual organizations, institutions that predated the arrival of the computer and that have provided structure to work and economic activities for at least two centuries—an idea introduced in Chapter 2. Today, there are many virtual organizations that exist only in the minds of people and surface in Internet-based chat rooms, conventions of like-minded people, publications aimed at these audiences, and in the statistics on economic performance produced by government economists since at least World War I; industries are one set of these. In the language of scientists and economists, they can also be labeled "communities of practice." Historians thought often of such communities as guilds in the Middle Ages and craft unions in the nineteenth and early twentieth centuries.

The Essential Manager: How to Thrive in the Global Information Jungle, First Edition.
James W. Cortada.
© 2015 the IEEE Computer Society. Published 2015 by John Wiley & Sons, Inc.

Industries are real, active, vibrant, and not to be ignored. Some provide an international alternative reality to that of national economies.

This chapter discusses how industries and their technologies affect the work of management in a globalized, increasingly connected economy. Make no mistake, the behavior of industries affects directly the work of many people. They set standards for how things are done, create processes by which people are credentialed through certification boards and associations (as happens with accountants, doctors, and lawyers, for example), provide information about best practices, and offer education and a sense of community. In some countries, government agencies organize these into almost mega-corporations to promote and implement a national economic initiative, as occurs often in South Korea, Japan, and China on a regular basis. They are real.

So, there are characteristics of industries that need to be understood within the context of how national economies are structured and the work of today's manager and his or her firm. In this chapter, we focus less on the mega-economic structures of industries and more on what the individual manager and his or her company does and must do going forward. Because the role of IT in the life of an industry has become extremely influential in how industries function, some of those features need to be described. I use the word *some*, because the expanding role of IT within an industry's context is still evolving and emerging. Also, with so much IT now being used, and in fact, still increasing, traditional managerial practices of having an IT organization responsible for implementation of technologies are being swamped by employees who are very comfortable in using, implementing, or hiring IT resources with which to carry out their work.[2]

We approach the issue of industries with four discussions by defining what an industry is, describing their behavior, cataloging risks encountered in being part of an industry, and how IT affects them, especially their overall strategies. In each discussion, the role and implications for management are presented. This chapter ends with a discussion of the implications for management, as they are significant, calling for specific actions on their part that are becoming essential components of the emerging new style of management.

WHAT IS AN INDUSTRY?

This may seem to be an odd question, because managers must obviously already know in which industry their company or agency works. But the answer is not always certain. For example, ask FedEx/Kinko's employees what industry they are in and they pause. Is it in package delivery? Or printing? Or are they in retailing, selling packing materials and office supplies? Are they in the copier business or in photography?[3] Newspapers, reporters, TV commentators, and many business writers routinely use the term *industry* in a sloppy manner, labeling groups of firms as industries that are not readily recognizable by companies or economists. Common examples include the technology industry, media industry, and entertainment industry. So, what constitutes the technology industry—IT, bioinformatics, space travel, or MRI manufacturing by GE? What is the media industry—newspapers and magazines, or also TV and the Internet, or radio and movies? What about Apple and its iPods and iPads; is that firm now in the media industry, or because of iPhones in telecommunications, or a manufacturer of electronics products? Apple managers still think of themselves as purveyors of personal computers, as manufacturers, yet now as major players in consumer electronics and the software business. In short, many people can be quite imprecise in their use of the word industry.

But why do we care about naming conventions? We pay very little attention in this book to defining terms because it is aimed at practitioners of management already familiar with the language of business. But in this particular case, it turns out, as suggested in Chapter 2, in what industry a firm operates has important implications for how it performs and on the careers and work of individual managers. In fact, there is a large body of empirical evidence in support of that statement, and the research reinforcing that notion continues to pile up on a regular basis.[4] Economists have led the way by describing the activities of specific industries to such an extent that there is considerable clarity about what a specific industry consists of in terms of member firms, business practices, rates of performance, and their roles in society and within an economy. Economists working for governments have also selected what industries to track and equally precisely, what firms *by name* are within those industries. Thus, for example, every firm in the United States that has to report income, pay taxes, and log employment data with the federal government is assigned to a specific industry. Data at the firm level is collected and summarized by economists at an aggregate industry level. When the U.S. government announces that the banking industry did more or less business in a particular quarter, its economists can go back and provide a list of every bank from which they obtained the data used in direct support of the public pronouncement.[5] Both in Europe and in the United States, government analysts have done this for nearly a century. Today, over half of all national governments, and every member of the OECD, collect data on economic activity about an industry to such an extent that the debates are never whether to do so, rather about if the Chinese are reporting accurate data, for instance, or why another country does not. So, by custom and law, firms are members of industries and these memberships are well understood by at least the senior management of those companies.

Yet, managers have faced a real problem since the 1980s with respect to industry identification and the effects that murky views of boundaries and roles have on their firm's business strategies. Part of this murkiness is caused by the role and effect of IT on an industry's work and position within an economy. Thousands of observers of industries have written articles and books commenting on how the boundaries of various industries are blurring, or have been radically altered in recent decades. For instance, hundreds of technology commentators have been announcing the desegregation of industry borders since the 1980s.

Photography is an extreme example. Kodak, which produced film, developed photographs, and manufactured cameras for consumers and professional markets and dominated the photography industry for a century, faced enormous problems in the 1990s and early 2000s as consumers and professional photographers moved rapidly away from film-based photography to digital photography. By the early 2000s, the firm's biggest competitors were Japanese consumer electronics companies that also sold the digital cameras that became the basis for digital photography. So, was Kodak now in the consumer electronics industry, which played by very different rules than the old photography industry? This company's experience in high end, consumer electronics was quite limited, instantly putting it in a disadvantageous position vis-à-vis its new rivals. Kodak's experience will undoubtedly be the subject of many business school case studies, but for our purposes, it provides evidence of the power of technology with which to change rapidly the fortunes of a firm or whole industry, and the importance of an industry's context to the well-being of a firm. In Kodak's case, management did not understand well enough the strengths of the firm within the ecosystem of consumer retail businesses nor of its technological capabilities that might apply in other industries. The result of this lack of insight was the near fatal collapse of the firm by 2012 and many tens of thousands of employee losing their jobs, including thousands of managers and executives in the space of a decade.[6]

While we have more to say about the role of IT on industries later in this chapter, it is important to point out that many non-technological factors also led to the obfuscation of industry border lines, most notably the global trend of deregulating many activities of firms underway since the 1980s all over the world. For example, in many countries, banks have been given increased latitude to offer services that previously were the exclusive domain of other financial industries, such as insurance and brokerage. In other nations, constraints increased, for instance in Japan, where the government has been stripping the postal system of its ability to offer customers savings accounts and other financial services. Some of these regulatory actions reflected the economic and managerial philosophies of a nation and its political leaders, such as in the United States where the impulse to deregulate many industries proved great in the belief that these would become more competitive in a globalized economy in the 1990s. Regulators working within the European Union also issued many regulations intended to foster competition (e.g., forcing Microsoft to share its software's design and content with competitors) and imposed significant environmental standards on all firms (e.g., regarding the return to a retailer of used PCs and printers). Regulatory practices influenced profoundly the ability of pharmaceutical firms to introduce new drugs (or to hold onto their patents), with often the difference in having a patent or not involving billions of dollars in revenue for a firm and, consequently, for the careers and incomes of individual managers. In yet other instances, the lack of regulatory initiatives caused havoc in an industry, as occurred in China in 2007–2008 when customers around the world and in China learned that its seafood was tainted, toys had been manufactured using lead paint, and some medicines improperly manufactured.[7] In subsequent years, there was a resurgence of regulators asserting new rules and defining boundaries across all financial industries in direct response to the global recession of 2008–2012.

Government financial subsidies and taxation also help define the contours of an industry, influencing the extent to which a firm might want to participate in one versus another. For example, it is quite common for national governments to influence what crops and animals farmers raise, either by paying them to grow or not to grow a particular crop, raise a certain type of livestock, or to prop up the price one gets for their products. The French do it for tomato farmers, the EU for vineyards, the Americans for dairy products. Thus, what gets a subsidy or not influences what crops a farmer will cultivate. The fundamental basis of the free trade movement of the past three decades, creation of regional trading areas such as NAFTA (North American Free Trade Agreement) and the EU, and global trading agreements via the World Trade Organization (WTO) are in direct response to what public officials want to have happen in the performance of specific national industries functioning within a local or globalized economy. Thus, for instance, within the context of the WTO, certain practices called dumping, in which goods from one country are sold at below cost or are subsidized by the exporting nation, can lead to international law suits and punishments of a firm or a whole industry within a country. Americans accused the Chinese of dumping computer chips and steel into the American economy to the competitive detriment of local chip and steel industries, while the Europeans have had issues with the United States regarding agricultural products competing against European farmers. Both went to adjudication in an international court that had the authority to order changes in the policies and law of nations.

Because of the proactive role played by all governments in determining what an industry can or cannot do, hence their boundaries, firms within industries and associations representing industries spend an enormous amount of time and money influencing decisions made by regulators, government agencies enforcing regulations, and legislatures passing laws or approving trade treaties. It is not uncommon, for example, for industries to maintain full-time lobbyists in major capital cities in the most advanced economies of the world. Senior management in major firms spends considerable time in places like Washington, DC, Brussels, London, Tokyo, Singapore, and Beijing, persuading regulators and legislators to take actions that affect favorably their industries and firms. If anything, the amount of time spent by a company's senior officers dealing with such matters is still continuing to increase, and in all likelihood will continue to expand in the years to come, because we have entered a period when globalized regulatory practices are being implemented as well and with NGOs become simultaneously quite influential too on regulators, legislators, customers, and firms.[8] At the same time, governments are working to rationalize (often referred to as *harmonizing*) the behavior of industries in the increasingly internationalized global economy.

One other trend not always so obvious or visible in the regulatory process is the role of middle and lower management and experts within a firm. Normally, a company does not allow its employees to talk to regulators or elected officials, preferring to use its government relations staff, media liaisons, lobbyists, and senior executives to do that. However, as employees across a firm became active as leaders in their national industry associations, or, became recognized as experts due to their work and publications in industry magazines, blogs and books, they influence the opinions of regulators and legislators, or are called upon to inform them. Over time young managers and young regulators have met and grown up in their two professions, remaining friends or at least well known to each other. Sometimes they even swap jobs as occurs frequently in the United States at fairly senior levels in such industries as defense, banking, and other highly regulated industries.

So, we come back to our question, what is an industry? It is important to have a model, albeit even if a simple one, since functioning successfully as a manager and a business is in part dependent on leveraging to one's advantage the ecosystem sustained by an industry. There is also another reason for a definition, because new ones appear all the time, some due to a new product, market, and business model (e.g., in recent years the video game business), and in other instances, because government economists are identifying clusters of businesses as constituting new industries (e.g., many of the information industries "created" by the U.S. government's economists in the late 1990s).[9] For our purposes, as a practical matter, an industry is a cluster of firms that compete with each other, and also against companies in other industries, with similar products, services, sets of customers, and often with more similar than dissimilar business models, firms, and business strategies. Members of an industry recognize fellow members of their part of the economy and take explicit actions to compete or collaborate with these companies. That has been an effective working definition for decades.

The competitive aspect is a fundamental building block and home to a set of assumptions about how firms interact and it is also relatively straightforward: these are members of an industry whose employees get up every morning and try to take away business from your firm. You know them well, the rivalry is personal, and customers know the relationships you have with each other. Collaborating with rivals is often also a reality within an industry and can range from being business partners pursing opportunities together (such as joint bidding on a project where each has complimentary skills) or working together as a lobbyist team to get a specific regulation or law passed or changed.

Another way to posit a definition is to characterize the elements of collective behavior similar to a group of industries. Those who have studied the behavior of industries tend to include the following features as shared by member firms:

- Common buyers and suppliers
- Competitive intent
- Technical platforms.[10]

Regardless of which typology one adopts, I find each one useful for this chapter and for managerial work, because they confirm the common practice of structuring one's thinking about an otherwise abstract, hard-to-define issue, in this case what should seem to be a relatively simple task, the identification of what industry one works in so as to figure out what strategies to deploy and how to perform. Later in this chapter, we discuss why placing too much emphasis on industry perspectives could limit your business strategies.

Today, industries have two other sets of characteristics that help define when an industry exists. They normally have associations, and industry-specific publications, not just magazines about a profession that may or may not be exclusive to an industry (e.g., *CFO Magazine* read by financial officers in many industries or *Chief Executive* aimed at senior executives also across multiple industries). Industry associations and groups of executives form task forces made up of managers and employees from multiple firms within an industry to address an industry-wide issue, such as a law or technical standard. Members of an industry also come together on a regular basis at national or international conferences designed to address the issues and needs of members of an industry. Everything described so far was true of industries in 1925, 1975, and today, except for the fact that IT and communications now is pervasive and practical, and the practice of attending conferences widespread easily, thanks to relatively inexpensive air travel. Such features of industry activities have made one's connections to an industry more concrete over time, hence more real and less abstract.

Another set of shared circumstances is that they no longer are largely rooted within a national economy; rather, they are globalizing. One goes to a conference and sees attendees from all over the world, most recently from India, China, other parts of Asia and Latin America. Subscriptions to industry magazines and other publications are increasingly international. Managers from around the world routinely listen to industry webcasts. These features of industry communications are incrementally becoming more common than ever before. One consequence is that managers are beginning to act like members of industries at an international level. Only in the area of advocacy of a firm's point of view do companies and national industry associations still work on an issue at a country level, persuading their local national standards communities or representatives to an international body about their point of view rather than directly having some international industry-wide conversation with an international organization, such as the WTO, OECD, or EU.[11] But, in time that may change too if international associations change their decision-making model of having national delegates vote on a policy on behalf of their national constituencies.[12] But in the meantime, national perspectives will dominate the attention of managers and their firms when they are lobbying or dealing with regulators.

What does all this discussion mean, therefore, for a manager? At all levels within an organization it means several things. Managers need to know what industry they are a part of while paying attention to what their industry is doing as a whole. If there was one action any manager should take relative to industries, it is to join one or more of its major associations regardless of whether their employer will pay the memberships fees or not; it is that important. Then, at least read regularly its trade magazines and when relevant, its journals. From time to time, attend their annual conventions and early in one's career at least participate in their education and certification programs. After a couple of years of membership in which you learn about the industry and its associations, become active within it to the extent time permits, presenting at conventions, joining committees, standing for elections, and setting agendas for the organization and the industry as your leadership authority increases. I would do these in the order just listed, from joining and presenting to leading. Not enough people do this yet, even by middle and senior managers with years of experience, so the opportunities to say grace over whole swaths of a national economy are there to be had. Environmentalist associations in Europe demonstrate this level of influence while in the United States chambers of commerce do so at the state level, and the American Medical Association (AMA) in national affairs. Not all the voices in these organizations are CEOs; many are lower level managers in their firms and agencies who have spent years volunteering within associations, earning their stripes so to speak.

In short, the role and structure of industries is not expected to change or go away in the foreseeable future. It is such a proven way of organizing within business that, if anything, we can expect to see more industry ecosystems appear in those national economies that become increasingly similar to those of the most advanced economies, first by opening chapters to large international associations, and second, local economists plugging into the data collection efforts of such organizations as the UN, OPEC, IMF, World Bank, and the WTO. Those two actions alone will stimulate industries to acquire rapidly identities in emerging economies all over the world. As with so many other activities discussed in this book, it will be an evolutionary process of expansion and change, which is all good news for today's manager who might be trying to figure out how to leverage industries and their infrastructures for economic benefit.

BEHAVIOR IN AN INDUSTRY-CENTRIC WORLD

If industries have individual personalities, how do these affect the work of managers? There are effects and they are caused in ways similar to what happens to managers today. Industries have *styles* of working that evolve over time. However, one can generalize too much about the behavior and attributes of industries for the fact of the matter is that banking industries are different from automotive industries, electronics from movies, and so forth. Economists and others have done much work to create various taxonomies of industries that can assist managers. Two relatively new models briefly introduced here suggest the kinds of methodologies managers are increasingly relying upon to organize their understanding of the industries in which they work. There is no doubt that others will be constructed during the working careers of today's managers, since we live in a time when processes and

Table 3.1   McGahan industry trajectories[a]

Progressive	Discount retailing, long-haul trucking, commercial airlines
Creative	Pharmaceuticals, motion-picture production, oil/gas exploration
Intermediating	Investment brokerage, fine-arts auctions, automobile dealerships
Radical	Overnight letter delivery, landline telephone manufacturing

[a]Derived from Anita M. McGahan, *How Industries Evolve: Principles for Achieving and Sustaining Superior Performance* (Boston, MA: Harvard Business School Press, 2004): 9.

systems are valued as part of the emerging *style* of management. What is important to remember, however, is that managers are increasingly becoming students of their industries, looking at them in some structured manner posed by some economist, sociologist, cultural anthropologist,[13] or professor of business management or public administration.

Table 3.1 describes a model, derived from the one developed by Anita M. McGahan, to help managers identify the styles of behavior of four types of industries so as to understand how they change. We can debate whether or not she "got it right," but the important point is that she developed a typology in order to explain how companies could change their business models, strategies, and so forth synchronized with core attributes of one's industry. In this particular instance, McGahan observed that "when a strategy is aligned with industry evolution, a firm's performance improves," in such areas as acquisition and retention of customers (which becomes easier and less expensive to do), relationships with suppliers "become easier to manage," while competitive threats diminish.[14] In fact, she is rather exuberant about her findings: "your strategy *cannot* succeed if it violates the rules of change in your industry," adding that "if your organization has the flexibility to redefine its strategy around the opportunities created by the trajectory of industry evolution, then the chances for improving your profitability are compounded."[15] This is strong language, yet borne out by her investigations and those of others. Her research takes to a more granular level insights developed a quarter of a century earlier by Michael E. Porter, when he introduced his now widely used Five Forces Models that today probably every MBA student in the world learns. He argued that for any industry shifts in five forces cause some of their greatest changes. These are shifts in technology, demographics, regulations, trade barriers, and political circumstances. Managers have found his model—again a simple one to explain yet complex to apply—useful in establishing an industry's average profitability, for example, and for assessing potential strategic options against a typology and set of targets. It also helped to define the features of an industry.[16] We will later in this chapter encounter Rita Gunther McGrath's work that says industries are not as important as just suggested, but both McGrath and McGahan deliver an important message: we have to be more granular in how we look at an industry and how management responds to specific influences flowing from it.

You should, therefore, dive deeper from a model of your industry, to moving toward identification of the kind of behavior needed to be effective in one dimension of your business, such as in the deployment of IT or some other technology. Figure 3.1 illustrates what happens if one positions various industries along two axes: the vertical describing the extent of required collaboration among members of an industry (e.g., in banking where they have to transfer money to and from each other) as compared to a second, horizontal axis, describing the extent to which practices and institutions within an industry define the nature of that collaboration.

Managers can then take that same matrix and ask themselves how they must alter their practices when selling goods and services into a particular industry. Figure 3.2 identifies what behavioral characteristics

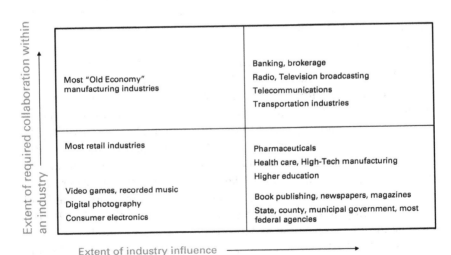

Figure 3.1 Industry collaboration.

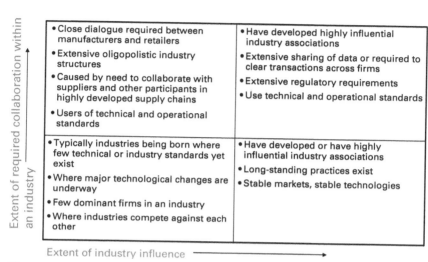

Figure 3.2 Industry behavioral characteristics.

are needed to influence decision makers on the acquisition of complex products, such as software or computers. Each of the quadrants in Figure 3.2 correlates to those in the previous figure. Then, if one extends the discussion to what a manager has to take into account when deploying whatever the technology they bought, using the same matrix, we can see that behavior has to vary depending on the kind of industry in which a particular firm operates. Those behaviors are illustrated in a simple manner in Figure 3.3. All three sets of quadrants are based on the behaviors of many industries over a half-century, proof that while much changes over time, some realities and behaviors evolve less so, or not at all.[17]

The Scottish economist and business management professor, John Kay, has commented for years on how globalization affects the behaviors of whole industries, consequently too, of managers in firms playing on a global stage. He has demonstrated that globalization of economic activities erodes national markets for an industry. It is a process that favors firms that leverage well their distinctive, but continuously evolving, competitive advantages. That leveraging process calls for an enterprise to exploit its distinctive advantages rather than to rely on the historical incumbency it had when ensconced in the comfortable zone of a national market. This line of reasoning makes a great deal of sense for managers today who deal with the wider market of the entire world. Market share or size of a firm is not a source (*cause*, Kay's word) of competitive advantage. Rather, it is success that results in large size. In a global

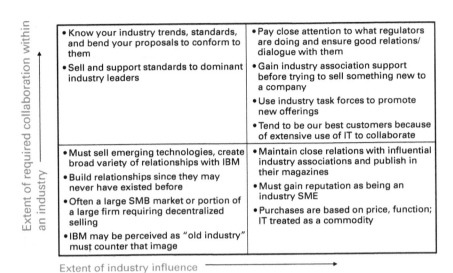

Figure 3.3   Management considerations within an industry.

economy, firms succeed when they match a capability—what Kay calls a firm's "distinctive capabilities," hence difficult for others to replicate—to a market's realities (read, industry too), what he simply labels as "market opportunities"; when they have a valued brand and reputation, because these cannot be reproduced so easily by a competitor; when they innovate in myriad ways, such as in the introduction of new products; are structured to optimize relationships with suppliers and customers (a variation of McGahan's notion of riding an industry's trajectory of change, Table 3.1); and have assets that are difficult to replicate, such as knowledge acquired over a long period of time and not available elsewhere, or possible to replicate within a cost justifiable period of time.[18]

The ideas developed by these various students of business realities represent useful and enduring insights for managers. They all suffer, of course, from the problem of being too generalized for many readers and for possibly discounting the cultural differences that exist in how work is done in various countries. That is where managers have to tailor such useful broad thinking into terms that are relevant to themselves and to the situations they face right now. So, the issue is not so much is Porter's views on competitive strategy too static, for example, but how to apply his five forces to specific circumstances. That is the task of managers, and why the work of people like McGahan and McGrath are so useful, but too must be embraced with prudence.

RISKS OF WORKING WITHIN AN INDUSTRY

Next, we can ask, what risks exist for managers and firms operating within industries that are global in nature? It is a topic fraught with emotion, new and changing circumstances, and relatively little empirical research. But, as a firm becomes a globally integrated enterprise (most commonly called a GIE), some obvious considerations come into play that, while not lethal, must be understood and mitigated. If a company cannot deliver value to its customers in a particular nation because of social unrest, a pandemic, war, or riots, for instance, that is classic business disruption. But, as a firm increasingly becomes dependent on its revenues from multiple nations, it perforce increases the number of potential points of failure. These circumstances are complicated by the fact that markets and opportunities are often significantly variegated, making it difficult to have a "one size fits all" strategy intended to optimize scale and scope as we traditionally think of the concept. Yet, managers of multinational firms always try to achieve that optimization. It is, quite frankly, a mistake repeated frequently and not called out loudly enough.

A second collection of potential risks come from the extended internal processes that straddle multiple nations, cultures, time zones, rates of productivity, and worker efficiencies. These are subject to variations in costs of labor for similar work, and the simultaneous clash of effective and ineffective practices in work and decision-making. The "talent war" has its own mitigating circumstances: rapidly aging work forces in Japan, Italy, and Germany, while burgeoning yet inexperienced young work-forces in India, China, Brazil, and parts of Africa. Significant gaps in capabilities can occur between experienced and junior workers, while pipelines of replacement managers can empty quickly (and that varies by industry as well) and that cannot be refilled fast enough, as is occurring in many rapidly growing emerging markets in Asia, for example.[19]

Managers are also beginning to ask, "How can I simultaneously achieve cost and value advantages?" Failing to execute enterprise-level priorities, while understanding and making practical trade-offs, is one manifestation of the problem posed by the question. Balancing resources with needs of customers around the world is a real and chronic early problem emerging from globalization that has yet to be resolved. Simply stated with a ridiculous example to illustrate the point—if everyone who wants a haircut lives in France and most of my barbers work in China, how do I take care of the needs of my customers? Poor process design is also a critical risk factor as processes are implemented with process steps executed in myriad countries. You would want to outsource haircutting to countries with the lowest labor costs for barbers, deliver consistently high-quality (read competitive) hair-cutting services, but you really cannot because no customer in France is willing to fly to Vietnam, for example, to get a hair cut. You can obtain cost advantages if you made hair clippers and barber chairs, but more people make a living delivering hair-cutting services than in selling clippers and chairs. So, while the question may seem too simple to ask an MBA student, it is a really difficult one to answer if that student is a few years later a product development manager in either a manufacturing company or in a services firm. The simple becomes complex, and the answers keep changing.

There is additionally the ill defined, most nebulous of all risk factors: the pace of globalization. The future arrives unevenly in all manner of work and circumstances, and nowhere is this lesson once again being relearned than in the world of internationalized firms and industries. Individual national markets will be more or less receptive to specific products, services, contractual terms, and conditions than a manager might want. For example, in the United States, a cell phone service provider can ask and get a 2 year contractual commitment for its service, thereby stabilizing cash flows and reducing marketing expenses. But in Sub-Sahara Africa, where demand for cell phones is equally keen, customers will not agree to a 2 year contract; they prefer buying time on a cell phone in monetary increments equivalent to a few cents or dollars. In some parts of Asia, the sale might be to a village that shares the phone among many residents. A corollary is that governmental regulations still vary enormously from one country to another, thereby inhibiting the ability of a firm to evolve into a GIE or an industry to become highly integrated on a global basis. While regulators and standards boards are collaborating more than ever before, they are, nonetheless, moving slower than managers might desire to harmonize regulations. Furthermore, a noisy public scandal for a firm or industry in one country will assuredly be publicized almost instantaneously around the world. Thus, if a firm or industry experiences legal problems because of bribes in Mexico, for instance, regulators in Europe will start investigating the same firm or industry to see if the same is going on in the EU, while U.S. government prosecutors will follow suit too, since American laws apply to all American firms and American citizens regardless in what countries they operate. And regulators share information about bad behavior as they are doing now in going after those financial institutions that they collectively believe caused the Great Recession of 2008–2012.

In short, the list of risks that managers face are real, are also somewhat familiar in that they existed in smaller variants within the context of a nation's economy, and either can be mitigated or will expand due to the behavior of an industry as a whole. A highly experienced executive might argue that the list is not new; however, their diversity and potential opportunities to rise up remain substantial. The message for management is simple: they will have to deal with these contingencies at the same time that they are enthusiastically figuring out how to sell more goods and services to ever-larger or changing markets.

Which are the most critical risks for an industry? It all depends, of course, on the industry, circumstance of a particular firm, and the geopolitical and environmental realities on a particular day. That said, a good list of the most severe would include inadequate supply of the right-skilled labor as the greatest risk to success; followed by inadequate understanding, trust among multicultural sets of employees, public officials, and customers; rejection by the public and, hence, their governments of where companies move their work seem to be the next level down of potential problems. A final tier of reasonable possibilities always include not creating firm-level or industry-level business models and practices that take advantage of those features of a globalized economy that seemed attractive to a firm or industry in the first place. An experienced manager knows to draw up such a list, rank their potential severity to his or her firm, and develop risk mitigation responses in advance of an actual crisis. That task has not changed since Peter Drucker and others began codifying managerial behavior decades ago. What has changed is the development of many tools and techniques that now represent important sources of revenue for all of the major managerial consulting firms.

Lest the reader think that these issues are only relevant to large international enterprises, such as to the *Fortune* 1000, several sobering statistics highlight the scope involved. There has been an enormous increase in international players just in the recent past. Between 1990 and 2005, the number of firms playing on the international stage rose from 35,000 to 70,000, while the number of foreign affiliates of existing firms did too, by 360% from 160,000 to 690,000. Translated into sales, foreign affiliates alone increased their revenues from US$4.4 trillion in 1990 to US$19 trillion in 2005. By any measure, these data reflect a significant expansion in international trade.[20] The opportunities for people to misbehave, to create problems, and to not be able to respond effectively to crises are numerous and diverse. That reality is part of the style of how today's industries work and management functions.

Useful practices continue to emerge; we summarized some of those in the earlier discussion about risk mitigation. Being cognizant that the work one does in any organization could become the conversation of millions is a reality driven by the wide use of social media tools, not just by the traditional press media of television and newspapers. Managers are rapidly becoming far more sensitive to the role of Twitter, in particular, and other similar messaging systems, because these are rapidly becoming sources of communities of interest around specific issues and problems and can be quick to pick up on a leaked problem from a corporation or individual and make it a national issue within hours or a few days. That is a very new reality for managers, from a first line newly minted one to a gray-haired 40-year veteran of management. My own research suggests that too many organizations and their management do not "get it," when it comes to the risks (and opportunities too) of social media. It now remains perhaps the single least understood circumstance affecting risks, the prospects of a firm, and the characteristics of an industry. So, it behooves managers to learn more about this new reality rather quickly as it transcends the kind of IT discussion that is next in this chapter.

HOW IT AFFECTS INDUSTRIES AND SHAPES THEIR STRATEGIES

Begin by recognizing what is obvious and true, before thinking of threats and opportunities that may change what is today's reality. The historical record indicates that IT, in particular, has long affected the construct and functioning of firms within an industry and of industries themselves. The technology, when applied concurrently with other nontechnical initiatives, such as business strategy, capital investments, and so forth, affects what is done or offered by an industry. Additionally, technology makes it possible for industries to scale up to more global-wide forms, as occurred most dramatically in the last quarter of the twentieth century in banking and in the sale of stocks and bonds. There has been much confusion and debate about the strategic value of IT in today's world, with some misguided statements that IT is no longer a strategic tool at either the firm or industry level;[21] a contention not borne out by the facts.[22] We sort out some of this confusion and then discuss four types of IT-dependent strategies that are in wide evidence as emerging ways of using computing in support of business strategies. These represent components of the new *style* of management. They are formed, articulated, and structured, and are bounded by systems and processes, evident and measureable. But first we need to understand some misconceptions.

An important misunderstanding about IT and industries involves the belief that technologies destroy or deconstruct industries. To state the obvious, IT does nothing of the sort, because much like a hammer lying on a workbench or a kitchen knife in a drawer, IT does nothing by itself. To damage a firm or industry, one needs incompetent managers or unforeseen economic or political crises. Only when used by people in support of some activity—such as hammering a nail to hang a picture on a wall or to cut a piece of meat to cook for a meal—does a tool become animated. Yet, there has been a substantial debate and even a body of beliefs created on the role of IT in transforming industries and firms.[23] Even historians, who are normally wise to the problem and reject the notion that technologies are intentional, life-like, and anthropomorphic, sometimes have to pause and ask themselves under the weight of so much rhetoric about computers and other technologies, if these are not more than inanimate artifacts of society.[24] One of the most widely held beliefs by managers, business school professors, economists, and regulators is that IT has the power to destroy industries much like earlier technologies were argued to have done, such as the refrigerator eliminating the need for ice cutters on lakes at the end of the nineteenth century.

Clayton M. Christensen's discussion about the innovator's dilemma is a quite interesting expression of the idea that technology can destroy firms and industries.[25] In his case study about the ice cutters, for example, use of refrigeration became an attractive economic and technical alternative to the older way of producing ice for sale outside of a local market, but someone had to use the technology first and in time the ice cutters were not able to continue competing against the effective use of that technology, such as initially in refrigerated train cars and later in industrial then home refrigerators. What he and others wisely have noted as economic destruction, or just varying degrees of change, did not occur without some other organization or set of products and technologies replacing them. In other word, a creative process is the cause of destruction of an old way and thus the destructive process's counterpart. Put in practical terms, as something is changing or falling apart, look for what is replacing it. That hunt for the new may be obvious (as in the case of digital photography replacing film, customers buying more goods online rather than by walking into a bricks-and-mortar store) or less so, such as when an industry transforms (as did the U.S. banking industry when it began selling securities and derivatives after 1998). Changes that cause transformations of companies and whole industries, however, tend not to be so obvious if they occur slowly, although they look clear and came fast when we read about them in hindsight. While in the "thick of battle" engaged in the daily work of our companies, we can lose sight of these destructive forces and so have to consciously keep looking for them. If there is an "a-ha" here, it is to assume there are disruptive forces at work which managers at all levels of an enterprise need to identify because they can be pervasive and varied enough to affect many activities of a firm in different ways so that even a perceptive colleague in another department might not see the evidence of change in the same way as you. It is the acceptance of the idea behind the old joke of the seven blind men trying to identify what the large object is in the park, and not knowing that an elephant had moved in.

Kodak at the moment is an interesting story, but only one of many that could be used to suggest the possibility of a new technology affecting profoundly an industry. It is useful because everyone understands what picture-taking is about, but perhaps not the effect on what happens at an industry level. If we define the photography industry as it used to be—selling film, film products, and cameras to consumers and industry—then it was largely destroyed, although there are still a few firms selling small amounts of film-based products. Rather, other industries benefited from selling products that supported digital photography, most notably consumer electronics through digital cameras and smart phones, and we could include telecommunications because the telcos and the Internet had to carry a great deal more data on their networks made up of digital images. In the ice cutters case, they were not an industry but small adjuncts to others, all of which survived: railroads, meat packing plants, and restaurants, while a new industry was nurtured in part, those firms that manufactured refrigerators along with other consumer appliances. In Kodak's case, the photography industry still exists as an industrial category measured by government economists;

one may want to question the relevance of tracking the declining sale of film products or buggy whips, but even these economists know not to accept the logic of destruction of an industry by IT without being cautious in their assessment.

The normal, and quite reasonable, view is that the use of IT makes it possible for firms in one industry to enter the domain of another with the ability to absorb, replace, subsume some of its work, or to take away customers. One good example of that process at work—finance—has been extrapolated to mean it can—and does—occur across many if not most industries. In the case of finance, computers made it possible to integrate a customer's various accounts—banking, checking, saving, stock brokerage, insurance, insurance investments, financial planning, and estate management—into one portfolio or account. But it was the regulatory practices of a nation's government that determined whether or not such integrated services would be offered. In the case of the United States, the technical capability of being able to integrate accounts using computers existed in the 1950s, but it was not until the 1970s that the U.S. Congress began to consider the notion of allowing banks, insurance companies, and brokerage houses to start competing with one another. To put a finer point on the discussion, decades after they could compete against one another the three industries still existed, in each instance with almost all the same major firms that operated in the 1950s, including their own associations, publications, conventions, and practices.[26]

Furthermore, all three industries had grown in size and as a percent of U.S. GDP, not because of the power of IT, but due to changes in laws and regulations, and the growth of their markets. The creation of the 401(k) retirement savings plan in the United States is an *uber* example of non-technological actions causing industries to grow and thrive. In short, computers do not destroy industries; instead, they have made it possible for managers and their employees to expand and change activities and offerings as the standard of living of the entire human population rose and their activities changed in many parts of the world.

At a more tactical level, digital computing made it possible for companies within industries to thrive, to integrate with one another, or to collaborate with firms in other industries (e.g., manufacturers with retailers as the Wal-Mart case illustrates). The role and purpose of industries did not change, just as the role of managers remained relatively consistent decade over decade. Automotive industries still made cars, banks still loaned money, hotel industries still rented rooms, and universities still conducted research and taught students. They just used a great deal of computing to do their work and they encouraged their institutional members to use more IT, routinely describing how best to do so. There is no reason to think that this process will not continue as new technical capabilities appear, such as we are seeing now with the use of mobile computing and social media. To be sure, borders of industries became less precise—in financial and media industries in particular—as firms either integrated cross-boundary goods, services, and shared customers or, diversified, as firms in one industry owned by those in others. This last circumstance had less to do with the role of IT than with other factors, such as the availability of capital to invest in faster growing or more profitable industries, or in newly formulating industries that eventually became subsumed in preexisting ones, or due to perceived opportunities by managers to enhance the value of their firms.

The case of newly forming industries is one that involves IT quite constantly, such as the software firms/industry becoming part of some other industry, as in the case of movie making, or information technology (for example, IBM, H-P).[27] The converse occurs too when, for instance, a part of an industry breaks out of an earlier one to become one relatively close to its parent, such as the electronics or computer chip manufacturing industry born out of the old computer industry of the 1950s and 1960s.

Finally, what industries did, but early in part due to the existence of IT, is to emerge from a previously fragmented collection of firms, because computers and communications made it possible to recognize each other and to collaborate. Examples include many small industries: bed and breakfast firms, restaurants, and baseball (fans tied to collectors, to vendors of sports memorabilia, and to sport teams).

What is not yet so clear is if these industries will eventually be as globally connected as they are normally at the national level. As this book was being written in 2013, one could have argued that the globalization facilitated by use of computers was still in an early phase of development, but that one could clearly see these industries were globalizing, because firms within these national industries were already expanding around the world. It will only be a question of time before the same occurs in many of their industries. This evolution will happen for the same reasons as industries had emerged in the first place as distinct social and economic entities of value to firms and employees within a national economy. The rate of evolution of an industry, and its use of technology, thus, originates largely from the actions of individual enterprises already members of an industry. For that reason, to understand how IT affects an industry, we need to appreciate what is occurring strategically at the firm level.

Picking up where Kay and Porter left off with regard to strategy, hundreds of studies have now been done that provide overwhelming evidence that managers within industries have been able to create competitive advantages by using IT at the firm level that subsequently spreads across entire industries.[28] IT-dependent strategies have been deployed to such an extent that I was able to argue in Chapter 1 that a new style of management was emerging. IT-dependent strategies are those competitive moves that cannot be executed without extensive dependence on information and communications technologies. Business process reengineering, use of Enterprise Resource Process systems, electronic commerce, Customer Relationship Management (CRM), supply chains that extend across multiple firms, industries, and geographies, and electronic communications are obvious examples. When IT becomes a critical part of a firm's strategic initiatives and subsequently the way an industry works, it always occurs because a group of activities and processes are implemented with IT such that they become the way "things are done around here," by a company or an industry. Put another way, these are activities that could not be done without extensive reliance on IT.

What was just described is not new; this is how IT and business have come to work together over the past several decades, so much so that it characterizes how business is done. And so for any manager, it remains important to understand that reality and be a student of it so as to continuously leverage that IT-business dynamic, because if there is anything new in this process, it is that which affects almost every corner of a business, a firm, and an industry. Firms are often slow to pick up on that idea, as we can see with the slow pickup on what to do about mobile computing and social media in so many industries today. So, what might seem obvious to a student of the process, such as a business school professor at MIT or Harvard, may not to a middle manager tucked away in some firm who is too busy to even read his industry's trade literature, let alone some publication like the *Harvard Business Review* or the *Economist*, two places where they might get early signals of changes relevant to them.

When done effectively, IT-dependent strategies tend to avoid erosion, that is to say, they sustain the competitive advantages desired by a firm for a period of time. To be sure, the historical record also shows that these uses of IT need to be constantly upgraded, changed, modernized, and otherwise altered to fit the market and competitive realities faced by an enterprise or a whole industry.[29] When done well, imitators (competitors) find that it takes a long time to replicate these advantages (as occurred in providing tracking of packages by governmental postal systems in response to those of private sector package delivery services). In the meanwhile, the originator of an IT-dependent strategy thrives and, in the process, so too does that firm's industry.

There are essentially four types of IT-dependent strategies that firms and industries deploy that create barriers to competitors, hence create and sustain some sort of competitive advantage. One form of strategy takes advantage of preexisting IT capabilities within a firm or industry which are so compelling that competitors simply cannot easily scale up to meet these. Wal-Mart's global telecommunications network linking its stores and suppliers is a good example. No other retailer in the world has as extensive a network as this firm. However, in the process of creating this network, Wal-Mart motivated many retailers around the world to use IT more extensively than before to communicate globally with their stores and suppliers. Many large enterprises went "high-tech" and global. Spain's Zara chain is spreading around the world, American retailers are popular in Asia, and so forth. As a result, the highly fragmented retail industry today has an increasingly global identity.[30]

A second IT-dependent strategy involves creating processes and organizations leveraging use of technology so as to optimize both the technology and the activities of a firm. This has become a core best practice evident in all industries today with respect to any process redesign and, as discussed in the Chapters 1 and 2, is how work, firms, and industries have increasingly globalized. Taking advantage of customers interacting within an industry through networking and e-mail, for example, makes possible cross-selling. Harrah Entertainment cross-sells to its patrons visiting its casinos; Amazon.com tells the buyer about a book others bought by people who acquired the volume that the purchaser is about to order. A competitor would have to duplicate both that specific use of IT and the processes and offerings around it just to be equal to a rival.[31] By then Amazon.com or Google would have introduced yet another new IT-based service unique to the firm, as Amazon.

com recently did with its Kindle and Google with its wireless phone services. The effects on a firm and industry are very consistent with conventional thinking about strategy. It can effect scale and market share; spread governance across wider parts of an enterprise, industry, or geography; extend or increase distribution channels that might also be shared across an entire industry; and promote an industry's image or the brand image of a firm.[32]

A third way IT strategically affects companies, hence, industries, is by doing something with IT that creates a new process so complex or difficult to replicate that it essentially serves as a barrier of entry to another rival firm or industry. American Airlines' (AA) travel reservation system is so extensive that no new airline attempts to create its own; thus, they have to rely on an existing one, which will not always display their flights first in possible options for a customer. AA's system lists its own options first on a screen. Another feature of these kinds of systems is that they can result in the creation of massive data warehouses of information about customer preferences, market patterns, and trends in costs that are classic marketing tools of extraordinary value, because they are not shared with competitors. Mail order houses were early users of such systems; large retailers are too. IBM may have been the first with a database system created in the 1960s to track the performance of every mainframe computer it made to know when to quickly and correctly fix malfunctions and to do preventive maintenance; the system proved to be a powerful selling point against rivals. If such a system is available across an entire market from one vendor, it is all the better too. ATMs from large banks used to be that way until whole networks of ATMs were interconnected on a global basis. Ordering books online was another example for many years. New networks are created all the time across most industries.[33]

The fourth IT-centric strategy is when a rival penetrates an established IT-based strategy. Often multiple firms and/or with customers will invest in new systems and processes to avoid becoming locked in and dependent on one supplier. Then the game is to come up with an alternative offering that is sufficiently attractive to warrant the usually high costs of creating them.[34] Online banking is an example of this strategy but once done can generate the kind of information useful in subsequently locking in customers. Customers often have to invest time in providing information on themselves to such an extent that it is not worth their time later to change vendors. When they do, it is because of so many new services or conveniences becoming available that making the move becomes worthwhile. If Apple creates an operating system or graphics package far superior to Microsoft's Windows products, this circumstance can lead to an assault on the industry leader and then a subsequent relocking in of a customer. But to accomplish that would require a vast improvement over a rival's incumbent offering. It appears that iTunes, iPods, and now iPhones and iPads may be steps in the creation of a new effort at such a strategy, because some users of these new products subsequently buy Apple's computers, which use software and an operating system not from Microsoft, the dominant PC software firm.[35]

The point to keep in mind is that there are many business strategies continuously implemented that extend the power of a firm or industry due to the use of IT and other technologies, many of which have embedded in them IT, such as automobiles and industrial machinery. One could argue that is true also for e-books, which is an IT-based rival to paper-based books. In recent years, such social networking software used in Facebook, LinkedIn, and Twitter, and a myriad of Internet-based offerings reminded managers that IT was very malleable and constantly being reshaped to meet new market circumstances. Instant billionaires continue to pop up because of another new use of information technology.

Some of the strategies are evolutionary as well. For example, computer-based games were played on PCs in the 1980s and early 1990s. Then they became available over the Internet. In the beginning, only individuals played such games; then, in the 1990s, they could be played with or against literally millions of people all over the world. In the beginning, one bought a game at a store, consisting of a cardboard box with CDs and a manual of instructions, possibly also with a digital gaming device. Today, one can do that or simply log onto some website and download a game onto a PC, laptop, or even a cell phone.

This last example suggests one additional feature of IT and industries. We have discussed it briefly before: networking. Networking allows customers, individuals, firms, and whole industries to function in multiple geographic settings as if they were in one country, around the corner, or down the hall. Two observers of the process defined it in the arcane language of economics and sociology as, "a multiscalar system operating not only at a self-evident global scale, but also at a horizontal global scale (the network of affiliates)."[36] This is an elegant way of saying that networks make it possible for industries to operate in a more integrated fashion anywhere in the world when it makes sense to do so. The key idea for today's manager to pull from what otherwise is an obvious statement of what they see today is not so much the notion of networks, but rather the concept of connections. Networks by themselves are useless, but are enormously valuable when they connect people and organizations, because then conversations and transactions can occur. Influence and presence can be exerted and felt.

Many observers have done a wonderful job in exaggerating the power of IT on enterprises and no doubt others will, in time, do the same about industries. To a large extent, industries remain grounded in individual countries due to several realities. Their constituent member firms are in one or few countries; they are still regulated largely by national governments, not international bodies; and they have yet to link up as intimately with sister industries in other countries as have companies within an industry. But that circumstance should change as globalization becomes more ingrained into the fabric of business. Already some industries are globalized—automotive, electronics manufacturing, and banking, for instance. By the end of a middle manager's career, he or she will have seen the IT power of connections create other integrated global industries, compete with their own practices, conferences, international magazines, and so forth.

We are headed toward a circumstance already evident at the firm level that will extend to industries made possible by IT: the imbrications of digital, physical realities, and social characteristics. Three patterns of behavior are becoming evident. First, because financial data can be digitized, capital, in effect, can be made highly mobile, moving rapidly from one country to another. Yet, the act of moving money still requires physical institutions—bank buildings and employees for example—which means the hypermobility has to be created, that is to say, a digital network must be established and used. Consequently, while connected to anywhere, industries and their firms will still be grounded in various nations and variegated markets. Second, goods and capital can be changed in the process. For example, the value of real estate can be converted into a digital form of capital (perhaps a mortgage) which can be fractured into pieces (securitized) and be sold all over the world with both positive and negative results as became publicly evident in 2007. Yet, simultaneously, there is a property that is physical, which remains the ultimate collateral of the digitized real estate investment. How all that is done is very much an industry-centered activity. A third feature of the imbrication underway in various industries is the influence of multiple social and industry-specific cultures: for instance, Indian and Chinese management often think differently than French or Americans. Within myriad social logics, all four societies and their managers influence what services and agendas are set as a result, causing processes to be organized in ways that would not have occurred in an unconnected market.[37] In other words, firms and industries are affected by physical realities, not simply by some digital circumstance, and by vagaries of multiple cultures. As a consequence, the pace with which IT affects the construct of an industry will continue to be driven more by physical human realities than just as a result of some powerful technological innovation in function, reliability, or cost.

There is more to the nature of industries, the strategies of firms, and the daily work of managers than grand discussions about how IT affects the world of business. To reinforce a message in this book that IT does not dominate what really happens, although a great deal of it is used, one only needs to turn to a long-lasting fascination of senior and middle management: strategy. Most if not all people who studied for an MBA degree since the late 1970s have been raised on the thinking of Michael Porter whose work suggests that one can acquire and sustain competitive advantages. While admirable and his work very useful to the work of creating strategies, the ugly reality is that nothing is permanent. Sustainable competitive advantages and sound strategies dependent on a clear understanding of how industries work, what customers want, what technologies are available, and so forth, are not permanent, not static. We know the world changes constantly, requiring, therefore, that strategy work changes. An American business professor, Rita Gunther McGrath, has documented both that painful reality, but also what managers are doing about it. She did this so one could move from the useful observations of an earlier generation of strategy gurus to actions one could take with the disruptive, uncomfortable rounds of changes that buffet managers today and that can be pretty certain to make their lives challenging for the rest of their careers.

Essentially what McGrath points out is that (a) changes in strategy and assumptions underpinning them occur quite frequently in those firms that truly are successful, (b) that those very firms actually recognize that reality through what they do, and (c) that rivals within an industry competing against them do not represent the biggest threats or sources of opportunity for success. Her research demonstrates that competitors are increasingly coming from other industries, as we saw with Kodak and its rivals in the consumer electronics industry, and how customers are shifting their expenditures from one category of products to another, such as buying fewer CDs and, instead, spending more on music through iTunes and other Internet-delivery channels. Particularly relevant for our discussion, she argues that, "using industry as a level of analysis is often not fine-grained enough to determine what is really going on at the level at which decisions need to be made." A new level of analysis that reflects the connection between market segment, offer, and geographic location at a granular level is needed, "what she calls 'arenas,' which are 'connections between customers and solutions, not by the conventional descriptions of offerings that are near substitutes for one another.'"[38] While the role of managers does not change—in this case they still have to develop and implement strategies—the work they do to fulfill their mission does, and to McGrath's point, it is not driven just by new IT but by the kinds of broader considerations discussed throughout this book. Again, context is king, a manager's personnel competitive tool that processes developed over time demonstrative are effective, indeed essential, to use while the targets of our attention constantly transform.[39]

IMPLICATIONS FOR MANAGERS

There is much debate about the role of managers, perhaps even intensifying: what constitutes their professionalism, work, ethics, the function of corporations, society's needs and the role of regulators, social values versus immutable laws of economics, and so forth. There is much confusion on the issue that derives from a continuing lack of consensus, possibly also clarity, about the functions of management, when compared, say, to those of doctors and lawyers, while in recent years, a series of scandals among businesses in the United States, Great Britain, and in China grabbed headlines all over the world. Even business schools are accused of losing their ways in defining the role of managers and training them.[40] Additionally, there is the rising tide of transnational business activities to deal with, what many characterize as globalization or globalized business, and the emerging role of such new business models as the GIE.

The complexities of the discussions are compounded by a couple of other realities. If one accepts the notion that two key constant roles of a manager are (1) to make decisions about what tasks are to be done and

(2) to allocate resources of an enterprise to those initiatives, does this mean that digital systems that do these kinds of things are, *de facto*, taking on the role of managers? For example, take a bank manager (a person) who decides that nobody will be given a mortgage to buy a home unless their credit score is a minimum of some number, and then programs mortgage software so that the computer looks at the score and if not high enough spits out a form letter to the applicant telling that person this bank declines to extend him or her a loan. The computer just made a decision, to be sure a primitive one, because other circumstances will not be taken into account in making such a decision, but, nonetheless, did what a manager in an earlier time would have done. Computerized simulations of decisions are also becoming *de facto* decision-making entities because of the enormous reliance managers place on such tools to arrive at a decision, frequently taking at face value the output of such digital exercises. Another fuzzy behavior is the practice of managerial decisions delegated to teams of process workers who are not managers. Using such teams is now a fundamentally essential way of working in firms around the world or where employees have more knowledge of an issue or technology than the manager in charge of their function. So, even the definition of the scope of managerial work is possibly in drift, because more than managers seem to be doing the work of management.

Now add in the role of industries and IT. Member firms in industries have long had a tradition of supporting associations that included within their mission to provide training to managers. If, as some critics are right in declaring that traditional centers of training of managers—business schools—increasingly are failing to do their job well enough or in relevant ways, then one can expect that association-based training of managers will increase both for newly minted managers and as part of ongoing life-long training for managers and executives, such as the IEEE Computer Society provides to its tens of thousands of members. Additionally, as the fashion of credentialing spreads around the world, one can expect that practices of certifying one's skills so evident in engineering, medicine, and law, for instance, will extend into industries. Indeed, that has already happened. This practice is widespread in industries that have strong needs for technical expertise, as in IT.[41] Industry associations and business schools are also providing industry-centric education while major corporations have done that for decades for their own personnel using largely internal training programs.[42] In short, the role of industries in defining the work of management will probably increase.

Business schools will continue to play important roles in creating new knowledge about how managers should work, although not all of this new information, since there are other organizations doing the same too. They will continue to shape discussions about the professionalization of managers and will train even larger numbers of them. In emerging economies, new business schools keep opening, or increasing in size, almost all of which are modeled on the American or European versions of these professional schools. They also often use translated versions of the same texts and case studies as the Americans and Europeans. Professional associations in the West are also exporting to these areas their versions of training materials, as do many of the technical societies in the IEEE. Both business schools and professional associations will also expand their outreach programs in their communities to fledgling entrepreneurs to provide pro bono coaching, often in collaboration with experienced or retired business management.

Many firms selling to other businesses and government agencies like to go to market through an industry-specialized model. For example, IBM's sales and consulting communities specialize by industry, even though they sell goods and services that are similar from one industry to another, such as computers, CRM software, or change management consulting. Almost all its key competitors do so. Clients of IBM and other consulting and services firms insist that their suppliers understand their issues (read, their industry and firm), or they want someone who is an expert in another industry, so that knowledge can transfer from one industry to an enterprise in another. It is one way that managers learn about new and differentiating practices from outside the imagined walls of their own industry.

So, what is the future of industries? For one thing, they are not going away; there are too many organizations vested in their remaining, such as government economists tracking their activities, national associations with members and publications, experts who identify with specific industries, and consulting firms that specialize in them. What this means for a manager is that they will have to be able to brand themselves to some extent as knowledgeable about how something is done in a particular industry, even if the task is done in a similar way in multiple industries. The point is, employers want managers who have experience in specific industries so to simply position yourself as a generalist—a good thing to do over time—will not be enough. At the risk of some gross generalization, it is not clear that young to mid-career managers understand this requirement. Senior managers want that in their staffs, but at senior levels, industry skills, while still relevant on their resumes, are superseded by other managerial skills of a general nature: knows how to turn around a failing company, knows how to do mergers and acquisitions, is effective in bringing out new consumer products, for example. The obvious task for a manager, therefore, is to acquire the industry-centric experience or position one's expertise within the context of an industry.

Industries will continue to have many of its activities transform, even profoundly on occasion, through new uses of IT. The successful implementations of some of the key information technology systems in the world were industry specific in their configuration because they made good business sense. The ATM in banking is an obvious example. Cases exist in almost every industry: bar codes and point-of-sale terminals in retailing; GIS systems in government; smart bombs in the military; kiosk registration systems in hotel lobbies; handheld MRIs and other scanners in medicine, retail, and law enforcement; capacity management software in manufacturing; tax preparation tools in accounting; the list is endless. What these industry-centric implementations of IT taught now the two generations of managers is that industry-specific functions, processes, technologies, and, routinely, knowledge are proven ways of making a firm successful. Moreover, in the case of IT, technology facilitated the transformation of whole industries.[43] In short, just as industries will play an ongoing, indeed, increasing role in the training of managers, so too will managers use technology to help them define the scope and work of whole industries.

All of these behaviors lead to one clear conclusion: managers are increasingly not able (or willing) to perform their work effectively without a solid body of knowledge about at least the industry they work in, not to mention that of other industries from which they can usefully learn. This is especially so among middle and senior managers. The notion that there are some universal managerial skills, some corpus, does not diminish in relevance. Rather, some of those skills and duties are redefined in terms relevant to a particular industry in our connected age.

To be sure, many MBA programs around the world have yet to tailor their courses to address that reality, while some have.[44] In the United States, those that did were physically located next to a major industry or were supported by individual firms in an industry. In Michigan, business students have learned about the automotive industry; in northern

California about computing and software; in the northwest of the country about forestry and the paper industry. A similar observation can be made about many other industries in North America, Western Europe, and increasingly in East Asia. But the universities have not picked up as quickly on this need as today's and tomorrow's managers will require. Since industry associations and consulting firms are willing to fill that gap, contemporary managers will continue to gain access to sources of formal training in their respective industries. Associations are also willing to collaborate with nearby business schools, as one sees, for example, with education provided about entrepreneurship and CRM that go beyond just having internship programs with local companies. One can reasonably predict that in years to come, more industry-specific managerial training will occur than in the late twentieth century.[45] In summary, since managers are more identified with industry-specific views of business than ever before, they will continue to add to their corpus of skills, acquiring insights drawn from the realities and experiences of relevant industries.

What is not clear, however, is how being industry-centric will affect the values and worldview of future managers. If the experience of IT is any indicator of things to come, the answer is that it will. Language will continue to become more industry-centered (just as academic fields have developed their own phrasing in economics, science, humanities, and professions too). Conversely, since we know that how one speaks influences their values, worldview, and the way they think, we can expect these managers to affect what happens within industries.[46] Many business schools require the use of English in part because of the power of language over our thinking. For example, the Copenhagen Business School teaches many classes in English and requires its 15,000 students to know English and be able to work in that language on business issues. Similar practices are evident in other European and in some Asian business schools too. Technologies facilitate the process because of their capability to make information available and to foster communications, hence connections. Thus, an industry can become more of an individual's *de facto* virtual neighborhood than was possible before the availability of such tools as the Internet and databases, both of which have proven so essential to the development of "communities of practice."[47]

The growing influence of technologies of all kinds on the work of managers, firms, and industries, and conversely, the rising importance of industries as transnational institutions influencing the behavior of its members, often in collaboration with parochial interests groups and even regulators and political leaders, should force managers to challenge some old assumptions and lead to relevant strategies and new managerial behaviors. Pondering several questions can begin to stimulate that process.

- If the norms are incremental, yet creative uses of all manner of technologies in an industry are valued, what might be of use to our firm that could emerge from our or someone else's industry?
- How well does our organization and our management team understand how our industry, and related ones too, are incrementally changing, not just radically transforming?
- What economic, political, and social risks can be mitigated by understanding our industry and uses of technology? While at it, how does our industry and its uses of technologies vary from one society to another in which we operate?
- Do we leverage that insight in the way we make decisions and how we manage?
- How can we improve that process?

Two key takeaways emerge from our discussion of industries and their use of IT. First, managers will need to continue to understand and participate in their one or more industries; indeed I would argue that they need to expand their understanding and involvement. Second, management at mid-career and mid-level on up have to pay considerably more attention to international political and economic issues affecting their industries than they have in the past, not just their companies. As part of that second observation, they need to monitor, manage, and mitigate new sources of risk to their companies, from social media incidents to political and regulatory decisions of governments. This requirement loomed in greater importance as the Great Recession unfolded and its consequences continued over many years. Events also pop up, such as the release of NSA (the U.S. National Security Administration) files that caused Chinese officials to pull back sharply in the use of American technologies within the space of two-quarters in 2013, or American firms to challenge their providers of cloud computing to beef up rapidly their data security protections. Flare-ups in Central African wars cut the supply of electricity too frequently, disrupting business unexpectedly, when in fact an understanding of local political conditions might have given managers forewarning to protect their assets. One cannot be cynical about this and say, "Oh we have always had these kinds of issues." The years from 1980 to 2001 were far calmer than what we are experiencing now. The end of the Cold War led to a period in World history of increased churn and uncertainty that we simply must deal with more aggressively than perhaps in the past. All of that uncertainty affects the deployment and use of IT. Whole industries at a national level are affected. In short, the knowledge sphere for management about IT expands to set into industry and national political and economic contexts their appreciation and use of technologies of all kinds.

While discussions of technological trends and global industries are interesting for some managers, and that I contend are obviously important, management is ultimately about operating an organization, be it a department, a branch, a division, an agency, a small company or a large global enterprise, or a government. Management styles, role of IT, and the behavior of industries all get converted into the actions of organizations. Therefore, it is to the role of organizations that we next examine to add to our argument that today's manager must work in a highly connected expansive business ecosystem to be successful.

NOTES

1 Anita M. McGahan, *How Industries Evolve: Principles for Achieving and Sustaining Superior Performance* (Boston, MA: Harvard Business School Press, 2004): 95.
2 By 2013, this variety of IT players in a firm had become a major managerial problem again, as this happened in the 1980 and 1990s, reported on in "Surfacing a Digital Wave, or Drowning?" *The Economist* December 7, 2013, pp. 65–66.
3 While doing research on the role of IT in various industries in the early 2000s, I asked a vice president of communications at Kinko's what industry her firm was in so as to understand the set of competitors they faced and the role of her industry. She was unable to answer the question crisply because the firm straddled so many different parts of the economy. There is now a memoir of the firm written by its founder, Paul Orfalea, with Ann Marsh, *Copy This!: Lessons from a Hyperactive Dyslexic Who Turned a Bright Idea Into One of America's Best Companies* (New York: Workman Publishing Company, 2005).
4 For a recent spectacular example of this linkage between the work of firms and the influence of industries, see McGahan, *How Industries Evolve*.
5 For details, see http://www.census.gov/epcd/www/naics.html (last accessed February 6, 2012).

6 In 2013, the firm came out of bankruptcy completely reorganized, including issuance of new stock to replace the previous moribund issues. It remains a shadow of its former self.

7 In 2007, the Chinese government began to address these problems. In a highly publicized trial, the head of China's drug regulatory body, Zheng Xiaoyu, was found guilty of corruption and was executed; Public Affairs Council, *Worldwide Government Relations Benchmarking Project* (Washington, DC: Public Affairs Council, 2006).

8 The subject of increasing attention, Rodney Bruce Hall and Thomas J. Biersteker (eds.), *The Emergence of Private Authority in Global Governance* (Cambridge: Cambridge University Press, 2002). One might also argue that their presence in such national capitals is also a by-product of the corrupting influence of contributions to the reelection campaigns of legislators too.

9 For a description of these industries, see http://www.bls.gov/iag/information.htm (last accessed November 6, 2012).

10 List drawn from Anita M. McGahan, *How Industries Evolve: Principles for Achieving and Sustaining Superior Performance* (Boston, MA: Harvard Business Review Press, 2004): 95–104.

11 Public Affairs Council, *Worldwide Government Relations Benchmarking Project* (Washington, DC: Public Affairs Council, 2010).

12 Peter Gourevitch, "Corporate Governance: Global Markets, National Politics," in Miles Kahler and David A. Lake (eds.), *Governance in a Global Economy* (Princeton, NJ: Princeton University Press, 2003): 314–315. Getting an accurate count on how many industry associations there are remains problematic, although estimates reaching 8000 are not uncommon. Hundreds already have the word international in their name, many of which were established before the recent surge of globalization of trade and commerce.

13 Social sciences are playing their part. For an example of a cultural anthropological of an industry, in this case the retail industry, see Paco Underhill, *Why We Buy: The Science of Shopping* (New York: Touchstone Books, 1999).

14 Anita M. McGahan, *How Industries Evolve: Principles for Achieving and Sustaining Superior Performance* (Boston, MA: Harvard Business School Press, 2004), 21.

15 Ibid., 27.

16 Michael E. Porter, *Competitive Strategy: Techniques for Analyzing Industries and Competitors* (New York: Free Press, 1980).

17 A key finding of my *The Digital Hand* (New York: Oxford University Press, 2004–2008), 3 volumes.

18 John Kay, *The Hare and the Tortoise: An Informal Guide to Business Strategy* (London: Erasmus Press, 2006).

19 We have looked at the disparities of ages within the ranks of government workers around the world which represent some of the most severe gaps between ages and experiences, James W. Cortada, Sally Drayton, Richard Lomax, and Marc Le Noir, *When Governments Seek Future Prosperity*. Maintaining Economic Strength and High Standards of Living (Somers, NY: IBM Corporation, 2005); Beth Axelrod, Helen Handfield-Jones, and Ed Michaels, *The War for Talent* (Boston, MA: Harvard Business School Press, 2001) was one of the first studies to begin laying out the modern crisis.

20 UNCTAD World Investment Reports, various years.

21 Nicholas Carr, "IT Doesn't Matter," *Harvard Business Review* 81, no. 5 (2003): 41–50.

22 F.W. McFarlan and R.L. Nolan, "Does IT Matter? An HBR Debate," *Harvard Business Review* 81, no. 6 (2003): 109–115. The overwhelming body of economic literature on the subject provides evidence contrary to Carr's contention. My own recent work does too, see Cortada, *The Digital Hand*, 3 vols. (New York: Oxford University Press, 2004–2008).

23 See for example the widely distributed, Don Tapscott, *The Digital Economy: Promise and Peril in the Age of Networked Intelligence* (New York: McGraw-Hill, 1996); Frances Cairncross, *The Death of Distance: How the Communications Revolution Will Change Our Lives* (Boston, MA: Harvard Business School Press, 1997). Scholars are beginning to look at the issues more dispassionately, see John Zysman and Abraham Newman (eds.), *How Revolutionary Was the Digital Revolution? National Responses, Market Transitions, and Global Technology* (Stanford, CA: Stanford University Press, 2006).

24 Merritt Roe Smith and Marx, Leo (eds.), *Does Technology Drive History? The Dilemma of Technological Determinism* (Cambridge, MA: MIT Press, 1994).

25 Clayton M. Christensen, *The Innovator's Dilemma: When New Technologies Cause Great Firms to Fail* (Boston, MA: Harvard Business School Press, 1997) but which should be consulted with its sequel written with Michael E. Raynor, *The Innovator's Solution: Creating and Sustaining Successful Growth* (Boston, MA: Harvard Business School Press, 2003). Christensen's innovator's dilemma: "the logical, competent decisions of management that are critical to the success of their companies are also the reasons why they lose their positions of leadership," xiii.

26 Dwight B. Crane and Zvi Bodie, "The Transformation of Banking," *Harvard Business Review* 74, no. 2 (March–April 1996): 109–117; for insurance, see the various Best's publications; Mary J. Cronin (ed.), *Banking and Finance on the Internet* (New York: John Wiley & Sons, 1997).

27 To illustrate the change, in 2007, IBM derived a rapidly growing percent of its revenues from the sale of software, IBM Corporation, 2007 Annual Report, available at http://www.ibm.com/ (last accessed September 22, 2014).

28 Gabriele Piccoli and Blake Ives, "Review: IT-Dependent Strategic Initiatives and Sustained Competitive Advantage: A Review and Synthesis of the Literature," *MIS Quarterly* 29, no. 4 (December 2005): 747–776.

29 A key finding of mine in looking at the experiences of dozens of industries, *The Digital Hand*, 3 vols.

30 R. Santhanam and E. Hartono, "Issues in Linking Information Technology Capability to Firm Performance," *MIS Quarterly* 17, no. 1 (2003): 125–153.

31 Barrie R. Nault and Albert S. Dexter, "Added Value and Pricing with Information Technology," *MIS Quarterly* 19, no. 4 (1995): 449–465; Danny Miller, "An Asymmetry-Based View of Advantage: Towards an Attainable Sustainability," *Strategic Management Journal* 24, no. 10 (2003): 961–976.

32 David F. Feeny and Blake Ives, "In Search of Sustainability: Reaping Long-Term Advantage from Investments in Information Technology," *Journal of Management Information Systems* 7, no. 1 (1990): 27–46; William J. Kettinger, Varun Grover,

Subashish Guha, and Albert H. Segars, "Strategic Information Systems Revisited: A Study in Sustainability and Performance," *MIS Quarterly* 18, no. 1 (1994): 31–58; the standard—now classic—statement is by Michael E. Porter and Victor E. Millar, "How Information Gives You a Competitive Advantage," *Harvard Business Review* 63, no. 4 (1985): 149–160.

33 James L. McKenney, Duncan C. Copeland, and Richard O. Mason, *Waves of Change: Business Evolution through Information Technology* (Boston, MA: Harvard Business School Press, 1995).

34 A core topic discussed by Carl Shapiro and Hal R. Varian, *Information Rules: A Strategic Guide to the Network Economy* (Boston, MA: Harvard Business School Press, 1999).

35 "Apple Computer," *BusinessWeek*, April 3, 2006; Julia Hanna, *HBS Cases: The Evolution of Apple* (Boston, MA: Harvard Business School Press, 2007), available at http://www.businessweek.com/magazine/content/06_14/b3978407.htm (last accessed December 6, 2009).

36 Robert Latham and Saskia Sassen, "Introduction," in Latham and Sassen (eds.), *Digital Formations: IT and New Architectures in the Global Realm* (Princeton, NJ: Princeton University Press, 2005): 23.

37 Ibid., 20–21.

38 Rita Gunther McGrath, *The End of Competitive Advantage: How to Keep Your Strategy Moving as Fast as Your Business* (Boston, MA: Harvard Business Review Press, 2013): 9. This is essentially a good "play book" on how to implement new strategies in support of her contention. As often occurs with such "how to" books, I think she has overstated her case by implying that earlier knowledge about how to do strategy work needs to be tossed out, which is clearly not something I would recommend any manager do. Rather, apply her suggestions where they make sense, taking into account her useful insights.

39 I like the elements of your "play book" and recommend that the reader look at them if a mid-level or higher manager in an enterprise. For a brief summary of these, Ibid., 18–20.

40 Rakesh Khurana, *From Higher Aims to Hired Hands: The Social Transformation of American Business Schools and the Unfulfilled Promise of Management as a Profession* (Princeton, NJ: Princeton University Press, 2007): 291–332.

41 Kenneth R. Bartlett, Sujin K. Horwitz, Minu Ipe, and Yuwen Liu, "The Perceived Influence of Industry-Sponsored Credentials on the Recruitment Process in the Information Technology Industry: Employer and Employee Perspectives," *Journal of Career and Technology Education* 21, no. 2 (Spring 2005), available at http://scholar.lib.vt.edu/ejournals/JCTE/v21n2/ (last accessed January 16, 2010).

42 In the United States alone, there are over 1600 corporate "universities," described by Richard S. Ruch, *Higher Ed, Inc.: The Rise of the for Profit University* (Baltimore, MD: Johns Hopkins University Press, 2001). They are also proliferating in Europe and in Asia.

43 Cortada, *The Digital Hand*, 3 vols; for a dramatic example from a globalized industry, see John Leslie King and Kalle Lyytinen, "Automotive Informatics: Information Technology and Enterprise Transformation in the Automobile Industry," in William H. Dutton, Brian Kahin, Ramon O'Callaghan, and Andrew W. Wyckoff (eds.),

Transforming Enterprise: The Economic and Social Implications of Information Technology (Cambridge, MA: MIT Press, 2005): 287–288.

44 Khurana, *From Higher Aims to Hired Hands: The Social Transformation of American Business Schools and the Unfulfilled Promise* (Princeton, NJ: Princeton University Press, 2010): 368.

45 Richard S. Ruch and George Keller, *Higher Ed Inc.: The Rise of the For-Profit University* (Baltimore, MD: Johns Hopkins University Press, 2001).

46 Adam Jacot de Boinod, "Say It in Style," *Guardian*, December 15, 2007, available at http://www.guardian.co.uk/money/2007/dec/15/businessjargon (last accessed December 20, 2007).

47 Eric L. Lesser and John Storck, "Communities of Practice and Organizational Performance," in Eric Lesser and Laurence Prusak (eds.), *Creating Value with Knowledge* (New York: Oxford University Press, 2004): 107–123; on the role of technology, see David E. Smith (ed.), *Knowledge, Groupware and the Internet* (Boston, MA: Butterworth-Heinemann, 2000).

CHAPTER 4

New Organizations: What Changes, What Does Not

There is nothing more difficult to take in hand, more perilous to conduct, or more uncertain in its success, than to take the lead in the introduction of a new order of things.

N. Machavelli

A manager of a call center in India, running three shifts 7 days a week with several hundred employees, spends his time recruiting because turnover is high, training all his people is continuous, and all while struggling to make his various call targets. Finding good people is difficult, morale is low, stress is high, as is turnover as people move on to other call centers that continuously offer higher salaries. Then he gets the call from his manager, someone in the United States, announcing that this Indian call center is going to be moved to Brazil within two quarters and that people would reach out to him to make the transfer quick and smooth.

An internal memo is issued by headquarters of another company announcing layoffs and budget cuts in the 5–7% range, effective immediately; people have to make decisions about taking a "package" or

The Essential Manager: How to Thrive in the Global Information Jungle, First Edition.
James W. Cortada.

being laid off within 45 days. The manager has to move quickly to implement these. Crisis, personnel angst, and a great deal to accomplish now kicks off. Then, 60 days later, a press announcement released by corporate headquarters announces that the division in which the layoffs occurred has been sold to another company, pending regulatory approval, which, of course, senior management expected to receive within the next 90 days. More crises for the poor manager as stress now skyrockets all over the organization. But this time, he is welcomed by the new owners, at least for the time being until consolidations take place, which frequently can occur within the next year or two.

These scenarios are all too familiar and reflect churn caused by a constant drumbeat of reorganizations, mostly in midsized to large firms, less so in government, and hardly in companies of less than 50 employees. These scenarios reflect the reality that institutional churn is now a routine activity. Media accounts of downsizings, layoffs, mergers, and acquisitions do not reflect what occurs to managers who either have to implement these or suffer the consequences. The widely available accounts about the lack of senior management's loyalty to its workforce and of high levels of employee job insecurity, hence understandable poor morale, while real and should not be disrespected, need to be set aside for our purposes in this book. Instead managers need to appreciate the larger picture, the macro trend of their careers—the restructuring of firms and industries alluded to in earlier chapters—because not surviving and thriving in that churning reality essentially means the destruction of a manager's career, and normally, loss of job, reduced income, and profound psychological stress (too frequently ignored by senior management and the press).

The purpose of this chapter is to discuss what is happening with the organization of businesses so that managers can develop skills and strategies for thriving in these, rather than becoming victims of some pretty substantial and dynamic changes underway. Following our overall theme that the world of management is built on systems and processes widely accepted by management and industries, and that knowledge of context and trends, are key tools for thriving, we turn to several, but not all, issues affecting organizations, or more realistically, constant reorganizations, more evolutions not revolutions. We first explore the structure of forms and organizations of change, next how enterprises are transforming today, and then visit the issue of how profits and value move around the enterprise, since these are the twin drivers of much of this churn. Since everything does not change, we will briefly catalog that circumstance; we end with a discussion about the implications of this chapter's messages. Through the chapter, suggestions are made for how management can deal with the issues at hand.

CHANGING STRUCTURE AND FORM OF ORGANIZATIONS

In recent years, it has become quite obvious to business strategists, academics, senior management, and observant employees that organizations were changing quite profoundly. That sense had become apparent before the rapid diffusion of the Internet to commentators like Drucker and Charles Handy,[1] both of whom predicted the ongoing transformation of the corporation beyond the forms it had seemed to have settled into by the end of the 1920s. Hardly a 6 month period of time passes without yet another observer publishing a book or article on the emerging next form of organizations, while bloggers do it everyday. Many commentators are widely read and discussed. For example, in recent years, it was Don Tapscott's ideas expressed in *Wikinomics* that seemed to be attracting attention.[2] In 1999, managers were reading Kevin Kelly, *New Rules for the New Economy*, and yet earlier, in 1987, Michael E. Porter's, *Competitive Advantage*, among others.[3] All of these studies have one thing in common: they acknowledge the growing influence of new business models, strategies, and most often, the effect of IT and other technologies on the work of enterprises, not just on employees and managers. To be sure, all subscribed to the business orthodoxy that form follows function, a business mantra taught to every business student since the 1960s. So, what do the tea leaves have to say about the ever-emerging "enterprise of the future"? There are no guarantees with any forecast, but some patterns are emerging that have been developing for well over two decades and, thus, can be relied upon with some confidence, because change in the structures of firms has historically taken longer to occur than commentators admit.

As enterprises evolve, along with industries and even whole economies, sources of revenues and profits transform too. Debates about green companies, corporate social responsibilities, and quests for innovation are noble and appropriate for corporations to pursue, but these will always be taken seriously only if profits are made. Underlying much work of management in the new century will be the hunt for profits and, therefore, any discussion about emerging business models and enterprises, or the use of IT must account for the role of profits, a major issue to keep in mind when trying to either understand why you are being "reorged," or why and how to transform an organization you run.

The term used to describe what many see as the actual unfolding of the enterprise structure is actually a useful one, the globally integrated enterprise, or simply GIE. It is a term introduced by the CEO of IBM in the early 2000s, Samuel Palmisano, which acquired traction among the *Fortune* 1000 companies, but that is not so radically different from other descriptions of changing enterprises. GIE will be used here because it is a short and convenient term. But it also has several more substantive attributes making it useful for describing what is unfolding now and that will probably take another two or more decades to play out. First, there is the integration of functions across the world within an enterprise or business ecosystem involving multiple firms. Second, the process is very global in scope. Third, it is being driven by market capitalism, that is to say, by the creative forces of entrepreneurs identifying and seizing upon economic opportunities. The tag for this transformation—GIE—is quite real and has been unfolding since the 1980s, but it has only been since the early 2000s that the trend finally acquired a name that energized what now can be characterized as a major one in the largest corporations in the world: their process of worldwide integration and restructuring the likes of which humankind has not seen much of in business. Make no mistake about the rigor of these evolutions: there is a growing body of knowledge, systems, and processes for doing these, and whole management consulting practices are devoted to these, along with staff at capital banks; rarely are they casual and *ad hoc* events anymore. These transformations involve hundreds of thousands of business partners of transforming firms and industries as well. There are a few exceptions, of course, but not in business, such as the structure of governments within the Roman and Chinese empires, and the Roman Catholic Church, although the latter is poised for some rapid transformation if Pope Francis implements his early pontifical messages; so even 2000 year old institutions change.[4] In long-enduring entities, such as the Catholic Church, Roman and Chinese empires, and British rule in India, while their institutional cultures were relatively homogeneous and stable within each ecosystem wherever these organizations operated, work was highly delegated to local management from the earliest history of these organizations. It was normally at that lower level that evolutions occurred incrementally, unlike in modern corporations where the initiation of change begins near the top of the enterprise. There are prior cases of this modern process at work too at the firm level: European wool trade in the Middle Ages and Northern European banking houses in the seventeenth century come quickly to mind, so too creation of large corporations in the late 1800s. Not until the conveniences of communications networking and speedy and effective flows of information, both brought about by electricity, then telecommunications, and finally IT linked in network fashion realistically after roughly 1980 that the GIE became realistically possible to create.

What is described in the next several pages is quite real today. It has been emerging for enough years now that we can point to them and say "these companies do not work they way they did in 1990," and by direct application, nor do their managers. Pharmaceutical companies are always a favorite example of this process, so too semiconductor electronics. Yet, it seems "everyone" is in the game: IBM in software and services, Nestle's in food production, P&G in consumer products, Oxxio in energy, and Yan Sha in manufacturing, to mention a few. In short, there is a profound change underway in the structure of corporations that no longer can be ignored, just as when managers were exposed to the concept of supply chains in the 1980s, they almost instantly realized that what they had been doing to tighten the development, manufacture, movement, storage, and disposal of inventories for the prior three decades had, in fact, been the presage of what today are best practices in the management of supply chains. The same is underway with globally integrated enterprises.

Before describing what these look like and how they are emerging, we need to dampen the hype and pabulum that so surrounds every new business model. This is not a revolution in how organizations are evolving. Revolution implies radical and speedy breaks from the past. Nobody is as conservative and cautious as a room full of middle and senior managers and they are the ones who are implementing the changes described here, doing it incrementally on a daily basis. Many of the examples touted of the GIE, when examined closely, reveal that the key initiatives already had a 7–10 year history from when a senior executive said, "let's do it" to the time they began bragging about it. In the case of the company I worked for—IBM that is seen as a model of how to do this, particularly in regards to procurement practices— embryonic, global steps were taken in the 1970s and 1980s that had characteristics of today's GIE: extensive use of IT, communications, technical and operational standards on a globalized, collaborative, connected, and integrated basis. IT uses contractual terms and conditions that are relatively new to the firm and innovative operational and governance models not deployed in earlier decades. Today this process is extremely well organized and globalized, integrated, and dependent on a techno-ecosystem that is complex and comprehensive. But it was a process, a journey to this point.

Most executives would probably argue privately (as some have to your author) that it is probably impossible to implement a global transformation—and integration—of a major function of any organization (public or private) with some sort of process reengineering initiative as naively described by many process transformation advocates in the 1990s. Process management and transformation techniques first need to be learned by individuals as a core skill ubiquitous with a management team. This knowledge must be applied and then enhanced and expanded to create what is emerging today. That exercise takes over a decade, requires incremental changes, and calls for fighting the nay Sayers who often either honestly disagree with the need (or form) for such changes or have personally much to lose in the process of creative destruction so busy at work. It is not clear at this time if any of the examples of successful GIE work is complete. I suspect not because as we saw in Chapters 2 and 3, whole industries need to evolve too for all this to work as an economically efficient system.

So, an initial forecast is in order: those that have started implementing GIE organizations have only just begun their journey; we will look back in 2025 or 2030 and see that much changed. We have history to learn from as the basis for this conclusion. For example, every major IT project that I have looked at from any industry that required expenditures in excess of over US$100 million took more than a decade to reach minimal stasis, normally ran over budget, proved different than desired originally, and required multiple generations of managers to accomplish. GIE is even more complex than large IT projects. However, this is not bad news, because like massive IT projects, or supply chains, they are an incrementally developed set of initiatives that can also be described as iterative in their formulation, normally by managers with an eye cast toward achieving positive economic benefits each quarter or year. So, one can expect that they will extract from their efforts financial benefits along the way for their corporations. Over time, these benefits can result in substantially new sources of revenues, profits, and cost avoidance. That is why the GIE transformation is underway and will probably remain the central transformative organizational work of management for many years to come.

This transformation is not being led just by small start-up firms with a radically different business model, which is always the perennial delight of professors, reporters, and consultants looking for "revolutions," or the next big trend. To be sure, there is much of that underway and, when successful, result in the emergence of large new enterprises, such as Bharti or Infosystems in India, Li & Fung in China, or Tetra Park and Oxxio in Europe, or Facebook in the United States. But those are the exceptions. In looking at hundreds of companies, Rita Gunther McGrath identified less than 10% that generated significant new business through their products and the structure of their organizations.[5] That is a very small percentage. The hard work of creating GIEs is currently being done by the largest enterprises in the world because they have the resources and the greatest incentives to do this. Budgetary resources allow them to invest in training and hiring around the world, while management experience and market demands create possibilities for change. Incentives come specifically from the fact that they are already dependent on their revenues coming from many countries, so they had acquired some capabilities to operate globally and thus instinctively understood the potential benefits of improving that capability. If they did not do this, their equally equipped competitors would.

So, what does this emerging enterprise look like? What are its features? The most underlying of all features is that GIE comes in two slightly different forms, often integrated into one enterprise. The first involves the physical localities where work is done. This is more than simply outsourcing manufacturing to Vietnam or operating a customer support center in India or Africa. It can also mean transferring management of those efforts to another country away from corporate headquarters. For example, the senior executive at IBM responsible for operating the company's procurement process in the early 2000s—itself global in form—physically moved his home and family to China, was not Chinese, yet part of the senior corporate leadership team headquartered in Armonk, New York. The second fundamental feature for many firms involves who does the work. It began with manufacturing, spread to customer services, next to software development, then to product design and data entry, and extended recently to managerial consulting. This combination allows a company not only to choose what to make and do, but also who, and how that should be done, all the while with a map of the world defining the physical limits of its scope. As one CEO described it, "the emerging globally integrated enterprise is a company that fashions its strategy, its management, and its operations in pursuit of a new goal: the integration of production and value delivery worldwide."[6]

As managers push the work of their companies to the places where these can best be done, three sets of activities prove crucial to the process. First, they impose open or technical standards and systems (processes too) across their empire. These can take the form of using the Internet and wireless communications, encouraging deployment of trade regulations by the governments which say grace over portions of a company's market, and collaborating and sharing intellectual property, also practices on how to use assets (such as software).

Second, they organize their work into components, the concept of children's building blocks—Legos—and take the form of global centers of excellence specializing in some facet of a firm's work, doing it for the entire company, for example, writing software in India for all parts of one enterprise. Partnerships with other enterprises are established for the purpose of outsourcing a body of tasks to one or more firms that can be added or dropped as circumstances warrant, while part of the company's ecosystem works within the context of pre-established technical and operational standards. The key managerial mantra here is to heighten and optimize operational flexibility consistent with the overall business strategy and intent of the corporation.

Third, there is the difficult task of integrating these various activities so that the whole supply, or value chain, works as plans and pundits indicate it should. The integration involves making these various pieces work in global markets that optimize finding resources needed to get the work done on a global basis, and that insures effective internal and external collaboration overlaid with a practical governance (read, managerial) process. Those three sets of activities constitute some of the most important work of middle and senior management in today's workplace. These are key components of the new style of managerial practices now emerging.

It seems no firm is immune from the process and it can be quite substantial. Lee Scott, president and CEO of Wal-Mart Stores, reported in 2007 that, "today we find ourselves operating 2285 international stores, buying products from 70 countries, and doing 20% of our business abroad."[7] This is a retail store headquartered in the state of Arkansas, United States, which is nestled in the upper South and Midwestern part of the country, a locale rather isolated when, in the 1970s, the firm began expanding across the U.S. market. Table 4.1 illustrates a sampling of the breadth of activities being performed by firms fashioning themselves into the new GIE enterprise in the early 2000s. This is not just a story of American or European companies outsourcing to Asia. Asian executives are doing it in reverse as well, even with Indian firms situating American workers in the United States.[8]

Firms listed in this table have various aspirations as they integrate their global operations, but they are nearly obvious. They want to transform from regional to global business units, from slow (or poorly)

Table 4.1 Examples of globalwide operational initiatives

Firm	Global initiative
P&G	Market development
	Shared services
Yan Sha	Supply chain integration
Li & Fung	Partner collaboration
Bharti	Partnerships
	Sourcing
Tetra Pak	Standardized supply chain
	Partner collaboration
Medtronic	Back office consolidation
	Supply chain optimization

executing departments and vendors to competitive in markets they serve, quick to scale up to meet global market opportunities, and from a mixture of manufacturing standards and performance to standardized and operationally optimized. The process has been underway long enough that some of these firms are beginning to comment on results in their annual reports. P&G and Li & Fung announced that they can offer 50% more stock around the world; Nestle saves money by producing food more efficiently; Yan Sha brags that its order accuracy moved from 80% to nearly zero errors; while Bharti grew its revenues by 60% in less than 2 years.

But because the process is evolutionary, the effort transcends the time of any one manager and thus has to be driven by a corporate-wide commitment. A.G. Lafley, P&G's president and CEO, reported that some of his company's global processes took as long as 7 years to develop, but it allowed his firm to get big enough to serve an ever-growing market.[9] To put a fine point on the matter of using numbers, between 2002 and the end of 2006, P&G grew its non-U.S. revenues by 20% compounded (CAGR), from US$17.3 to US$36.1 billion. To appreciate that performance with more perspective, his North American revenue grew at a slower rate, by 9% CAGR, from US$22.9 to US$32.1 billion.[10] While the North American performance is impressive, it is not as exciting as what happened when the company took seriously the need to scale up to global proportions.

In many ways IBM is emblematic of large corporations, with all the attributes and eccentricities of any giant firm. It has operated around the world for a century, with employees and even senior executives coming from scores of nationalities, although it was normally considered culturally essentially an American company. It has been on a GIE path since the 1980s, and rather than tell the story of that journey,[11] look at Table 4.2 to see the various types of work its managers changed to improve IBM's global reach and to optimize its operations. Some of these processes are very mature and effective, such as procurement and research, while others have been undergoing change for fewer years and thus are still emerging in a GIE form, such as human resource (HR) management. In IBM's case, billions of dollars of operating expenses were permanently eliminated; new sources of intellectual and operational innovation became possible in part, thanks to the hiring of an ever more diverse workforce; while net earnings per share rose continuously with net income climbing

Table 4.2   IBM's globalized processes, circa 2010[a]

Function	Pre-GIE	Current
Research labs	Individualized and specialized	Eight integrated
Product development	Separate/non-standard	Integrated
Supply chain	Multiple/local	Integrated/global
Procurement	300 centers	Three centers
Marketing	100s/individualized	One global framework
Sales	Local/varied	One standard sales process
Finance	Local/multi/non-integrated	Integrated
HR	Local systems	Global plan/standard skills
IT	155 data centers	10 data centers
Networks	31	1

[a] IBM Corporation.

from US$2.4 billion in 2002 to US$9.4 billion in 2006, US$16.6 billion in 2012.[12] Now that we understand the type and scope of these evolutions and the possible benefits to be harvested, there is the inevitable necessary conversation about execution in large enterprises, to which we now turn.

TRANSFORMING LARGE ENTERPRISES

How do managers systematically transform such large components of their companies? Historians have yet to weigh in adequately on the question—business school professors, some executives, and management consultants have. A growing body of anecdotal evidence points to issues of a new managerial style. First, leveraging what they learned about process reengineering in the 1980s and 1990s, the most senior executives pick a crucial area of the business with which to begin: inventory management, supply chains, and procurement were (and are) the most popular as they affected directly the internal costs of operations and offered a path to global markets. They assign a senior executive skilled in organizational change, often having engineered a number of them within that or another firm, who is given responsibility and held accountable for lashing existing pieces of the puzzle together, then reorganizing work. Second, these executives cascade responsibility right down the various organizations involved and promote collaboration among the managers who, in actuality, will have to change the flow of work, and ultimately craft new organizations. So, collaborative activities and deployment of tools and processes in support of such coordinated activities become very evident, more importantly, essential. Third, managers realize quickly the power of having open standards, or some standards, and other channels of sharing of information so as to promote innovative thinking and working, such as the use of social media.[13] As one executive put it, "real innovation is about more than the simple creation and launching of new products. It is also about how services are delivered, business processes are integrated, companies and institutions are managed, knowledge is transferred, and public policies are formulated."[14]

At the task level, it seems almost *de rigueur* for management to engage the services of consulting firms to do two things: first, to shepherd them through a transformation to some new organization and workflows in a structured manner, and second, to do some of the actual work of the change (such as running meetings, documenting "as-is" and "to-be" processes). Every new managerial priority or fashion creates a spike in the demand for consultants, seen as experts. Managers rely on this two-pronged approach because, on the one hand, they have to continue running the business the old way while it is being transformed (hence the need for additional resources to invent the new work and structures), yet on the other want to take advantage of expertise that probably does not exist within the firm itself. For instance, experts on supply chain management are engaged, as might software experts to install tools that allow for greater collaboration among managers scattered around the world.

On a more strategic level, the transformative process is increasingly made more rigorous in part, thanks to the nature of how consultants work and by how middle and senior managers have been trained by business schools. Common to the formality of the process is often for management to ask and answer several questions before taking any significant action. Today the ones most asked are as follows:

- What is a global integrated enterprise?
- Why would such a model be relevant to my firm?

- What are the various levels of integration that we should consider implementing?
- How do I do that?
- How will I know that I am achieving the goals I set for this set of changes?

These sound simple enough, and they are very familiar to those who have managed process changes over the past quarter century. Implementing this order of magnitude change requires many years to such a point that one can now think of these transformations as actually being the way firms are managed in an ongoing way today.

These various activities are leading to a new style for how whole organizations are working, reflecting an accumulation of the changes in the work practices of managers in total. While many observers are always commenting on how organizations are changing, none has yet linked the changing style of managers as being the specific origin and, hence, aggregation of practices that are resulting in specific changes at the organizational level. Table 4.3, therefore, is an early list of some of

Table 4.3 Sample of evolving features of corporations[a]

As of early 2000s	Evolving to...
Deal/operations/capabilities led	Market-driven, repeatable services
Line of business focused offerings	Product-based offerings spanning lines of business
Focuses on delivery requirements	Focuses on market/customer requirements
Country focused	Global focus
Customer services/offerings	Standardized/taxonomy-centric
Offerings developed bottoms-up	Configured from standards
Labor-based	Asset-based
Fragmented development	Tops down funded development
Optimized geographically	Optimizes brand and life cycle
Deal-oriented creation of capabilities	Targeted investments in chosen markets

[a] IBM Corporation.

This list also reflects many of IBM's priorities as it continues transforming from a largely hardware firm (1970s–1980s) to a largely services firm (1990s) to a combined services and software enterprise (2000s).

the features of the proto-new style of enterprises and government agencies derived from the evolving work patterns of their managers. Although not definitive, and still in need of rigorous research across hundreds of enterprises, it illustrates how they are evolving. The underlying data behind this table came from several surveys involving nearly one thousand firms, so it is a credible start.[15]

Small- and medium-sized firms are not immune from the process nor should they be. Often these firms are run by managers who grew up in larger enterprises where they learned the hard lessons of leadership and transformation. They learned how to plug into the larger business ecosystems of globalizing firms in order to scale up sufficiently to find the resources they need to make products and service them around the world and to reach larger pools of customers. In a study of some 600 biotech firms working with the largest pharmaceutical companies, there were very few exceptions to this rule: all had to make the kinds of adjustments and changes described earlier. What is most interesting about the pharmaceutical example is that of all the major industries of the world, it is the one that has perhaps the most extensive experience operating as globally integrated enterprises, particularly when it comes to product development (normally R&D), testing, manufacturing, and working with government regulators.[16]

Are all processes of a firm being evenly globalized? If not, what is holding up the transformation? Every wave of fundamental change of businesses since the start of the First Industrial Revolution occurred unevenly in piecemeal fashion as new technologies emerged and became effective, consequences realized, old thinking retired, and legal and social impediments eliminated, and so it is today with this current round of substantive globalization of enterprises. Manufacturing is the most advanced in its evolution and, thus, companies within manufacturing industries. Additionally, because of the pervasiveness of IT and communications, the movement of information and the consolidation and integration of information handling work are also far advanced. That is largely why software developers, video game manufacturers, consulting firms, and all manner of financial industries are also far along in their transformation. However, other functions within firms across all industries are further behind, such as sales, finance, and HR, despite the fact that one can identify many examples of GIE-style innovations underway in each of those areas.

SPECIAL ROLE OF HUMAN RELATIONS IN THE TRANSFORMATION OF CORPORATIONS

Looking at HR management suggests what causes the cadence of corporate evolutions to move faster or slower, despite the fact that those implementing global HR practices are already experienced in doing so with supply chains or purchasing, for instance. HR issues are some of the most complicated faced by management. The majority of discussions about the role of HR over the past two decades centered largely on outsourcing work to less expensive pools of labor, such as to India or Russia from the United States and Europe, and now to Vietnam, Indonesia, and the Philippines, about the rising tide of knowledge management as the ticket to prosperity in the twenty-first century, and dealing with myriad labor laws from one country to another. All are important themes; none has diminished in relevance to executives and managers striving to create highly integrated global enterprises. There are other issues at work too that affect outsourcing, KM, innovation, and personnel practices that receive less attention yet can slow the pace of innovation.

Since the late 1970s, there has been a slow heating up of a problem that by the 1990s began to be called by various names, all of which had the word *talent* in them. By the 2010s, it had become central to the rising popularity of two other ideas: improving innovation as key to corporate success and another round of attempts to drive down operating costs as often the primary way to increase profits. The central HR issue is about having the right skills at the right salaries. In South Korea it was, and is, about skills to manufacture electronic components; in China and Japan often about finding people who spoke English or were trained in engineering and market capitalist business practices; in the senior ranks of corporations, hiring executives with experience running P&L operations in other countries; the list is endless. If one cannot find enough workers with the right skills, expansion is not possible. By 2006, concerns began to surface that India and China might be running out of the kinds of workers corporations in more advanced economies liked to hire.[17] In the case of China, there is still a dearth of experienced senior executives which time will fix, as middle managers mature in the context of their nation's current economy.

Ideally, one would like to hire ready-trained workers; it is faster to put them to work and is a less expensive approach than training them within the enterprise. Yet, all large corporations still find that they have to train them. Governments have the same experience. In the United States, the U.S. Department of Defense is the largest educational institution in the country. It would not be a surprise if someone were to argue that the Chinese army was the largest school system in the world. Both have to train millions of people in basic administrative functions, about the particular work they do (e.g., fighting wars), such "soft" skills as leadership, verbal communications, and how to use PCs and the Internet, even reading and writing. Vast numbers of these militarily-trained individuals only spend a few years on active duty, even in the all-volunteer American military, before entering the private sector where they apply what the government and experience has taught them.

A chronic impediment to integrated workforce management is the myriad of local (national) laws governing labor practices, compensation, roles of unions, vacations, and so forth that became ensconced in local practices and legislation in every country in the world over many decades, if not centuries. These often stand as nearly immutable barriers to the creation of uniform operational HR practices around the world that would make it possible for managers to have highly adaptable work forces. In Europe, for instance, laws dictate how many hours an employee can work per week and how many weeks of vacation they must take. All of these features of daily work vary by country, even though most Europeans are members of the European Union. European labor laws are also at variance with those of the United States, where firms can more readily hire and dismiss workers at will. In fact, economists routinely comment that European labor practices are uncompetitive when compared to those of the rest of the world.[18] Despite attempts to change those laws, to make work force management more flexible, suggestions for changes are routinely met with stiff opposition, including strikes and riots, as the French experienced intermittingly in 2005–2007, and many parts of Europe in 2010–2013. Productivity is often hampered by local religious and national holidays as well. American managers giggle at how many such national holidays Europeans have while the Europeans are amazed at how few the Americans enjoy.

If you are a manager working in a large international corporation in which your work depends on synchronizing the activities of a workforce spread across the world, it can be a messy business. One office can be closed on Monday in one country while almost all the others remain open, yet another holiday in yet a different country on Friday closes a facility for a day (e.g., in the Middle East), essentially giving the manager 3 days in which his or her globalized integrated work process is working as intended. Then there is the frequently annoying reality of time zones, often one of the most frequently heard about topics for grousing. Only too much traveling away from home could top the complaints about time zones and conference calls. Probably only a few managers in a global enterprise have managed to avoid 5 or 6 A.M. or 11 P.M. conference calls. American managers quickly learn that Sunday in Philadelphia is Monday in Sydney. If their manager happens to be Japanese and holds Monday morning staff meetings, well one understands where this line of reasoning is going. These are all real problems that face the modern manager. Some of these realities they live with—the 5 or 6 A.M. conference call is usually one of them—but others they attempt to work around or alter.

There is the related more serious issue that is clearly not receiving enough attention: the role of different cultures around the world and the effect they have on managerial behavior. So far in this chapter, we have discussed process reengineering and global supply chains as if they were homogenous, highly integrated activities that function in some Newtonian machine-like efficiency if only management was properly educated and trained in Total Quality Management (TQM) or Knowledge Management (KM), or some other management practice. But managers and customers come to work every day with different perspectives and values. For a manager to function in a globalized economy, he or she must come to understand deeply the nuances of multiple cultures one over another. Remember the problem of a national holiday on 1 day is a workday for another? Extend that notion to differences in language, even in how some idiom like English is spoken, or to how people function from multiple countries in a conference call, let alone over the dinner table, and one begins to get a sense of the complexity of cultural influences. Today's manager cannot sell a product in India the same way as in the United States, even to Indian customers who were educated at an American university. The same is true all over the world. Every manager with international experience has a collection of funny and sad war stories to prove the point.

Extant evidence suggests firms have not worked out well how to factor national, social, and religious cultural differences into the ways business must operate when involved in multiple environments. The world is not necessarily becoming culturally more homogenous, but it is partially in what technologies and products people use, and incrementally in its entertainment.[19] To use a fashionable New Age management term, this reality means we have a "disconnect." Doing a job rotation in India for 2 years by a German manager will not fix the problem she might face in dealing with the Chinese, Saudis, the Latin Americans, or emerging markets in Southeast Asia—four major emerging markets for everything. There is no obvious solution to this problem; it is a conundrum that will probably be partially mitigated over time more through trial and error and participation in management by citizens from those regions than by organized research and some innovative managerial practices.[20]

Although in some instances, other realities are helping. For example, until the 1990s, it was customary in all of Spain for workers to take 2 hours off for lunch. They would go home, eat, take a nap and then come back to work, while their colleagues in other countries took a 30–60 minutes lunch break. When large Spanish cities expanded and chocked with automotive traffic (most notoriously Barcelona and Madrid), it was becoming difficult to make the roundtrip home and back and still have lunch within the 2 hours. So, work habits began to change such that today there is a growing number of business and government agencies that maintain office hours more consistent with what one finds in Amsterdam, London, or New York.

At a basic level, we must ask, what are managers concerned with regarding HR in largely transforming companies today? They worry, of course, about what skills they need and where they have those today, as suggested before. The latter point speaks to the issue of finding these skills at the right time. This can involve identifying quickly experts within the company about oil rig management to address a problem at a drill site in one location, while most of the experts are situated at another. It can involve identifying enough people around the world available to be assigned to a project, a thorny problem faced by all services and consulting firms. This is why managers in many international enterprises are investing in what they call locator systems that identify where variously skilled employees are working, describing their availability. Never have systems that help in assigning people to work been so important; hence the plethora of online employee directories, resume repositories, skills tracking databases, personnel help desks, and online repositories of frequently asked questions.

One of the biggest challenges facing the modern manager is overcoming barriers to collaboration among employees. A survey conducted of some 400 companies in 2007 identified in descending order as obstacles organizational silos as a continuing problem dating back many decades, individuals too busy to assist others in disparate parts of the enterprise, and performance measures insufficiently aligned to reward individuals for collaboration. Far lower on the list were inhibitors that while important, simply proved less significant: inadequate IT tools to facilitate effective collaboration (yet this issue gets much attention), some individuals treating collaboration as unimportant, and concerns about protecting intellectual capital.[21]

Senior executives have much to say about managers in general worth reporting. Skills in general are the leading collections of business issues in HR followed closely by the lack of sufficient leadership skills and experience. This second issue is both a comment on leadership capabilities and about the right skills given what a transforming corporation would need in the future. Senior executives complain that managers below them do not collaborate enough for the same reasons cited in the previous paragraph. As recently as 2007, they were still reporting in descending order the paucity of leadership and skills that existed in Asia Pacific (exclusive of Japan), followed separately by Japan, and then Europe.[22] These problems remain severe across all manner of industries, with manufacturing leading the way, followed by distribution and communications.[23] We will come back to this problem again later in this chapter, summarizing what successful executives generally recommend be done by managers.

Training people remains a process that reflects ways of teaching during the years of the late Second Industrial Revolution: on-the-job-training remains the most widely applied method, followed by classroom instruction within the firm and instruction outside the company or agency. Other commonly used techniques include job rotation, reimbursement for education, self-managed training over the Internet, and self-study by other means.[24]

SPECIAL ROLE OF FINANCIAL AND ACCOUNTING FUNCTIONS

In addition to HR issues, finance and accounting constantly attract the daily attention of managers at all levels of an organization. For hundreds of years, the mortar holding together the building blocks of business consisted of budgets and financial reporting—that reality has not changed and probably will remain crucial far into the future, even in economies that are not seen as capitalist or market-driven. So, we might ask, how is the new style of management working in the world of finance? It is an issue subject to many similar localized regulations and practices one sees with labor, so a logical topic to discuss.

Financial systems in companies that operate around the world have not made as much progress in becoming integrated globally the way manufacturing and procurement have. Financial and accounting systems remain highly fragmented and tied to various corporate legal entities, which often is how a national company's organization is structured in any given country. Many, but not all, in the financial community still operate as if in a traditional multinational corporation while other functions in the firm have become far more integrated across organizations, partnerships, and nations. In a survey of over 1200 financial officers conducted by colleagues of mine, of those firms with over US$1 billion in revenue, only one in seven had redefined their financial processes to operate as an integrated global function.[25] Inevitably, however, that functional distortion with respect to how corporations is evolving will have to be fixed because, if for no other reason, regulators and stockholders are increasingly seeking more clarity and transparency in financial reporting, not just of the banking industry.

What would that transformation look like? For one thing, an early step would involve establishing globally mandated standards for how information is collected, presented, and analyzed, leading to a common standard Chart of Accounts global in scope. For another, financial systems would continue the current trend of moving from just reporting historical data on what happened in the past to also providing headlights for current and anticipated conditions, risks, and other financially measurable realities. The governance structure will mimic that of other global processes in that the CFO will have global responsibility for the integration of all financial data, not merely for preparing the myriad country-specific reports or doing corporate-level reporting. Increasingly, there is debate within the financial community and among government regulators and their political leaders about what role CFOs should play in identifying and mitigating various risks to corporation—a role these financial managers historically played with regard to cash flows, finances, and corporate assets—but now increasingly for other risks traditionally not quantified, such as political, environmental, and other threats to the economic well-being of a company's operations. That debate about the role a CFO in mitigating risks has not been resolved; however, it is indicative of the changing nature of a senior manager's duties in this new age of management that risk analysis is being codified, formalized into risk mitigation processes, and are expanding into a global arena.

As this was being written in 2013, a growing concern over the availability of employees attracted the attention of management at all levels of the enterprise in the most developed economies of the world. CFOs, HR executives, and general management were engaged on the issue. It proved so riveting that it could not be ignored. The problem was that most large enterprises and government agencies in Japan, North America, and in Western Europe were just facing the start of the retirement of the Baby Boomer generation; it is an historic break with the past anticipated to be in full play by 2017. It is historic because of the magnitude of the anticipated size of the transition in leadership and the exodus of experienced employees at all levels of the enterprise. Conventional wisdom has it that many firms will starve for qualified replacements. However, as firms transform into GIE, they will be welcoming into their organizations a massive workforce that at the same time have been entering the job pool in emerging economies over the previous 15 years, such as those in China, India, Malaysia, Indonesia, parts of Africa, and Latin America. So those firms should be in far better shape to replace their Baby Boomers than others whose operations are rooted in one or few national economies, such as those dependent on labor markets where populations are not only relatively aged but also shrinking, as in Japan, Germany, Russia, and Italy.

Additional to the GIE phenomenon is the propensity of managers working in the new style to blend technology and innovative work practices and processes, with a mixture of employees from around the world, which should allow them to optimize these variable assets to avoid the already appearing problem faced by national governments which, for political reasons, find it challenging to outsource existing work to other countries.

Since we live in a period of transition from the way managers worked in the 1970s to early 2000s to a new style, we should ask if there is a breach developing between new practices emerging in management and their beliefs? Said another way, are beliefs in the new style of management racing ahead of the slower process that always exists in how organizations change? Little research has been done on this very important issue. However, some recent evidence on the matter involving hundreds of CIOs suggests that there is a riff developing between beliefs and practices with beliefs transforming faster than practices. Those who have studied change and revolution will smile knowingly as this is a well-understood phenomenon. A survey done of 170 CIOs from around the world in 2006 reported that what should be (belief) and what was (reality) are not synchronized. Furthermore, they are not aligned across a variety of fundamental managerial issues.[26]

Finally, we must ask, does every firm and manager become part of this new order? The answer is simply no. The small shop or restaurant may not, unless, of course, such an enterprise is scooped up into someone else's value chain, as has increasingly occurred in the restaurant industry in such areas as North America and Western Europe and did many years ago for book sellers around the world. Service firms are often small, operate in local markets, and, thus, avoid being hard-wired into some larger specific firm-based ecosystem, normally because they either do not need to scale up or cannot. Obvious examples include lawn care services, barber shops, housekeeping, or building construction, all very large segments of the work force in advanced and developing economies. There is much debate among economists about the role of such smaller businesses, which replicate existing offerings rather than invent new ones. A dry cleaning establishment is an example of a replicated form of capitalism. The owner does not need to invent something new; rather, he offers a service to a community that could afford this service. Often, affordability is driven by the existence of someone else in the economy innovating, such as inventing Apple Computer's iPad, because that inventor then can afford to have her clothes dry cleaned.[27] So, there is a mutually reinforcing circle and interdependences that include the crucial element of entrepreneurship, manifestly evident when an economy is vibrant, open, and expanding.

PORTRAIT OF THE NEW MANAGER

There is an emerging image of the new manager with common characteristics shared by all levels of management. All of the activities of management described so far in this book shaped the modern manager. So, before discussing the evolving hunt for profits and values, a brief view of this new manager seems in order, because the reader can measure themselves against this profile and then develop a plan for bridging gaps in their knowledge and skills. While there is little consensus on what this manager looks like, some features are obvious enough.

What skills do they need to be successful? Today, we can accept as given that at all levels they have a solid grounding in basic business principles acquired at a university: accounting, finance, organization, strategy, HR management, marketing, and a modicum of labor and other local laws, rarely anymore "on the fly"; the subject has become too complicated and subject to so many laws and regulations for untrained managing to widely be the case. Managers will know how to use various IT tools for fact searching, spreadsheet work, modeling and simulations, and e-mail. They are increasingly facile with social media tools, young and middle managers the most. Very quickly in their careers, they are expected to acquire several more skills: team-based work, formal project and process management knowhow and experience, an ability to measure and quantify without recourse of statistics, algebra, or calculus since there are software tools to do all of that but with the ability to analyze data these display. As they move into middle and senior management, they will have acquired skills in networking, how to learn about other parts of the world, and will have acquired the habit of staying current with business, economic, and political issues broader than whatever is immediately affecting their company. They will continuously expand their analytical skills, learn, respect but then accept with a cautious tone a general approval of new forms of management practices as they will see many of them in their life times. Already, they know to read key publications in their profession and to be more cerebral about their work than were their fathers and grandfathers.

Their attitudes are changing. Loyalty to a firm is far less than loyalty to a profession and a career. They want less direction and more freedom of action, and increasingly willing to do their work around the world either in person or through the use of communications. In large corporations, it is already not uncommon for managers to understand more than one language, while English continues to spread through developing economies within management ranks. It is my sense that future managers will be more willing to move from one industry to another because their knowledge of a major business process or body of knowledge will make that attractive, as occurs today with financial officers, all levels of IT management, and in such specialties as marketing and supply chain management. They all share one feature: each has a body of knowledge and experiences about systems and processes that are transferable and applicable across different firms and industries. Surveys for a half dozen years are signaling that future and young managers in Western economies desire to spend less time than their parents working, with more time for holidays and family, so they and their employers will need to find new ways to improve productivity. In emerging markets, however, young managers are still willing to work very long weeks in order to move ahead.

While this emerging profile may seem more like a collection of tidbits rather than a full picture, it is a broad one calling for proactive personal development that extends beyond prior practice. One cannot depend on their employer to invest in their personal skill development; those days appear to be disappearing, and already essentially gone in many large American corporations, even in the face of these enterprises grousing that someone else should be training their workers, such as schools and universities. It is a debate that should not distract a manager determining how to develop their portfolio of skills; rather, they personally need to constantly assess what skills they need, create a plan to acquire them, and implement it. That has to be a lifelong behavior, because there will be too many new things to learn that cannot be acquired from a class or experience; both are needed. Also, knowing what jobs to hold is increasingly important. These should include in them opportunities to do the following:

- manage ever larger projects (activities with a beginning and end)
- engaging in the use and management of processes that have a high IT content
- redesigning and implementing ever-larger processes.

Managing workforces operating in multiple countries is absolutely crucial to one's development, while it will also be essential to spend days, weeks, even several years, working in another country, ideally in an emerging economy.

Part of the internationalization of work, hence of managers, will call upon a skill many already have today: social networking. However, now the need is to maintain those members in a network for longer periods of time regardless of one's current job. That diversity in one's network is needed because of the variety of jobs, companies, and industries one will work in over the next several decades. The days of maintaining contacts with 100 or so professional colleagues ended a long time ago, so too the wide practice of maintaining such connections with 200–300 people. Now the number has to be larger and the community more diverse. One by-product of that networking that does not seem to get adequate attention is for management at all levels of an enterprise to use their network to seek diversity of opinions. Already mentioned in this chapter is the need for differing points of view, not simply a collection of employees of different sexual orientations and ethnic and national backgrounds. The sweet spot in diversity is in the variety of perspectives brought to an issue, problem, or opportunity. Learn to acquire those proactively. Then the hunt for new sources of profits could be made easier.

MIGRATIONS OF PROFIT AND VALUE

Because in a capitalist economy businesses exist to create profits, much of what management does should be in direct support of earning profits. Yet it is also quite amazing how few managers even understand the profit profile of their employers; those operating in small enterprises do, however. Various perspectives float around, some accurate, others less so, and all always subject to constant morphing. When manufacturing firms dominated the ranks of the largest and mid-sized firms, conventional wisdom held that if a firm was to gain market share over a competitor, then profits should follow. Increasing the volume of business has also long been seen as a path to profits. Services sector businesses subscribed to similar beliefs. However, as customers acquired increasing access to information about products and services and could compare suppliers one to another, the old mantras came under siege. Who in a company was making profit was also obscured in many instances, not the least of which by complex, multilayered hierarchies in large enterprises that had their own little-known political-budgetary ecosystems where careers were made and broken based, for instance, on whether products came into or stayed in the product line, with less regard to their contribution to profit than should otherwise be the case.

Much has been written about the increased power customers gained in the past two decades and now about their use of social media, as they acquired more knowledge about the features of goods and services, and range of prices they could pay for these. By the early 2000s, their market power had grown sufficiently that the old saws about how to be profitable were indeed challenged. To be sure, there were many signs along the way that this was coming, not the least of which was an important book published in 1999 by economists Carl Shapiro and Hal R. Varian, in which they stated the obvious: that the laws of economics had not been abrogated because of the arrival of the Internet, Dot-Coms, and so forth. Rather, they outlined myriad ways that the Internet and market realities dictated that business models and services had to be closely tied to the desires of customers.[28] Two years earlier, consultants Adrian J. Slywotzky and David J. Morrison had delivered a similar message in very blunt terms: that the old ways of earning profits were eroding in the face of rising consumer knowledge and that traditional forms of organizing businesses along product and service lines no longer made as much sense as structuring enterprises by types of customers.[29] Today, both publications read as so obvious that one wonders, how could they get away with publishing books that should have insulted the intelligence of any normally competent manager or executive? But hindsight is very clear, foresight not so. The expansion of the Internet, product orientations, exuberance favoring bureaucracy, and inwardly focused corporate cultures limited the ability of managers to understand, let alone be aware, of changes underway around them. So, these authors proved insightful and did a service by delivering important messages.

What these and other observers pointed out at the time, and subsequently reinforced by others, was that how profits were generated was *shifting* within an enterprise, even within industries. It is incumbent on us not to over-generalize about the sources of profit today, because each firm is unique. But because emerging behaviors among managers in response to shifts are part of the new style of early twenty-first century management, some of these have to be understood. Briefly listed, managers increasingly use analytics and extensive data about customers to select which ones they want to do business with, based on their profitability from one class of customers to another. For instance, a person who pays off their credit card bill every month is not a desirable customer; one who maintains a balance owed, yet pays regularly, is highly prized. So, an important element in the design of a modern business model is to segment potential customers, appeal to those who can generate the most profit, and try to walk away from the others. That mindset would have been challenged and been seen as alien as late as the mid-1990s and difficult to implement without extensive use of computers and massive collections of customer profiles that could be analyzed applying information technologies.

A second element in the design of a modern profitable business is to determine where profit is to be found in a value chain. Simply put, if a service or product has 10 steps, and steps 3, 8, and 9 are profitable, but all 10 have to be done to get any profit out of even activities 3, 8, and 9, then today's management tries to figure out how to outsource the other steps to someone who can make a profit on those activities and concentrate on 3, 8, and 9, but still lashing everything together in an integrated value chain. That is why understanding how processes are run, understood, and changed has become such an important body of knowledge for any aspiring manager.

Third, today hardly any business of any consequence is designed to operate without taking into extensive consideration in highly organized ways what customers demonstrate are their greatest priorities.[30] For managers who came into the workplace after the mid-1980s, they probably do not recall a time when this was not the case, a moment when a company could simply offer a product or service with a nearly "take it or leave it" attitude, with minimal market analysis when compared to what happens today. But now, since competition can come from within and outside one's industry, "customer intimacy," as it became known, is a way of life. This all sounds very much like what is in any marketing textbook; however, there is yet another facet to customer services not always acknowledged. Both customers themselves and the dynamics of the marketplace change constantly. It is a key—if in hindsight incredibly obvious—observation made by Slywotzky and Morrison: "The game is *never* over."[31] Understanding why customers would buy from a particular vendor became a near-science, supporting substantial uses of market data, databases, surveys, and so forth, all of which are so much a part of today's managerial style of behavior. Social business practices today continue the game.

The intensity in the use of these tools varies by industries. Management is increasingly aware that how various technologies are applied in their firm often mimics uses elsewhere in their industry. They know that such uses affect their competitive performance relative to other rivals within that or some other industry. Industries with large firms tend to have automated extensively routine or repetitive tasks, such as manufacturing activities or the processing of account information and cash handling in insurance, banking, and brokerage enterprises. In fact, all financial industries are the most extensive users of computing for all manner of activities, even in developing economies in some of the poorest nations.

Yet, computing seeps into all industries as specific uses are identified. It is that rate of identification of relevant uses that dictate cadence of adoption. When a use becomes justifiable and effective, it spreads, as occurred with ATMs in banking and "apps" tailored to industries through use of smart phones. But in higher education or K-12, use of computers as teaching devices has only just started to make significant inroads for many reasons, not the least of which is the lack of sufficient evidence that they are effective in teaching. As a rule of thumb, the more industry specific a technology is, the more attractive it is to members of that industry. Computing continuously enters an industry and is adopted for sound business reasons by their rivals. Managers learn about new uses from adopters in other industries, since no application enters all industries at the same time, and there are competitive advantages to be gained some times in adopting a use before one's rivals within an industry. Industry associations and publications tend to be good sources of information about a use and concerning the rationale for such an adoption.[32] From such uses then come changes in how organizations structure themselves to exploit advantages of such applications when combined with an industry's business realities.

There are over two dozen recognized ways to structure a corporation so as to focus on customers and sources of profit that were not widely used prior to, say, the 1990s. Put in other words, there are many paths to profits in the modern corporation; so, the old ways of thinking about market share and product-centric strategies do not play out quite the same way as, for example, in the 1920s–1980s.[33] This is not the place to describe these myriad approaches; it is enough to say that when designing a product, service, department, division, company, or large corporation, managers increasingly go to great pains to understand where profits are really made in their enterprise and work out how best to extract it. The variety of measures of processes and customer performance, massive computerized market and industry databases, and so forth are today's most popular weapons of choice in solidifying or restructuring a business.

The process has become relentless with CEOs constantly admonishing their employees and bragging to shareholders and analysts about how they are "reinventing" their enterprises. Increasingly, that is less rhetoric and more reality as competition and new customers come and go around the world. Recent surveys reaffirm that how one builds a business, what role innovation plays in offering new products and services, and the way a firm "goes to market" does stimulate highly profitable operations. The same data also demonstrates that management today understands that reality of dynamic operations, because they report being unhappy with their organizations' ability to change fast enough nor as effectively as they need to do.[34] But, let us not overstate the case for everything changing and churning.

WHAT DOES NOT SEEM TO BE CHANGING

Consult widely read business publications such as the *California Management Review* or the *Harvard Business Review* for the period from the early 1980s to the present, and one remarkable feature stands out, namely, how little variety there is in the topics discussed. The consistency of themes with what Peter Drucker and others described as core managerial practices in the 1960s and 1970s is striking. It suggests that despite enormous hype, and publication of thousands of business books touting new managerial precepts, there appears to be a core set of activities that remain constant. This is so regardless of the introduction of some new technology, like the Internet, or fundamentally restructuring of an ecosystem, such as that created by intense economic globalization or recession. It is an important observation to make because there is a constant debate (and complaints) about what business schools teach their students, while it seems there is very little quality control over who publishes on business practices. There is more than a tinge of the huckster and clear amateurism involved. For example, regarding managerial leadership practices, every year several books are published on leadership principles according to some American general or president, or wife of a president,[35] or those from a military academy, or sports coach, all of which are purported to be directly transferable to business. The consistency in the themes of the two business journals remind us that a series of journal editors remain grounded in what is important to the core functions of a manager.

Perhaps the most important and consistent activity is leadership. To be sure, one can learn about how a successful American president or

British prime minister led, and there is a rich body of thoughtful research-based literature on the subject. But, the truth is that the characteristics of great leaders in the 1930s or 1960s are the same today. They have a clear vision (or purpose); they understand the need to take personal responsibility for leading their people to great achievements; they are superb in communicating verbally and in writing; they execute strategy and tactics well; they hire and fire effectively employees with sensitivity yet with decisive boldness; they are often liked (sometimes not) but respected; they are smart, hard working, and serve as effective role models. Most have a worldview and set of ethics, although the examples of some of Enron's senior executives, for instance, suggest that strong leaders do not always have socially acceptable ethical principles of behavior, but those are the exceptions that prove the rule. Moral of the story: leadership is a practice, not yet a science; it is a very human act of communications and motivation with confidence and purpose. Today's manager has to practice these same virtues to be effective.

Next is strategy, which, as a managerial priority, is not diminishing in intensity of interest. Austrian economist Joseph Schumpeter elevated strategy as an issue critical to management in the 1930s and 1940s, while Peter Drucker confirmed its importance as a managerial function between the 1950s and the 1990s. Michael E. Porter and Henry Mintzberg added flesh to the bones in the 1970s–1990s. Today strategy seems always to be on everyone's lips when it comes to discussing what managers should do.[36] Despite the vast amount of material that has been published about strategy, with a great deal of it in response to the availability of new software modeling and analytical tools and technologies (e.g., the Internet), the core function of strategy is what it was when Schumpeter talked about it as an economist and Alfred D. Chandler, Jr. as an historian.[37] It was about identifying new opportunities for generating revenues and profits, and investing enough in manufacturing, distribution, and services in an organized manner to convert an opportunity into cash flows. The continuous "creative destruction" of capitalism that Schumpeter spoke of in how new products, firms, and whole industries came into being is largely about strategy and its execution. Questions raised are essentially the same yet become more pointed as one focuses on today's immediate realities. Answers are not obvious and they keep changing. Often problems are overstated, but solutions are offered as we saw with Rita McGrath's work on strategy, "strategy is stuck," but then shows us how strategy has to address "transient competitive advantages."[38] The key message is that just as leadership is a core competence of a successful manager—still a skill and not a science—so too strategy is a body of knowledge that has yet to reach a level of practices that would qualify it as near-science. However, with all the attention it has received over the past half century, one can expect new tools and methods to continue to be created which apply nicely to the globalized networked world of most businesses today.

People management—HR—is another core activity that transcends eras. How one treats their employees, what they pay them, career opportunities they offer them, how they are trained and groomed for additional responsibilities, and hiring and firing are all tasks that every manager performs in any decade. The actual activities are highly influenced by a manager's attitudes toward employees, corporate culture in which they work, and national social and regulatory practices imposed on the workplace. To be sure, there are changes underway, not the least of which is how one can best motivate and leverage employee work in a world in which workers are better educated, increasingly like to work in peer groups (teams), and are a blend of individuals from different cultures, genders, and ages. All of this is happening at a time when scientists and psychologists are learning more about human behavior and their findings are slowly making it into the corpus of managerial practices. Today, for example, Howard Gardner, a leading authority on how people think, is as popular with managers in business as he is with students of the human brain.[39] His kind of work points to the expanding trend of companies integrating scientific findings about human behavior with training and tool kits for managers. One can anticipate with reasonable certainty that managers in the years to come will apply growing amounts of such insights in their work as a normal course of events.

As organizations have stretched around the world, the need for managers to lead, to set and implement strategy, and to work with their employees is as critical as in any other period in modern times. In fact, one can argue that these three core functions of a manager are more complex today, far exceeding in nuance the equally sophisticated work of creating global supply or value chains, or managing financial processes. Doing all of these things require ongoing development of skills, leveraging tacit knowledge of individuals and of the enterprise as a whole. It is a set of skills still very much under development. It is why so many experts on business call management a profession, not a science.

Our discussion of what does not change leads to several pieces of advise. First, beware hype about change; precisely understand what is changing and what it is not transforming any circumstance. Be suspicious when someone reports a "revolution" underway in which everything is going to be "blown to bits," two phrases used too often. Yes, there are many evolutions, which actually are more difficult to identify than revolutions. Second, no matter what changes a manager encounters or desires, the reality is that one can make all the changes they want provided they continue to bring in revenue and do the work of their enterprise without severe interruption—a very hard thing to do. How hard? One needs to change flat tires on a car without stopping the car from moving down the road. This entire book is about doing just that. Third, the reason "the basics," or things that do not change exist is because they are relevant. One needs a good strategy more than a great computer, skilled motivated employees more than a collection of business partners, while the art to persuade (lead) is the single most important skill any manager can have. Fourth, competition is effective, to be feared and respected, and to be taken seriously. Fifth, management is hard work, requiring long hours, great passion, and good intellectual skills. These five observations would have been true a century ago; they are relevant today, and they show no signs of not being so over the next few decades. Finally, there is the requirement to do these informed by a body of ethics that value obedience of laws and regulations, fair deals for employees, customers, and shareholders, respect for the physical and social environment, and candor within one's business ecosystem.

Senior executives, particularly CEOs of companies that have been very successful or turned around from the brink of economic disaster, have gotten into the habit of writing "how-to" management books in which they distill their secrets to success. There are hundreds of these books; American CEOs, in particular, like to publish these. Many are not particularly insightful, others more so. But if you read enough of them, you see that they generally share some common features. Table 4.4 summarizes the thinking of one such executive, Gerard Greenwald, who is credited with "turning around" Chrysler and United Airlines. His list of rules mixes business ethics, capitalist values as manifested in the United States, and various managerial practices, which are both obvious and, if you read the memoirs of other business managers, effective. They are as relevant to today's aspiring manager as they were for him in the four decades of his career. While hard to obey, values and practices designed to sustain them apply in any period and across one's entire managerial career.

Table 4.4 Gerald Greenwald's "Rules of the Road" for management[a]

Rule One: Place the teams' interest before my own.

Rule Two: Listen fully and respect each individual.

Rule Three: Speak with candor and humility.

Rule Four: Include all who have a stake in an issue.

Rule Five: Provide complete and impartial information.

Rule Six: Define the objective and establish a plan before acting.

Rule Seven: Reach closure on decisions.

Rule Eight: Address a conflict with a team member before mentioning it to anyone else.

Rule Nine: Keep my promises to the best of my ability.

Rule Ten: Establish a common agenda and mutually agree upon priorities.

Rule Eleven: Call a time-out when any of these pledges are violated.

[a]Gerald Greenwald with Charles Madigan, *Lessons From the Heart of American Business: A Roadmap for Managers in the 21st Century* (New York: Warner Books, 2001): 205–212.

CHALLENGES AHEAD

Despite all these activities, organizations, new styles of management, and innovative uses of IT, are senior executives structuring their firms to thrive, let alone to optimize their performance? Sadly, despite all our knowledge about management, there are problems. We discussed the lack of performance of many firms once inflation and other economic influences were stripped out in the Chapters 1 and 2, now we probe further. Symptoms appear all around us. An IBM survey of midmarket companies report that over half do not yet have an integrated digital strategy.[40] The 2013 Drucker Forum was lined with speakers complaining that organizations were in trouble, not able to carry out their objectives.[41] Business gurus complain as well. Don Tapscott thinks we have the "wrong organizational models" and so have "run out of gas," while Charles Handy criticizes "helicopter parenting" practices as false management, while Tim Brown, CEO of IDEO, argues that executives have injected too much fear into the workplace for employees to risk being innovative and personally responsible. There is a tinge of hubris here, to be sure, but not as much as we normally see in so many business books that promise to fix our problems.

Yet the future is always a combination of existing ways of doing business, challenges that are old and new, and emerging ways of addressing all of these, such as the move caused by the use of current information technologies to transform an organization from the old command-and-control hierarchical forms to various permutations of self-forming self-learning structures. For decades, business students and managers have had it hammered into their heads that how one structures and runs an organization is their central task from which all goodness flows to the balance sheet and to customers. Running organizations cuts across the five dimensions of establishing goals and structures, then coordinating work, maintaining values, and communicating—all elements found in Greenwald's rules. Purpose becomes important when customers increase their influence and shareholders become more militant. Current thinking holds that now and probably will into the future that making money for shareholders *per se* should not be the over-arching objective (as it is for so many firms today, such as IBM proclaims) but rather the result of working well with customers (as evident at Apple and Amazon). Having a strong sense of purpose attracts talent too. Possible goals that have proven effective and will in the future include attracting customers, in medicine in helping patients, in government citizens, and so forth. Customers provide the feedback necessary to create roadmaps of activities. IT enables employees, customers, and business partners to work together so in the future, good managers will strive to create organizations that operate that way. Gaming and modeling software tools help in defining options.[42]

A great deal of a manager's time, therefore, will be devoted to coordinating the work of various groups. The literature and conference talks are populating our language with terms to try and capture the essence of this task: agile, scrum, light footprint, mission command, strategic agility, learn and adapt, testing, and dynamic rules of the game, among others. What is quite new is the slow evolution away from hierarchical, very bureaucratic organizations, although too many of the world's most distinguished firms still operate this way—but not for long if they wish to stay in business. The problem with these old approaches is that they essentially consumes a third of an employee's work time and do not make it possible for the organization to respond quickly enough to changes in the market. What is proving to be more effective is work done in short iterative bursts around a problem or opportunity, delegating quite low in the organization considerable authority (and not just responsibility) for getting things done, and for insisting on the collection of market and customer feedback in considerable detail as one rotates through cycles of business activities. This environment aligns very nicely with the ideas of some of the more thoughtful observers who speak about temporary competitive advantages and the need for continuous evolutions in strategies, offerings, and terms. That is how managers get tactical in running effective organizations today and tomorrow. In this new world, transparency is about making sure relevant information gets to the right parts of the firm's business ecosystems, which is where communications (both IT and what one says) and computing play crucial roles as technology keeps evolving, affecting behavior (e.g., how we innovate or sell goods) and our values (e.g., how much we share with customers and employees).

IMPLICATIONS FOR THE FUTURE OF MANAGEMENT

The profession of management continues to change in substance and not at the margins. There is now a massive body of knowledge, insights, sound practices, and cases about how managers function. This material covers all aspects of managerial practices. It is no accident that the requirement within so many enterprises that managers be formally trained in a business school is widespread around the world, not merely in Western Europe or in North America, as there is so much now to learn. Growth in information about management parallels what happened simultaneously in so many other professions, so it should be of no surprise. For managers, their profession keeps acquiring new knowledge to keep up with more intensely than in prior decades. Each line of work, every industry, and all major processes, it seems, has its own academics doing research, its own journals and trade magazines, and, of course, its own conferences and trade shows. It is a characteristic of the modern manager that such an individual must remain a part-time perpetual student both formally trained and as an inquisitive self-taught and intellectually precocious entrepreneur seeking new insights.

Because of the increasing turnover of management moving from one firm to another and across industries, managers are put in the situation of having to create their own personal brand. That means adding to their personal core competencies and knowledge in order to make themselves attractive to a market both inside and external to their current employer. In other words, just as in the medical and engineering professions, having attended graduate school 10, 20 or more years ago did not fully prepare an individual for contemporary realities, so too the same circumstance applies to business and public sector managers. Today ongoing learning remains as crucial for managers as for a doctor or engineer. That is a new and important component in how management has to work.

A second reality concerns the continuing infusion of information technology, and its uses in data collection and analysis, to do the daily work of an enterprise. These technologies show no signs of slowing down either in their transformation or deployment. For the rest of all managers' careers, they will have to pay constant attention to changing technologies, learn when to move to new software, how to make those decisions, and how to create business structures that optimize the work of systems and processes enmeshed in various forms of IT. It was a point made in Chapter 3 and that will be reinforced in subsequent ones. For the truth is, everyone has to be a CIO of sorts. This is less about understanding how to use the latest version of Microsoft's operating system, spread sheet software, Facebook or Twitter, and more about how to function in a techno-intensive business ecosystem. Very few managers are trained to live in that kind of world. Look at a typical MBA curriculum in North America or Western Europe and the paucity of formal IT training becomes evident. Offerings to the contrary are exceptions and are even presented as degrees different from a traditional MBA. Eventually, business graduate schools will come to realize that their students need as much training about acquiring, using, and disposing of technology as they do about accounting and finance. But until then, assume managers do not know enough how technologies are acquired, even less about the effects they have on customers and the organization, or when to replace them and act accordingly.

A subtext to that needed training is the revamping of curricula regarding organizational management to reflect the techno-intensive features of the modern enterprise, such as those of the GIE. Executive MBA programs need that kind of content immediately. To suggest key issues, Table 4.5 lists those faced by CIOs; these are variants of the same ones senior executives and line management encounter frequently as well. Note that already senior executives support IT to such an extent that CIOs ranked "lack of support or authority" as the least of their concerns. Their biggest ones relate more to the chronic problem of people not

Table 4.5   How chief information officers ranked problems they faced as business leaders, 2006, percent ranking an issue as their number one barrier from making them influence business decisions[a]

Issue	Percent ranking this no. 1
Misconceptions	35
Lack of business skills	26
Failures of management to understand value of IT	12
Lack of time to focus on strategic issues	12
Poor collaboration with line management	8
Limited support from senior executives (CEO/Board)	7
Insufficient authority or responsibilities	4

[a]IBM Corporation, *The New CIO: Change Partner and Business Leader* (Somers, NY: IBM Corporation, 2007): 14.

always understanding their role or about their own sense of inadequacy in dealing with general business issues.

Because enterprises are increasingly global ecosystems, other skills are needed that are at least as important as an appreciation of how to appropriate information technologies for the betterment of the organization. It almost does not matter what surveys or interviews with senior executives one picks up to study, they essentially say the same things. They want managers good at teaming, who collaborate well with others inside and outside the enterprise, demonstrate a work habit of networking, and are sensitive to cross-cultural behaviors. Knowing English is not enough, other languages help, along with experience working and living in other countries. The requirement for these skills will only intensify. In 2010, there were approximately 85,000 transnational corporation affiliated with 850,000 international business partners and affiliates. By 2020, we can expect to see over 120,000 international corporations affiliated with 1.6 million business partners, a growth driven by declining tariff barriers, expanding trade, and intensified global competition.[43] Personally, I think that forecast is too low because of the agreement reached in December 2013 by 160 countries to facilitate world trade. This was the first major trade agreement reached in nearly 20 years when the World Trade Organization (WTO) was established in 1995; the forecast just cited above was prepared before this agreement looked as if it had a chance to be signed. Participating nations expect this agreement will add an additional US$1 trillion in trade each year by cutting costs of trade by 10–15%, increasing trade flows, collection of revenues, boosting investments, and increasing participation of developing economies in the world economy. As an example of change, it is remarkable because 2 years earlier, conventional sentiment held that there was no way such an agreement would be passed. What so many business and economic pundits overlooked was the fact that senior government officials kept telling them they would work diligently to promote trade as one of a half dozen initiatives to boost recovery from the Great Recession. Public officials too are motivated to do their jobs well in response to changing global circumstances.

It would be difficult to exaggerate the importance of personal leadership within the environment just described about the work they do within their organizations and in the international market realities in which they must perform. While managers are gaining more authority and accountability for their work, and operate in flatter more dispersed organizations, so too are their employees becoming better educated, more impatient for authority and respect, and capable of functioning with peers in the management and change of processes. It is increasingly common to even hear that perhaps management as a profession is on its way out. That line of thinking is nonsense, because someone will always be needed to create organizations, allocate resources, and lead people in a particular direction. Employees today need to be persuaded, trusted, and delegated to rather than be ordered about, whether they are managers or not. Add in the social and psychological complexities of having employees and business partners of multiple generations working side by side, and one quickly realizes that leadership skills need to be exercised in ways quite different than 20 or 30 years ago and within a very different work environment, one in which employees usually know more about a work process (or subject) than his or her manager, which is why Greenwald's list of rules is so practical. How people behave and think as understood by the scientific community will increasingly have to be part of a manager's tool kit. Because science changes, this means managers will have to learn more over time about the thinking practices of their human employees. They will have to do this in the context of diverse cultures as their work continues to spread around the world and move frequently from one national workplace to another. In short, leadership continues to be vital, complex, and in great demand, especially when employees and customers are more tightly connected, hence dependent on each other.

As businesses become more dependent on each other in what clearly are still very fragile supply chains around the world, managers increasingly have to be knowledgeable about political conditions, and potential disruptions due to war, natural disasters, and international economic crises, able to mitigate other non-business-related risks to their business. A bad harvest in one country or a weather change in another can affect a high-tech firm like IBM or Cisco, or a massive industrial conglomerate comprising many businesses, such as Tata or Samsung, just as much as a falling currency or labor unrest can cause management to move work rapidly in or out of a country or region. Thus, managers trained in the humanities and social sciences are increasingly needed, not just those with MBAs and engineering degrees. Diversity of skills, education, culture, language abilities, gender, experience, and political views are increasingly essential to the effective functioning of a firm in such an ecosystem. They make up the emerging world of the connected manager. If we can make one prediction with some certainty, it is that just understanding business practices will only get a manager so far, perhaps up to middle manager ranks, but no further in this emerging managerial ecosystem.

Questions to ask oneself in order to test where you are on this continuum from a multinational or national firm into an enterprise aligned with your opportunities and capabilities are difficult to answer, but essential to explore continuously.

- How well is my organization structured to seize the economic opportunities that exist, given what we can and have to do? How do I know how well I am doing?
- Where is my competition going to come from in the next 3–5 years? How am I going to deal with this challenge?
- What skills does our organization need in particular to begin developing and acquiring?
- What skills do I still need to acquire personally and within my enterprise or department?
- Where am I going to get these and how am I going to afford them?
- How effective is my process for keeping up, for learning from other enterprises?

In this chapter, we have suggested four broad answers to these questions and the rationale for these choices. Summarized, they are as follows:

- Managers need to become perpetual students of many topics
- Managers need to pay attention to changing technologies
- Managers need to develop skills in teaming, collaboration, networking, and sensitivity to cross-cultural behaviors
- Managers need to develop personal leadership for this new environment.

This has been a very long chapter, indeed, the longest in the book, because it is here that we get to the core of what managers worry about at all levels: their role in the organization and how to shape it to meet their will. That requires discussions about work activities, ethics, competition, global realities, and, of great interest to managers, required personal skills.

If managers operate in complex profit-hungry enterprises operating in a changing global environment, using the practices and values of their industries, yet affected profoundly by the events in the larger world, what does a manager need to know about emerging economic and business realities? Answering that question is our next topic of discussion. It can be skipped, if you think you understand modern economic realities, keep up with political events on a worldwide basis, and are comfortable operating in many cultures. Surprisingly, many managers have those qualifications; too many do not.

NOTES

1 For a brief moment, Charles B. Handy seemed to catch the attention of many managers with his book, *The Age of Unreason* (London: Business Books, 1989); he subsequently wrote another half dozen volumes on organizational changes.

2 Don Tapscott and Anthony D. Williams, *Wikinomics: How Mass Collaboration Changes Everything* (New York: Portfolio, 2007).

3 Kevin Kelly, *New Rules for the New Economy: 10 Radical Strategies for a Connected World* (New York: Viking, 1998); Michael E. Porter, *Competitive Advantage: Creating and Sustaining Superior Performance* (New York: Free Books, 1985). Two others popular at that time doing the same thing were James Brian Quinn, *Intelligent Enterprise: A Knowledge and Service Based Paradigm for Industry* (New York: Free Press, 1992) and John Henry Clippinger III (ed.), *The Biology of Business: Decoding the Natural Laws of Enterprise* (San Francisco, CA: Jossey-Bass, 1999)—both remain relevant for today's managers.

4 In the fall of 2013, the Pope announced a reorganization of the Vatican bank, and appointed a new leader to run it; he also had two task forces made up of cardinals to suggest major reorganization and decentralization of the Church's administration (called the Curia), and he launched a worldwide survey among Catholics regarding social issues and the Church's position on various sexual topics. He is acting very much like a private sector CEO doing a business turnaround, and at about the same speed and actions.

5 Rita Gunther McGrath, *The End of Competitive Advantage: How to Keep Your Strategy Moving as Fast as Your Business* (Boston, MA: Harvard Business Review Press, 2013): 15–18.

6 Samuel J. Palmisano, "The Globally Integrated Enterprise," *Foreign Affairs* 85, no. 3 (May–June 2006): 129.

7 Chairman's letter, Wal-Mart, *Annual Report, 2006.*

8 "Jobs to the USA," September 19, 2007, available at http://yakovfain.javadevelopers-journal.com/congratulations_india_is_outsourcing_jobs_to_the_usa.htm (last accessed January 12, 2011).

9 Chairman's letter, Proctor and Gamble, *Annual Report, 2006.*

10 P&G *Annual Reports, 2002–2006.*

11 Normally described by the firm as a recent initiative, see for example, Palmisano, "The Globally Integrated Enterprise," 127–136; IBM Corporation, *Becoming the Premier Globally Integrated Enterprise* (Somers, NY: IBM Corporation, 2007). However, IBM had operated globally integrated manufacturing and product development since the 1950s and had integrated support on the sales side for its largest international customers by the early 1980s. I was a sales manager at IBM in that period and dealt routinely with such integrated accounts.

12 IBM Corporation, *Annual Reports* (Armonk, NY: IBM Corporation, 2002–2012).

13 Publications on innovation in business have become a veritable growth industry. For an introduction to the concepts introduced in my text, see Tony Davila, Marc J. Epstein and Robert Shelton, *Making Innovation Work: How to Manage It, Measure It, and Profit from It* (Upper Saddles River, NJ: Wharton School Publishing, 2006).

14 Samuel Palmisano, "The Globally Integrated Enterprise," *Foreign Affairs* 85, no. 3 (May–June 2006): 132.

15 For nearly a decade, the IBM Institute for Business Value has been interviewing senior executives around the world, having talked to over 19,000 by the end of 2012, and publishing the results in its CX series; available at http://www.ibm.com/iibv (last accessed August 21, 2014).

16 Sinead B. Clarke, James W. Cortada and Heather E. Fraser, *Learning the Biopartnering Game: How to Achieve More from Your Biotech Alliance* (Somers, NY: IBM Corporation, 2004), available at http://www-935.ibm.com/services/us/index.wss/ibvstudy/imc/a1005825?cntxt=a1000060 (last accessed October 16, 2012).

17 Saritha Rai, "India's Outsourcing Industry Is Facing a Labor Shortage," *New York Times*, February 16, 2006, available at http://www.nytimes.com/2006/02/16/business/worldbusiness/16cnd-INDIA.html (last accessed January 12, 2008).

18 See, as a typical example, Alan Greenspan, *The Age of Turbulence: Adventures in a New World* (New York: Penguin, 2007): 285–286.

19 These issues are of considerable significance and yet are not being seriously examined by researchers.

20 For a recent discussion of this issue, see Pankaj Ghemawat, *Redefining Global Strategy: Crossing Borders in a World Where Differences Still Matter* (Boston, MA: Harvard Business School Press, 2007).

21 IBM Corporation, *Unlocking the DNA of the Adaptive Workforce: The Global Human Capital Study 2008* (Somers, NY: IBM Corporation, 2007): 13, available at http://www-935.ibm.com/services/us/gbs/bus/html/2008ghcs.html (last accessed October 16, 2010).

22 Ibid., 20–21.

23 Ibid., 21.

24 Ibid., 29.

25 IBM Corporation, *Balancing Risk and Performance with an Integrated Finance Organization: The Global CFO Study 2008* (Somers, NY: IBM Corporation, 2007): 10, available at http://www-03.ibm.com/press/us/en/pressrelease/22499.wss (last accessed October 15, 2011).

26 The full study is IBM Corporation, *The New CIO: Change Partner and Business Leader* (Somers, NY: IBM Corporation, May 2007) available at www-935.ibm.com/services/us/cio/pdf/wp_cio_leadership_forum_g510-6605-00.pdf (last accessed December 20, 2011).

27 William J. Baumol, Robert E. Litan, and Carl J. Schramm, *Good Capitalism, Bad Capitalism and the Economics of Growth and Prosperity* (New Haven, CO: Yale University Press, 2007): 104–113, 234–247.

28 Carl Shapiro and Hal R. Varian, *Information Rules: A Strategic Guide to the Network Economy* (Boston, MA: Harvard Business School Press, 1999).

29 Adrian J. Slywotzky and David J. Morrison, *The Profit Zone: How Strategic Business Design Will Lead You to Tomorrow's Profits* (New York: Times Business, 1997).

30 Today anthropological techniques are widely used to study customers. For a wonderful discussion of this process, see Paco Underhill, *Why We Buy: The Science of Shopping* (New York: Simon & Schuster, 2000).

31 Ibid., 13.

32 But not always the earliest to provide early warnings. One can reasonably assume that by the time your industry trade literature is writing about a particular use of IT that (a) early adopters are far ahead in their use in your industry and (b) that they learned initially about a use from another industry. That is why it is crucial to be aware of what is occurring elsewhere.

33 Described, Ibid., 35–70.

34 IBM Corporation, *Global CEO Survey 2006* (Somers, NY: IBM Corporation, 2006), available at http://www-935.ibm.com/services/uk/bcs/html/t_ceo.html (last accessed November 15, 2011); IBM Corporation, *Global CEO Survey 2012: Leading Through Connections* (Somers, NY: IBM Corporation, 2012), available at http://www-935.ibm.com/services/us/en/c-suite/ceostudy2012 (last accessed April 15, 2013).

35 Robin Gerber, *Leadership the Eleanor Roosevelt Way* (Upper Saddle River, NJ: Prentice Hall, 2002). In fairness to the author, who has written on non-business leadership history, her publisher marketed the book extensively in the business book market, a market most familiar to Prentice Hall, a publisher your author is familiar with having published eight books with that organization.

36 It should be recalled that Michael E. Porter also commented on global competitive issues before the recent resurgence in discussion about the topic. See his book, *The Competitive Advantage of Nations* (New York: Free Press, 1990). Also influential on management's thinking about strategy was Henry Mintzberg, *The Rise and Fall of Strategic Planning* (New York: Free Press, 1994).

37 Joseph Schumpeter is difficult to read, but for an excellent biography and explanation of his thinking, see Thomas K. McCraw, *Prophet of Innovation: Joseph Schumpeter and Creative Destruction* (Cambridge, MA: Harvard University Press, 2007); the key work on strategy by Alfred D. Chandler, Jr., *Strategy and Structure: Chapters in the History of the Industrial Enterprise* (Cambridge, MA: MIT Press, 1962).

38 Rita Gunther McGrath and Alex Gourlay, *The End of Competitive Advantage: How to Keep Your Strategy Moving as Fast as Your Business* (Boston, MA: Harvard Business Review Press, 2013): xi, xv.

39 Howard Gardner has written a series of books relevant to the work of management. Key works include *Creating Minds* (New York: Basic Books, 1993), *Leading Minds* (New York: Basic Books, 1995), *Extraordinary Minds* (New York: Basic Books, 1997), *Good Work* (New York: Basic Books, 2001), and most recently, *Changing Minds* (Boston, MA: Harvard Business School Press, 2006) which discusses how to persuade people of one's point of view based on scientific understanding of the workings of the human mind.

40 IBM, *The Customer-Activated Enterprise* (Somers, NY: IBM Corporation, 2012).

41 Schumpeter, "It's Complicated," *The Economist*, November 23, 2013, 68.

42 Adam M. Bradenburger and Barry J. Nalebuff, "The Right Game: Use Game Theory to Shape Strategy," *Harvard Business Review* (July 1995), as also HBR reprint # 95402, and also available as a reprint (Boston, MA: Harvard Business School Publishing Corporation, 2009).

43 Data from UNCTAD World Investment analysis, estimates from IBM Institute for Business Value.

CHAPTER 5

Emerging Economic and Business Realities

If the story of the past quarter of a century has a one-line plot summary, it is the rediscovery of the power of market capitalism.[1]

Alan Greenspan, 2007

A problem for managers and their employees at all levels of an organization is the variety and complexity of "the market." If you are a product manager at an automotive company coming up with the name of a new car to be sold around the world, you pick a name and then you find out that in Arabic or in Japanese it is a filthy word. With hundreds of widely used languages, this should be of no surprise. One cannot be expected to know all the possible problem words, but today's marketing manager has to be aware of that possibility and do the due diligence to make sure they do not run into this problem. Use of marketing materials and social media also are exposed to potential social *faux peaux* too. Another manager, an American man, flies to Saudi Arabia to participate in a business negotiation that goes well, and afterward the Arab hosts hold the hand of the American much the way a man and a woman might do in the

The Essential Manager: How to Thrive in the Global Information Jungle, First Edition.
James W. Cortada.

United States, offending the American since that is not a custom in the United States. Yet another manager, this time a British negotiating with Japanese colleagues, keeps seeing these Japanese smiling and nodding their heads up and down, which leads the Brit into thinking that all is well, when in fact the Japanese behavior does not necessarily indicate agreement, just understanding of what he is saying. Two hour lunch breaks in Spain, the Indian penchant for not being precisely on time for a meeting the way Westerners expect, and business practices and local laws that are derived from the English Common law system, French Napoleonic traditions, capitalism, socialism, Confucian heritage, and others complicate matters even further.

These are not rare events; with hundreds of thousands of companies now part of international markets and supply chains, these are the experiences of millions of managers, experts in every field (not just consultants), buying agents, sales personnel in business-to-business (B2B) enterprises; all encounter these. One can expect to see even more of these kinds of issues faced by a manager. Yet, they must navigate economic, cultural, and varied legal circumstances on a far more frequent basis than in the past, if for no other reason than because they will participate in more conference calls, today so easy to have and so widely used in lieu of traveling from country to country, although millions of business people do that every year with air traffic continuing to rise.

So, a fundamental recommendation to managers is to be aware that cultural and legal differences exist, seek them out if dealing with individuals not of your culture, and keep up with the so many more activities going on than simply those narrow tasks articulated in your performance plan. The work of managers and their world consist of far more moving parts than even a decade ago, made more intense by the larger number of immediate connections that exist. The more senior a manager or executive becomes, the larger the number of issues to track and factor into their planning, decision-making, and work. This chapter represents part of that new body of knowledge managers must understand. The global economy is increasingly evolving in ways that directly affect the majority of small- to mid-sized companies and all multinationals around the world. It is morphing in ways that is creating a more tightly connected global economy than the world has seen since before the world wars and Cold War of the twentieth century. It is also a very dangerous world, with corruption, wars, political unrest (or gridlocks) all making the process of doing business difficult and possibly growing in intensity. That is why the material in this chapter is so crucial for managers to understand, particularly by middle managers and senior executives. Equally essential, it is crucial that they keep up with these topics in the years to come. This is not an issue of "nice to know" or "interesting," it is vital to the personal success of managers and to their enterprises. The same applies to public officials even at the city and state level because they now compete directly for businesses, economic development, and talent with other cities, not simply with other nations. That last forum of international competition—city-to-city—is a new development just unfolding, so we have less to go on than one would like.

The evidence of increased changes in the world's economy, and the business activities comprising so much of it, had been piling up rapidly since the collapse of the Berlin Wall in 1989. Central planning in Eastern Europe and the old Soviet Union gave way rapidly, replaced with expanded market capitalism over the next quarter century, and in that process was joined by the "third world," indeed the latter collection of nations growing their economies more rapidly than such stalwart capitalist countries as Great Britain, the United States, and Japan. Yet too, in the advanced "free economies," capitalism experienced a great surge, characterized by rapid growth in wealth, trade, and technology-based products all fueled by vast supplies of capital and technologically-driven increases in productivity. But nobody was immune from the shock of the unknown or unexpected as the Great Depression demonstrated, and not just 9/11. In fact, while Americans in particular were stunned by the attacks of September 2001, and they were dramatic, such acts of violence have been common in every year since the end of the Cold War in Western and Eastern Europe, across all of Asia and Africa, and in pockets in Latin America. Western readers need to remember bombings in Madrid and London, earlier terrorists in Rome, while European and American business people were trapped in an Indian hotel under siege. The point is, violence is stalking the land but the pestilence of economic crisis is too.

Alan Greenspan, who chaired the American Central Bank (Federal Reserve Board) during the last two decades of the twentieth century, noted that there were other changes closer to the mechanics of business and economics of a more positive, yet international form also was underway. Such changes resulted in "the spreading of a commercial rule of law and especially the protection of the rights to property," which "fostered a worldwide entrepreneurial stirring."[2] He argued that the forces of the marketplace superseded many of the prior controlling influences of government, leading to a global-wide decline in regulations and to increases in the specialization of the work of firms, industries, and economies—in short, to the extension of Adam Smith's original notion of the "invisible hand." For one of the world's most well-known economists, it had become *The Age of Turbulence*, the title of his memoirs, just as much for the business manager as for the central banker or economist: "the world of a global capitalist economy that is vastly more flexible, resilient, open, self-correcting, and fast-changing than it was even a quarter century earlier. It's a world that presents us with enormous new possibilities but also enormous new challenges."[3] He wrote those words before the global recession arrived in 2008.

Into this turbulent world of expanded capitalism and prosperity stepped two generations of managers not well prepared for the shock of the new that met them, but nonetheless, in which they thrived. On their watch, they saw the deployment of information technology (IT), for example, in such unprecedented amounts that as early as the 1980s, pundits were prematurely labeling their era the Information Age.[4]

Indeed, by the end of the 1990s, there was hardly a senior executive anywhere around the world who had not personally led some implementation of a new process fortified by new technologies, most notably software. Already discussed in earlier chapters was the nearly invisible network of business processes (e.g., supply chains and common international regulatory practices) and, in effect, systems of IT networks and business practices.

This chapter describes current key features of the international economy as they exist today, such as some of its hot spots, sources of capital, labor, and profits. Although many industries have gone global, no longer merely national as was more often the case through the 1980s, local economic considerations remain profoundly important. Because industries have become some of the key institutional structures within which many businesses and governments—hence management—function today, their role has to be understood within the context of global economic trends. To a large extent, managerial activities have become so bounded together, thanks to the capabilities of computers and telecommunications, which managers rely on the quick movement of vast amounts of information around the world now embedded in all manner of industrial equipment and telecommunications, and in their work. This chapter discusses the "big picture" of the world's economy by describing important "nuts and bolts" elements of the global economy. This is followed by a discussion of how governments leverage IT for national development, because public agencies play an enormous role today in how the global economy works. We then examine possible future characteristics of the global economy since most managers will need to thrive there, not just in the present, and conclude with a summary of the implications for management. While the topics discussed in this chapter are of enormous interest to senior management, and increasingly is to middle management, even first- and second- line managers should be paying attention to the subject as well, as I have suggested several times in earlier chapters.

"NUTS AND BOLTS" OF THE GLOBALIZED CONNECTED ECONOMY

The evidence that international trade has expanded enormously over the past half century has been well-documented and need not detain us here.[5] Nor do we need to engage in a discussion about what economists have learned about its features so far, although it is those that management recognizes as important to take into account as they run their enterprises.[6] Various features should be highlighted that affect directly the work of managers.

Perhaps the most important one to call out is the growth of the global economy itself, despite recessions. Economists have long known that the more markets one had, the greater the opportunity to increase revenues. The larger the market, the more competition one could also experience as rivals sought out the same sources of revenue. The bigger a market is, the more specialized one firm can become as a way of increasing profits, of being competitive, of gaining market share (revenue), and of improving productivity, key ideas originally described by Adam Smith in his book, *The Wealth of Nations* (1776), and most recently expressed as the idea of the long tail.[7] The population of the world increased from three billion in 1960 to over seven billion by 2012.[8] Equally important, the size of the global economy, as measured by gross domestic product (GDP), expanded from US$8.5 trillion in 1960 to nearly US$70 trillion in 2012.[9] Productivity of firms grew enormously as well, which translated into either more profitability or better price-competitiveness. Figure 5.1 is one example to make the point; it shows the acceleration that occurred just within manufacturing industries in the United States in recent decades. Productivity sped up from an average of 2.9% between 1988 and 1996 to 4.7% between 1996 and 2005. These dramatic occurrences floated the boats of many Second Industrial Revolution industries and new technology-based ones too.

The current Chinese experience will eventually be shown to have probably been similar. China demonstrates that a less-developed economy can go a long way quickly to catch up with more advanced economies in a global market—in this case with annual GDP growths of over 10% per year. Older "advanced" economies in North America and Western Europe were expanding at rates closer to 2.5–4% per annum. By 2004–2007 some of the largest, fastest growing companies had names unfamiliar to

Americans and Europeans, such as Sinopec (China) and Wipro (India), while the world's largest firm was Chinese (PetroChina).

If one looks at the volume of goods and services moving across borders, not only are the volumes increasing, as the growing global GDP statistics suggest, so too the percent of totals. In 1990, roughly 40% of all goods and services were traded in the world economy, that is to say, outside the borders of nations in which they were created. That volume increased to 58% by the end of 2005, representing a significant speedup of an already large amount of commerce. This situation remained essentially unchanged during the next five recessionary years.[10] To spur that to potentially greater amounts is why the new global trading pack was embraced by 160 nations in December 2013. The pattern of world trade demonstrates that the global part of the world's economy was growing faster than even the overall economy of the world. Figure 5.2 illustrates that all regions of the world are involved. While this is not the book in which to explain why this is happening, clearly a global reduction in tariffs spurred the expanding globalization, not simply because of more computing or telecommunications (see Figure 5.3).

American firms were some of the most aggressive in exporting their manufacturing to countries with lower labor costs, beginning in the 1980s with automotive manufacturing, next with computer chip

Figure 5.1   Rise in U.S. manufacturing productivity, 1987–2005. From Bureau of Labor Statistics.

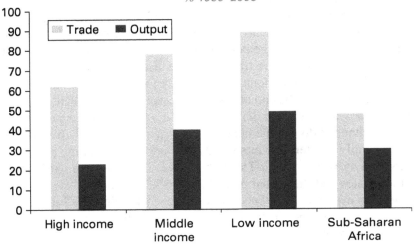

Figure 5.2 World trade growth. From United Nations.

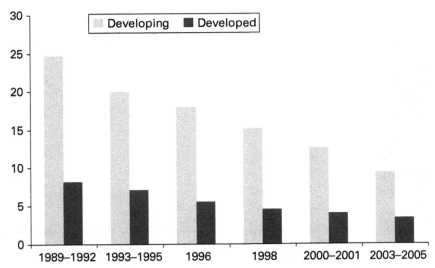

Figure 5.3 Average tariff levels. *All products, unweighted average most favored nation tariff, %, 1989–2005.* From United Nations.

production, and ultimately services, such as insurance claims processing, call centers, even medical x-ray analysis. Figure 5.4 shows what happened, using the example of costs and volumes of U.S. freight, a function essential in moving goods made in one economy through another. The cost of physically moving goods around the world dropped over the past several decades, despite recent increases in the cost of fuel. Additionally, goods move more quickly today because many items can be transported cost-effectively by airplanes, for example, freshly cut flowers grown in Asia or the Netherlands rushed to North American markets, creating additional opportunities for sales and competition. What is also important to point out from Figure 5.4, however, is the fact that volumes increased substantially while costs dropped significantly over the long period relative to inflation—two of many trends that proved essential in motivating manufacturers to plug into the global economy, enhancing connections and their underlying systems and processes. This observation applies to incentives provided by the relative differences in wages for labor, which often is the only factor observers seem to focus on when identifying reasons for the movement of work around the world. Finally, these trends and benefits are being experienced and enjoyed by firms all over the world, not just by those operating in the United States.

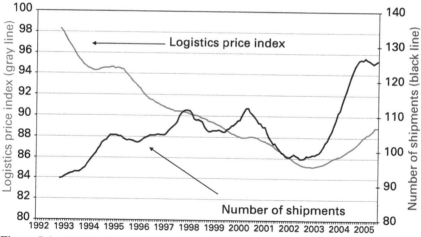

Figure 5.4 U.S. freight—volume growth, cost efficiency, 1992–2005.
Note: Price hikes in 2004–2006 were probably due to surge in petroleum-based fuels.

Another feature of the globalized economy is the speed with which new products are introduced and accepted by customers. Many managers are exposed to the experience of new technologies coming into their workplaces, particularly in those economies that are mature users of IT in North America, Japan, and Western Europe. Many American managers have seen variants of those listed in Table 5.1 as well and have drawn the obvious conclusion: occasions to sell new things emerge quickly and so require rapid response or they risk the loss of opportunity and market share.[11] This is a global observation not limited to the experiences of managers in the United States or East Asia. Furthermore, the less expensive a product is to buy the faster it often can be diffused around the world. An important recent widespread example is the mobile (cell) phone that went from being first introduced in Japan in 1979 as an expensive product for the wealthy to where in less than 30 years it is widely used in every country in the world, with over 2.7 billion users by 2007, today over 3 billion (2013).[12] In underdeveloped economies, as in Africa and parts of Southeast Asia, adoption of this technology occurred faster than in the most advanced economies, such as in the United States for various reasons often unique to a local market. Apple's iPad and iPhone, and their many serious competitors, are two of the most recent stunning examples of this process at work. Not the least of these developments (particularly for mobile phones in general) is the fact that in many communities there were no preexisting telephone networks to compete against, such as the landlines in the United States, where over 90% of all households had a telephone by the time mobile units first came on the market.

While many trends and patterns of contemporary behavior affect the growth of global economic and business growth, a few critical ones are quite important. First, governments around the world have generally promoted domestic practices that encouraged competition at home and within the global economy. For instance, European, Japanese, and American officials reduced regulatory inhibitors to competition and trade, while simultaneously facilitating global trade through regional arrangements, such as the North American Fair Trade Agreement (NAFTA) in the Americas, in Europe through the European Union (EU), and on a global basis via the World Trade Organization (WTO). In these instances, managers played important roles in the shaping of national economic policies and regulatory practices, often in collaboration with competitors within a country and increasingly within the

Table 5.1 Pace of introduction of consumer goods in the United States, 1890–2007

Invention	Household penetration starts	Years to reach 75% of U.S. households
Telephone	1890	67
Automobile	1908	52
Vacuum cleaner	1913	48
Air conditioner	1952	48
Refrigerator	1925	23
Radio	1923	14
VCR	1980	12
Television	1948	7
Personal computers	1976	
Cell phones	1982	24

Start dates are years when widely available commercial or consumer versions existed. In most instances, there were earlier products, prototypes, or predecessor technologies (such as the telegraph before the telephone).

context of the growing power of these international organizations in recent years. We come back to their role in this process later as it remains an important one. Countries that lagged in promoting competition either experienced lower growth or slower integration into the global economy.[13]

A second collection of emerging facilitators of trade are the institutions that evolved in support of global transactions, most notably the massive and dramatic modernization of the world's financial institutions, from government banking and regulatory organizations, such as the U.S. Federal Reserve System, to banks in all countries using IT to facilitate the accurate and rapid flow of funds from one firm to another, from one nation to another. The examples are everywhere: ATMs accessible around the world; global diffusion of credit cards such as American Express, Visa, and MasterCard; and international access to credit and capital. Between 1990 and 2005, cross-border flows of capital grew by 10.7% each year, more evidence that both the volume and speed of globalization were increasing. While the volumes of capital moving about declined during the global recessionary years that followed, by 2012–2013 the quantities being moved began rising again.[14] As before the recession, this movement of capital involved the whole world. In fact, since 1990, capital inflows into emerging markets have grown at twice the speed as inflows into more developed national economies. These kinds of institutional innovations transcended national borders and linked vitally together through shared practices, regulatory guidelines, and IT systems that communicated and shared information with each other. These are the kinds of nuts-and-bolts features of modern markets that proved essential to the expansion of firms around the world and in collaboration with each other.

Additionally, there has been an expansion, albeit slower, in the creation of local laws to protect property rights for businesses. It is an issue of enormous concern to software firms and all media industries, for example. The more developed an economy is, the greater the property protections that exist in law and practice. One reason some national economies are still characterized as "developing" is because they have not yet put into force effective property right protections. One of the conditions that the WTO places on a nation that wishes to participate in its trading sphere is the establishment of laws and regulations that protect such rights. Democracies with free presses tend to do this sooner and easier than societies with censorship and authoritarian public administration.[15] While much work remains to be done, enough has essentially been accomplished to make it possible for firms and their managers to be highly entrepreneurial in more than half the countries around the world, with appropriate economic and legal incentives to facilitate the process of further expansion of capitalist economic conditions.[16] The other half is small economically, so caught up in conflicts in the Middle East and Africa, for example, that many enterprises have written them off for the time being as too dangerous and ineffective in which to operate.[17]

Finally, the overall ability of a national economy to allow the "creative destruction" so diligently described by the Austrian economist Joseph Schumpeter more than a half century ago has been essential in the shaping of the modern economic landscape. His idea was essentially that as innovations appear, they lead to new goods, firms, and industries that generate more economic advantages (read, revenue, jobs, and profits) than older firms and industries. Older ones are destroyed as their economic resources shift to newly emerging opportunities.[18] That process of economic evolution described by Schumpeter required whole economies to become more flexible, calling, for example, for labor laws that allowed hiring and firing to occur easier than before, for the establishment of new businesses with less government bureaucracy, and development of appropriately skilled workforces capable of functioning in emerging industries. Table 5.2 catalogs well-accepted economic features that influence the competitiveness of a nation in the

Table 5.2 Economic ecosystem of an advanced economy, 2001–2006

Political environment	Economic environment
• Liberated, pro-competition regulation in the product market in most Tier-I countries	• Very strong macroeconomic environment with GDP per capita (PPP) in the range US$ 30,000–35,000
• Large part of the economy open to foreign investment and ownership	• Quicker and fewer procedures with average number of days for registering a firm in the Tier country at around 18–20
• Labor market is well developed with very flexible laws on permanent and temporary employment contracting	• Associated compliance costs for business are low
• Fairly advanced and well-developed e-government strategy	• Minimum or no regulatory impediments for firms to downsize/expand in most countries
	• Multiple sources of funding and capital available for new start-ups

Social environment	Technological environment
• Very low population growth rates across countries in the Tier	• High internet literacy at around 50–60% of population and very high mobile penetration at 80–90%
• High life expectancy observed at birth	• High per capita ICT spend at US$ 2000–2500
• On average more than 10 years of schooling	○ 55–45 breakup between Telecom and IT spend
• Most of the countries in the Tier also lie within the top 20 ranks on UN's Human Development Index (HDI) for 2003	○ Developed telecom infrastructure and a greater outlay on IT services as compared to Tier-II and Tier-III countries
○ Points toward a high correlation between social development and advancement on ICT	• Strong e-services market with the Tier containing many of the countries that are leaders in the field of technology playing a leading role in defining internet laws and management of intellectual property

world economy.[19] Senior managers in many large organizations (both public and private) recognize that doing well in each of these categories is absolutely essential for the welfare of firms, industries, and national societies. Thus, a CEO today engages routinely in working with governments and other influencers of public policy in his or her markets to promote modernization, evolution, or expansion of a nation's performance in each of these mega-categories of human activity.

A healthy understanding of the basics of how the global economy works is now an essential element in the education of a modern manager; it should also be a required course for MBA students. Managers and business students in developing economies in particular do not know enough; those individuals working in countries that have long histories of international trade have less of a knowledge gap, such as Dutch and British managers who are better sensitized to global issues; but others working in India and China do suffer from this lack of understanding. Not all emerging markets have this problem, however. In Brazil—clearly an emerging economy—many of its middle and senior managers were educated in the United States and acquired their MBAs at such distinguished schools as Harvard, Wharton, MIT, and Stanford, to mention a few. Asian students have been rapidly acquiring Western education over the past two decades, but there clearly remains a knowledge gap with respect to the nuts-and-bolts functioning of the global economy that needs to be filled. Academics and their universities will need to take leadership in addressing this problem because corporations do not see that as their role.

HOW GOVERNMENTS USE IT FOR NATIONAL ECONOMIC DEVELOPMENT

A general theme in this book is that IT has permeated almost every corner of a manager's life and, therefore, as economies have become more globalized, and a firm's work and sources of income more intimately connected to the economies of many countries, it should be of no surprise that much of the increased intimacy of international trade and commerce would be influenced by the role of governments. To remind about the obvious: during the second half of the twentieth century and to the present, governments at all levels have either profoundly influenced the development and/or deployment of IT and the evolution of national and international economies. Indeed, they remain central players in these developments. Senior business managers become involved in that process to optimize conditions in which they operate. Today almost all governments play a proactive role in making their economies competitive within the global economy. They use their regulatory and taxing authorities to protect national industries and to make them more productive. In almost every nation, one can find proactive governmental policies and programs designed to enhance local economic performance. With just a few exceptions, mainly in Africa and parts of what used to be the Soviet Union, governments are promoting use of information technology either to improve the productivity of their economies internally or to make them competitive in emerging high-tech markets. In short, globalization of economic activities is not happening by accident, but rather with rational push and encouragement on the part of senior public officials.[20]

In recent years, nearly all OECD (Organization for Economic Cooperation and Development) countries (and others as well) integrated IT into their national economic development strategies. Governments see IT as a way to improve the quality of life of their citizens. Companies are increasingly participating in the deployment of such strategies. The intensity of IT-influenced national economic strategies increased in the twenty-first century.[21] Strategies are often novel, a result of the spread of relatively new technologies, such as the Internet and wireless telephony. The rapid spread of the Internet, in particular, stimulated much new activity, with public officials recognizing that businesses and individuals were using this technology, along with mobile phones, to change the way they conducted business and socialized.[22] The Internet is rapidly becoming the world's *de facto* public network, with well over one-third of the world's people routinely using it and another one-third to join in before 2020. Even economies not seen as plugged into the global communications world to any significant degree is now a badly dated view. Figure 5.5 provides examples of the rapid diffusion of the Internet in several countries that might fit the image of being behind the curve to illustrate the expanding connection of people. Figure 5.6 suggests the share of growth in people connecting over the Internet.

One fundamental strategic trajectory is the effective use of IT by government agencies themselves to improve their own internal productivity, such as in lowering the costs of doing work or enhancing their ability to serve citizens (as in providing 24×7 service or greater access to information). A government's internal deployment of IT promotes directly use of IT by business management and their firms. For example,

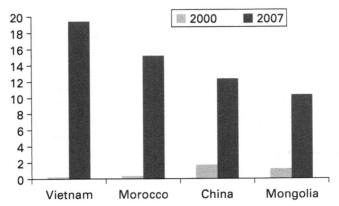

Figure 5.5 Rapidly advancing to the frontier. *Internet usage (%) for select countries, 2000 and 2007.* From International Telecommunications Union.

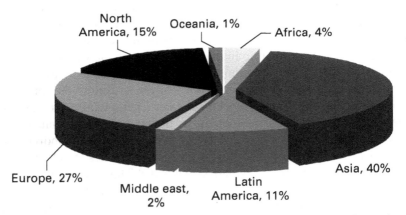

Figure 5.6 Share of increase in Internet users. By region, 2000–2007. From International Telecommunications Union.

by giving citizens access to information around the clock over the Internet, a government encourages citizens to access public services, data, and application forms using PCs, kiosks, mobile phones, tablets, and the Internet. That action strengthens the knowledge citizens have of how to use the Internet and, by inference, encourages them to leverage that technology elsewhere in their private and professional lives, including in the way they purchase goods online.[23]

A second set of publicly initiated strategies involves promoting use of IT outside of government in the greater national society and economy.

We hear of these most often: funding installations of Internet access in classrooms, passing copyright laws to protect digital forms of media content, and implementing regulations governing monthly costs of telephony, wireless communications, use of the Internet, and so forth. These actions tend to be facilitative as they are designed to create the technical, social, political, and regulatory infrastructures that make it more attractive for managers and customers to use these technologies in economically and socially intended ways. Such actions make their economies more competitive and their societies attractive to live in, particularly for those who Richard Florida has dubbed the "Creative Class."[24]

Managers are being asked to help craft these public policy initiatives. In turn, these efforts lead to business opportunities for firms, such as in supplying IT-intensive national identification cards, or radio-frequency identification tracking of goods, boxes, pallets and container cars.[25] Firms worked closely with their national governments for many years to nurture indigenous industries and emerging new ones relevant to global economic competition. Many are increasingly IT-centered, such as IT services (e.g., consulting) in North America and in India, IT-based telecommunications, such as broadband and wireless in Europe, and in rapidly advancing economies the sale and use of modern telecommunications (for instance, in Chile, Latvia, Taiwan, and Israel).[26]

Management increasingly expect their governments to shape local economic policies to make indigenous firms more competitive in a global economy.[27] One way to accomplish that is to participate in transnational initiatives by joining and supporting the work and practices of the WTO, EU, and NAFTA among others. By conforming to the requirements of these clubs, officials often have to reform local laws and regulations regarding border management, tax laws, and property protection. They have to improve local infrastructures, ranging from better roads to providing more electricity, to new labor laws and children's education to prepare them for modern work forces. Each government crafts policies and programs that take into account local political and economic realities as well as indigenous cultural, religious, and historical circumstances, which is why national policies are so varied, yet important. This also explains why management in large and small enterprises playing on a world economic stage have to take into account such localized circumstances as a normal part of their work.

While firms and governments want to make it possible for their nationals to participate in the global economy, no government wants to surrender the ability of its local enterprises and industries to remain competitive as well on the global stage.[28] Economic rivalry among (and within) nations remains a reality, increased most recently as a by-product of the global recession.[29] What is different today is that the use of IT is contributing in new ways to intensified economic competition. This is particularly the case with highly advanced communications and computing, and with a similarly fast, inexpensive, and reliable transportation network to move goods and people. Shipping flowers from Asia to North America, manufacturing computer chips in Asia, or providing consulting services sourced from around the world are common examples. So too is the integration of global supply chains with steps in the process scattered around the globe.[30] Management today routinely has to worry about managing workers in multiple countries and must understand how to move their work too, such as shifting call center work out of India, where salaries have risen substantially in the past several years, to less-expensive English-speaking Africa. The movement of data entry to various low-cost countries continues to be an ability managers hone in such industries as banking, insurance, and medicine, to name a few.

Compounding the complexity of remaining competitive, yet also open to international trade, is the fact that both public officials and private sector managers have to deal with larger groups of interested parties. It is not a clean or precise process. Richard R. Nelson, a leading authority on economic development, rightfully calls the effort "complex" in part because IT-centered economic development involves "not only the actions of private firms competing with each other in a market environment, but also organizations like industry associations, technical societies, universities, courts, government agencies, and legislatures."[31] He observes that to be effective both management and public officials require "a set of institutions compatible with and supportive of" the dominant technologies and industries of their age.[32]

What governments do to promote use of IT as a major component of their national economic development that has proven productive can be quickly summarized:

1. They facilitate expanded connectivity and availability of technological infrastructures.

2. They nurture business environments conducive to the use of modern IT.

3. They motivate consumer and business adoptions of myriad IT tools.

4. They establish and nurture legal and policy environments friendly to work and play involving extensive use of information technologies.

5. They protect and expand social and cultural environments that incorporate and make possible use of such technologies as broadband Internet and cell phones.

6. They encourage the emergence of new high-tech services.

Many of the strategies in evidence today in the most advanced economies are also in others rapidly catching up to earlier adopters of IT. The actions of both types are summarized in Table 5.3.

At each step along the way, senior management expresses strong views about what they need. Typically, they request that workers enter the labor market with more years of education; they want employees that can be hired and fired easily; workers who have computer skills; economies with strong property rights protections; simple and quick ways to register and open new businesses; easy and fast access to capital and tax schemes in support of entrepreneurial initiatives; and excellent transportation and telecommunications infrastructures. Public officials have widely embraced each of these requests as part of their economic development strategies in those nations that have the highest GDP per capita and also among a second tier of rapidly advancing economies, such as those of Central Europe and many parts of Asia.[33]

Table 5.3 Economic development strategies for most advanced and rapidly advancing nations

Most advanced economics	
Political environment	**Economic environment**
• Reduce or maintain product and labor market regulation at low levels to sustain economic growth	• Focus on increasing cross-sector and cross-community linkages to enable sharing of best practices to help increase the overall effectiveness of ICT in the economy
• Government e-strategy to be better coordinated to provide a more consistent and integrated experience for all government services online	
• Market reforms to reduce the costs of new technology to facilitate access for people excluded due to high costs	• Digital channels for governments and businesses need to be made more convenient and cost-effective to encourage higher adoption among consumers and citizens
	• Strengthen governance for e-commerce and internet security with industry to promote online trade

(continued)

Table 5.3 (*continued*)

	Most advanced economics

Social environment

- Focus on improving quality of secondary and tertiary education and reduce school drop-out rates
- Improve access to education and employment opportunity for specific sections of population deprived due to geographical constraints or ethnic background
- Improve participation of minorities in the labor force and specific groups not represented adequately
- Better sharing of demographic data across government agencies through integration and automation of systems

Technological environment

- Government vision for creating a strong ICT environment with a clearly articulated digital strategy to be implemented against measurable targets
  - E.g. governments target of ICT in New Zealand contributing 10% of GDP in 2012 up from 4.3% in 2003
- Formally coordinated government-industry programs to enable efficient rollout of new technologies
- Develop efficient technology commercialization and transfer rules for faster diffusion

	Rapidly advancing nations

Political environment

- Establish coherent and far-reaching government "e-strategy" providing citizens with incentives to conduct online, government-related transactions
- Reform product market regulation to enhance competition
- Relax labor market legislation to make temporary and permanent employment contracting more flexible
- Push public services like filing tax returns, car license renewal, and registration of new business online

Economic environment

- Promote the public–private approach to infrastructure development and roll out
- Provide more affordable and varied financing options to new start-ups to foster innovation
- Reduce the lead time and simplify procedures for new business registration in the country
- Subsidize consulting services and provide tax incentives to help firms to put their businesses online

Social environment

- Increase linkages between the education system and the labor market to keep up with demand
  - Technical training to facilitate up-skill of workforce to keep up with the demand of technically skilled labor
  - Increase access to and improve quality of tertiary education attainment among population
- Improve transport and housing infrastructure to increase labor transfer toward areas with higher levels of employment and better-paid jobs

Technological environment

- Need for community access programs to provide ICT access to people or enterprises with no access due to geographical constraints or affordability
- Greater scope for experimentation for firms facilitated through low regulatory burdens may enable new ideas and innovation to emerge more rapidly, leading to faster technology diffusion
- Improve trust in online payment systems using targeted legislation to promote online trade

A VIEW INTO THE ECONOMIC FUTURE

Nothing seems to be so insisting to a manager or executive than a credible forecast of things to come. While there is some question as to whether they act on such information, the highly experienced ones value these as a way of enriching their views. Forecasts inform decision making, help management to mitigate risks, and to promote confidence in future plans. It is also risky business because nobody knows all things, as we learned about the bad real estate loans and the extent of sovereign debts between 2007 and 2011 around the world, while unpredictable events frequently disrupt plans, such as natural disasters and wars. However, some trends are clear enough that they should be taken into account and be kept up with by any manager who wants to operate successful in a connected world. These are trends not enough managers understand well enough, but to list them at least provides an agenda for adding to their required appreciation.

The Middle East will remain unstable for years to come, while the nuclear arms race will disrupt events in different parts of the world, despite progress by the United States and Russia to reduce the threat from these weapons. Limited supplies and rising and falling prices for energy will continue to be a problem since alternative technologies are close, but not fully capable of replacing and adding to the supplies of oil. Recent increases in the worldwide supply of oil and gas in North America and soon at the North Pole will defer adoption of alternative forms of energy to any massive extent for at least another decade. There are questions about how long China can grow as rapidly as it has, if for no other reason than its political system is now so antiquated as its economy becomes more market driven and its middle class expands in size and influence. The real estate bubble that burst in the West, and earlier in Japan, has yet to pop in many emerging markets, making it a lingering threat to global economic health for years to come. What are the possibilities of a major health crisis, such as a pandemic in an emerging or mature economy? How many managers and their organizations are ready for that? These are a few uncertainties, so management should always have a list relevant to their organizations, and that can inform the decisions they take.

We have alluded to the fact that this is still a very dangerous world. Large swaths of the Middle East and Africa remain in a state of war and with no viable public administration. Sporadic outbreaks in Asia and Latin America also disrupt currencies, economic activities, and supply chains. Kidnappings are now a serious concern for many corporations, with nasty incidents occurring in Latin America, Nigeria in particular, and in several Arab nations during the 2000s alone. Violent regime changes will continue to disrupt lives, possibly increasing in number and involving as much as a quarter of the national governments over the next 10–15 years. Globally, there seems no respite to the deadlocks of political parties and legislatures, inhibiting the creation of laws and regulations governing commerce. Russia is following a Cold War strategy for national security in an age when Eastern Europeans want to integrate more closely with Western Europe. Iran remains an enigma for governments and businesses; it is a powder keg in the Middle East while North Korea plays a similar role in Asia. Very disturbing are the trilateral military tensions brewing among China, Japan, and South Korea, reminiscent of tensions in the area going back literally hundreds and hundreds of years.[34]

Businesses will not be immune from the Asian rivalries, in particular, because they either are headquartered in the region or rely on it. India and China have a technological race going on; Indian officials launch rockets into space to demonstrate their technological prowess to the Chinese while poverty remains India's biggest problem. So, instead of resources going into economic development that would benefit domestic and international businesses, managers have to watch a nervous situation develop. Chinese officials are becoming nervous with American spying activities and the aggressive behavior of such firms as Google and Amazon bristling at local regulations. The Chinese can be expected to increase their desire to be completely self-sustaining in key industries, such as in IT, by reducing their dependence on IBM and Cisco, for example. Extensive turnoffs of foreign exports can occur in less than 100 days, as IBM discovered in 2013, for political strategic reasons having nothing to do with the quality of products. Indian political and economic instability raises question: should Western companies rely on tens of thousands of workers in India to do their work worldwide? A prudent manager would do well to remember the old adage of not putting all one's eggs into a single basket, for fear of dropping it.

Finally, Western managers are perhaps too in love with the potential of business in Africa. Caution and deeper understanding of the opportunities and risks with these four-dozen nations are needed, yet the West continues perhaps to overstate opportunities in this continent.

The entire continent is still in the process of reordering precolonial boundaries that make sense to them, while struggling with poor public administration, and an inability to invest effectively in human capital.

There are, however, certainties that can be counted upon. The most obvious is demographic. Standards of living, health, and education continue to improve in many nations, although the bulk of the growth in population will still come from the poorest countries on earth for several more decades. The process of massive transfers of wealth from the West to the East, underway now for two decades, shows no signs of ending; indeed, one can reasonably expect that to continue, particularly as underdeveloped economies spin off higher per capita GDPs, resulting in over a billion people joining the middle class who today are poor. Rising standards of living will increase faster in the East than in the West. Water wars, price competition over oil, access to minerals and other raw materials will become more intense as the human population continues to grow and to move into the middle class. We are on the verge—within just a few years—of essentially having the entire world connected: people-to-people, machines-to-people, and machines-to-machines. Language barriers are dropping as larger numbers of people speak English, Chinese, or Spanish, and as translating software becomes more effective, indeed ubiquitous, over the next decade. And, of course, terrorism will remain a chronic destabilizing reality, possibly for several decades, as happened in earlier times when the world experienced bouts of such violence.

Figure 5.7 summarizes the expected performance of the world economy to 2025. Advanced economies grow slowly, emerging markets rapidly. These emerging markets could account for over two-thirds of the total worldwide growth in GDP during the same period. That means many managers are going to have to major on Indian and Chinese markets because over one-third of the growth in the economy of the world will probably come just from these two nations, which combined will have over 2.8 billion potential customers. This will occur even though both will experience a slowdown in consumption, requiring structural reforms to reenergize consumer spending.[35] Because over half the world now lives in cities, business activities are going to be largely urban-based since the largest 100 cities alone should account for one-third of the global GDP growth. Out of these 100 cities, some 45 will be Chinese; the world has over 5000 cities. Services will grow, while manufacturing

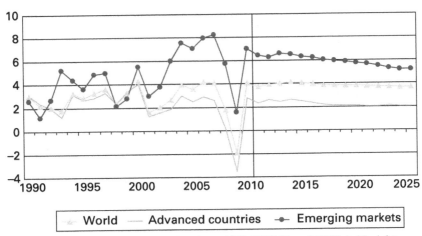

Figure 5.7 Global GDP history and projects, 1990–2025. From IHS Global Insights, IBM Institute for Business Value, OECD.

is expected to expand too, only at some slower rate, perhaps at half that in evidence in 2010–2012.

But the most important trend to watch worldwide is the growth in the middle class. These people will need to spend a great deal of money to acquire the goods and services that middle classes consume all over the world. To put a fine point on the matter, in 2009 there were 1.8 billion people in the middle class worldwide—that number jumps to 3.2 trillion in 2020. Then by 2030—still in the working lives of over half the managers today—it climbs to about 4.9 billion.[36] In short, the world could experience the largest economic boom of the past 200 years in the next 30 years! Now imagine 4.9 billion connected, educated, and financially capable consumers. To be sure, populations will shift around in their wealth and capabilities. The percent of populations of working age—when they can most afford to be consumers—will ebb in China and Russia as is now happening in Japan and Europe, while those of India, Bangladesh, Nigeria, and Egypt will grow.

There are many forecasts available to suggest what different industries will do in terms of growth and where. Industry associations, the OECD, and national banks in many countries routinely produce these and certainly for any half dozen years going forward are quite accurate, losing a bit of their quality the further out in time one goes. Managers should routinely study these and factor them into their product development and market coverage plans in 3–6 year horizons. Some are obvious, such as the growth in demand for industrial products, wholesale and consumer goods sales, travel and transportation, energy, electronics, healthcare, government, and banking. All are driven by this surge now underway in the expansion of the middle class. Some will grow more in one society versus another, which is all the more reason to pay attention to the details behind such forecasts.

Finally, what can we say about health? This is a nagging question that managers outside the health and pharmaceutical communities do not understand, and so remains enigmatic. We read snippets of concerns that should draw management's attention. Blue flues are obvious examples of pandemics that do disrupt work. But, how serious is the growing ability of infectious diseases to resist existing drugs? The Western press in particular is increasingly sounding the alarm. European governments are banning the use of antibiotics in cattle and other animals used for human food; the American government announced similar, yet limited, regulations at the end of 2013. The problem with infectious diseases is that they can affect the wealthiest countries in the world, and not just the poorest. Polio has resurfaced, while AIDS and Malaria are still with us. A growing concern will have to be lung diseases and cancer in China over the next two decades as the nation experiences the twin issues of an aging population and the consequences of environmental pollution, which have already occurred. Future attempts to minimize pollution will not completely eradicate the consequences of what has already been done to the bodies of currently living Chinese citizens. We can only guess what the consequences will be of medical problems on the work of management around the world.

The same applies to global warming. Highly controversial in many parts of the world, some facts cannot be denied. Temperatures are rising and if they were to stop tomorrow morning, that process and its consequences would take time to reverse or do something different. This includes what happens to weather, sea levels, and health conditions of living creatures, including customers and workers. I am not aware of any major corporation, for example, having taken action to avoid risks of being in future flood plains, like downtown New York City, or pulling out of Bangladesh because of the same problem. Increasingly violent storms as a possible working condition do not yet seem to be a factor in business strategy. However, one can surmise that future managers now being educated at universities and hence being sensitized to climate change issues will begin to take this problem into consideration in due course of time as they move into positions of authority in their firms. But until then, natural disasters will be treated as exceptions to the work of management, not the norm.

IMPLICATIONS FOR MANAGEMENT

A bank in China could easily develop a consumer credit card, market it in the West, offer it for half the cost in interest for unpaid balances, process transactions for a fraction of what they cost in either the United States or European Union, and make major card vendors like Visa and American Express look like tiny operations. They could buy a Western bank, like BankAmerica or Barclays, to promote their offer and within a few years potentially dominate the credit card business, assuming, of course, that American and European regulators did not get in the way. Exporting services is not a new idea; India's high-tech industry is all about services, not manufactured goods. So, models for how to do this already exist. For today's manager, the technology can already bring competition quickly and cost-effectively and offer that individual the opportunity to do the same in reverse. But that manager would need to know what the Chinese financial markets looked like and understand the rising tide of the middle class, one that still saves more per capita than almost in any other country, making that credit card opportunity not so obvious yet not impossible to achieve. Partnering with that Chinese bank would also be an opportunity, a services version of product supply chains in a new form. The point of this little scenario is to suggest that the future manager has to think in more global terms about possibilities and threats that were not realistic to ponder as late as the early 2000s. The higher up in an enterprise one is, the more they must pay attention to what is happening in national economies of the world.

At a minimum it means more than subscribing to *The Economist* or the *Financial Times*, although not a bad start. Personally and as an institution, managers and their organizations have to increasingly monitor global economic activities in some organized and structured way. Large corporations, for example, normally have one or more economists on staff reporting regularly on their findings to the rest of the enterprise, such as through bimonthly reports to a mailing list of managers and participating in corporate strategy planning. But more than ever before, managers who want to remain connected must read, visit other countries, and develop a network of colleagues around the world who they can learn from. By the time someone has reached the senior ranks of a *Fortune* 1000 company that had better be the case.

One of the most interesting implications for managers is what is happening with demographics, specifically the increasing numbers of new members of the middle class, and, to a lesser extent, new members of the upper classes of their societies. That phenomenon bears monitoring and is better understood more by personnel in other sectors than the manufacturers who produce consumer goods, as it will drive so much demand in banking, finance, real estate, transportation, consumer goods, and electronics, among other industries. This generation of the new middle class comes connected to the Internet to buy goods from around the world, and many societies are so fashion conscious that they will pay more for the "right brand," as we have seen with American automobiles in China, perfume and women's accessories in Japan, and Apple products in dozens of countries. That cohort is already moving into its new financial domain and is affecting businesses around the world; it is a trend that must be understood quickly by the reader, if not already done. Watching the evolution of the Internet, which is what we would have suggested a decade ago, is now simply old news; it is the middle class's expansion that is the issue to engage with today.

Despite globalization, and its institutional underpinnings, such as the operation of the WTO, regulators and public officials still roam their countries finding ways to protect local businesses, what a reporter at *The Economist* cleverly called "gated globe."[37] You can enter a gated community, but only if approved to do so, a modern version of old fashion protectionism even with WTO being reenergized. This is both a risk and an opportunity for all involved. For a savvy public official, it is a way of nurturing a local industry until it is fit enough to compete globally. That is what the Asian Tigers did to nurture their IT manufacturing capability, for example. Firms outside those countries bent their strategies to take advantage of this circumstance, such as investing in local manufacturing capabilities in Taiwan and in Indonesia. Connected managers and public officials work together, not always against each other, each to optimize their own position. But the point must be clear: public officials on the one hand will work to protect their citizens and nurture their economies while on the other simultaneously currying international trade. It is a delicate balance, a dance, but one done the best at this time by Asian governments, with eager students in Latin America. Capitalism, global trade, and the role of governments, thus, vary in style and definition from one part of the world to another. It would be a mistake to assume practices and values transcend overwhelmingly the world in some universal manner, even when officials and managers have been educated at the same universities, have similar operational practices (e.g., how they manufacture a specific product), and are cosmopolitan and fluent in other languages. Understanding specific cultural variances in the work of management must be prized as a valuable body of personal and institutional knowledge.

Finally, one could easily surmise that sets of customers will be displaced by new groups as whole national economies reach a point where they can afford your products and services, find them fashionable or essential. While much of the economic literature is about the disruptions caused by the arrival of new technologies and business models, too little is said about the disruptive effects of new customers. Would an established business know how to deal with them, such as a West European firm that finds demand for its products rapidly expanding in the middle of China? Would such a company be able to seize upon the opportunity or simply see it melt away in the face of more alert connected managers in an Asian country? It would not be a surprise to see the creative construction of new markets caused by rapid communications, crowd sourcing behaviors, and, of course, rising standards of living. This observation is not limited just to firms that sell to individuals and their families; it also applies to the B2Bs that sell to those companies, which in turn sell to the emerging middle and upper classes. Many firms will simply not know how to deal with these potential opportunities, or the problems that come with these. They would not know how to scale up fast enough or how to extend their reach, while surely others will understand perfectly well what is required.

All of this discussion leads to a number of uncomfortable questions to be asked and answered by management teams, but also by individual leaders:

- To what degree do you and your organization understand how your business fits into the global economy?
- How well does your enterprise monitor international events that could help or hurt your business?
- What role do international trends play in your business strategy?

- How sound are the reasons for you even having an Indian strategy, Chinese strategy, or any other international strategy? Do you have a strategy for foreign markets? How do you know if it is any good?
- How do you keep your middle and senior managers trained and current on global economics and world trade politics?
- To what extent is your workforce a reflection of the cultural diversity of your customers and markets?

In short, the message is simple: few managers will ever be immune from the ebbs and flows of the global economy, unless they run a single barber shop and buy only locally manufactured hair products. Even their cutting instruments are made around the world. Answers to these questions are not generic; they must be specific, tailored to your time and business realities.

It should be obvious what the individual manager must do—understand their global ecosystem—but just as important, their employer—meaning their company and not just their senior management—would find it useful to institutionalize keeping up with international affairs. Resident economists, in dialogue with government relations staffs who deal with regulators and legislators in countries important to the firm, and line management in those nations should converse regularly. Shared insights, information, and dialogue should also take place with those responsible for developing corporate strategies, marketing, advertising (even their agencies), and products.

There is also a special role to be played by graduate schools in business administration insistently in educating young business students and also mid-career management in seminars and executive MBA programs about the new realities. The same applies to industry and trade associations, even if they think of themselves as highly parochial to the needs of one nations' industry, because no industry is immune from the effects of international economic activities, let alone competition. The academics are well positioned to help immediately, some industry associations with chapters in other countries too. So the poor harried manager of the future who we are suggesting needs to keep up with so many new issues can—and should insist—on obtaining help to filter out the irrelevant, so that he or she can focus on their short- and long-term needs.

We should also keep in mind a key theme of this book that the modern manager lives in a world filled with complex systems and processes. They extend beyond the confines of one's department, firm, industry, and nation, rapidly even becoming quite uniform in many critical ways around the world. These include financial, banking, regulatory, and legal business practices; supply chains that involve multiple countries and their local industries and firms of different sizes, all bound together by collections of shared IT, systems, and practices. But, it is also a world where the exceptions to systems, processes, and practices in management are sufficient enough for managers to recognize variants and be able to adapt to them. Look for them, embrace them as potential sources of useful practices, and respect their importance where they are practiced.

As odd as this may seem, on a personal note, I have run into too many managers who did *not* have a current passport. We can talk all we want about international trade and opportunities, but today's manager has to be prepared to get on airplane tonight to seize upon an opportunity in another part of the world, and that quite simply requires a passport, not just enough budget to fund an airplane ticket. Passports are not expensive but they can take months to acquire. If you do not have one, finish reading this book, then apply for one. Without one, you cannot participate well in the global economy; consider it your driver's license to be a modern manager along with your university degree.

The next chapter (Chapter 6) pulls together many of the findings and recommendations described in this book. It calls attention to the fact that the manager today and in the future is and will be tightly linked to a larger collection of issues, opportunities, and risks than prior generations of management. How they can thrive in that situation is the key takeaway from the last chapter.

NOTES

1 Alan Greenspan, *The Age of Turbulence: Adventures in a New World* (New York: Penguin, 2007): 14.

2 Ibid., 15.

3 Ibid., 10.

4 I discuss this issue in some detail in James W. Cortada, "Do We Live in the Information Age? Insights from Historiographical Methods," *Historical Methods* 40, no. 3 (Summer 2007): 107–116.

5 For statistical evidence, see Angus Maddison, *Monitoring the World Economy, 1820–1992* (Paris: OECD, 1995): 232–239; for an economist's explanation, see Robert Brenner, *The Economics of Global Turbulence* (London: Verso, 2006); and for a perspective written by a business management professor, see Richard H.K. Vietor, *How Countries Compete* (Boston, MA: Harvard Business School Press, 2007).

6 William J. Baumol, Robert E. Litan, and Carl J. Schramm, *Good Capitalism, Bad Capitalism, and the Economics of Growth and Prosperity* (New Haven, CT: Yale University Press, 2007).

7 Chris Anderson, *The Long Tail: Why the Future of Business Is Selling Less of More* (New York: Hyperion, 2006).

8 http://www.census.gov/ipc/www/img/worldpop.gif (last accessed November 27, 2011).

9 http://web.worldbank.org (last accessed November 27, 2011).

10 Various statistics from World Bank.

11 The concept that first-entrant advantages suffered a major blow with the Dot-com bubble and bust, largely because the normal disciplines of controlling expenditures and actually generating revenues, and so forth, was not as adhered to. Bad management practices simply could not be covered over by first-entrant advantages, reminding management that even in an expanding market for some new service or good, sound managerial practices were still required. On the bubble, see Robert Brenner, *The Boom and the Bubble* (New York: Verso, 2003).

12 http://www/itu.int/ITU-D/ict/statistics/ (last accessed April 27, 2012).

13 IBM and the Economist Intelligence Unit have collaborated for a number of years to document these trends. For an overview of recent trends, see James W. Cortada, Ashish M. Gupta, and Marc Le Noir, *How Nations Thrive in the Information Age* (Somers, NY: IBM Institute for Business Value, 2007), available at http://www.ibm.com/services/us/gbs/bus/pdf/g510-6575-01-infoage.pdf (last accessed August 14, 2014).

14 Various statistics, World Bank.

15 Baumol, Litan, and Schramm, Good Capitalism, Bad Capitalism, 226–276.

16 A conclusion shared by all the economists cited in this chapter's endnotes and documented even for the highly regulated economies of Europe, Barry Eichengreen, *The European Economy Since 1945* (Princeton, NJ: Princeton University Press, 2007). To be sure, the whole issue of protecting digital products remains to be resolved by the most "advanced" economies first, and hopefully endorsed by the proverbial "everyone else," probably through the vehicles of international law, international boards, and industry practices.

17 Corruption is another example of the instability of so many national economies, BBC, December 3, 2013, available at http://www.bbc.co.uk/news/business-25193877 (last accessed December 19, 2013).

18 Thomas K. McCraw, *Prophet of Innovation: Joseph Schumpeter and Creative Destruction* (Cambridge, MA: Harvard University Press, 2007): 351–352, 503–504.

19 In this particular case, these are criteria used by IBM and the Economist Intelligence Unit (EIU) to rank various capabilities of nations in their role in global economics, use of the Internet, and so forth.

20 James W. Cortada, *How Societies Embrace Information Technology: Lessons for Management and the Rest of Us* (Hoboken, NJ: John Wiley & Sons, 2010).

21 There is hardly any government in any advanced economy that today avoids tracking the volume of IT in their nation or that does not have important IT policy initiatives underway. While the United Nations, OECD, and the European Union are the most

obvious sources for such tracking—all available on their web sites—individual government agencies also collect this sort of data, such as U.S. Department of Commerce and similar agencies in Japan, United Kingdom, Australia, and Germany to mention a few.

22 Literature on the topic is vast in quantity. But see, for example, *The 2007 E-readiness Rankings: Raising the Bar* (London: Economist Intelligence Unit, 2007), published annually since 2000; Kimball P. Marshall, William S. Piper, and Walter W. Wymer, Jr. (eds.), *Government Policy and Program Impacts on Technology Development, Transfer and Commercialization: International Perspectives* (New York: Haworth Press, 2005).

23 Mark A. Abramson and Roland S. Harris III (eds.), *The Procurement Revolution* (Lanham, MD: Rowland and Littlefield, 2003). E-business means use of online systems with which to conduct business, such as purchases, or to communicate and share information, such as e-mail or collaborative Internet-based tools.

24 Richard Florida, *The Rise of the Creative Class* (New York: Basic, 2002): ix.

25 For more detailed description of these dimensions, see James W. Cortada, Ashish M. Gupta, and Marc Le Noir, *How Nations Thrive in the Information Age* (Somers, NY: IBM Corporation, 2007).

26 Richard H.K. Vietor, *How Countries Compete: Strategy, Structure, and Government in the Global Economy* (Boston, MA: Harvard Business School Press, 2007).

27 A key point made by Thomas L. Friedman, *The World Is Flat: A Brief History of the Twenty-First Century* (New York: Farrar, Straus and Giroux, 2nd ed., 2006): 457–504.

28 Which is why rankings always show disparities in the performance of nations and regions.

29 "The Gated Globe," Special Report, *The Economist*, October 12, 2013, pp. 3–20.

30 Clair Brown and Greg Linden, "Offshoring in the Semiconductor Industry: A Historical Perspective," in Susan M. Collins and Lael Brainard (eds.), *Brookings Trade Forum 2005: Offshoring White Collar Work* (Washington, DC: Brookings Institution Press, 2006): 279–322; Jan Mazurek, *Making Microchips: Policy, Globalization, and Economic Restructuring in the Semiconductor Industry* (Cambridge, MA: MIT Press, 1999).

31 Richard R. Nelson, *Technology, Institutions and Economic Growth* (Cambridge, MA: Harvard University Press, 2005): 108. A point also made by an equally distinguished team of economists, Baumol, Litan, and Schramm, *Good Capitalism, Bad Capitalism*, 35–59.

32 Ibid., 111.

33 James W. Cortada, the chapter "How Governments Leverage Information Technology to Improve Their National Economies," in *How Societies Embrace Information Technology: Lessons for Management and the Rest of Us* (Hoboken, NJ: John Wiley & Sons and IEEE Computer Society Press, 2009): 71–127.

34 One of the most respected global analyses of global political, economic, and military risks is done by Maplecroft each year. Their latest report is Political Risk Atlas 2014,

available at http://maplecroft.com/portfolio/new-analysis/2013/12/12/instability-and-conflict-mena-and-east-africa-drive-global-rise-political-risk-maplecroft-bpolitical-risk-atlas-2014b/ (last accessed December 20, 2013).

35 I am grateful to IBM's economist, Dr. Martin Fleming, for these insights.

36 Projects by OECD. Definition of middle class: households with daily expenditures of between US$10 and US$100 per person in purchasing power.

37 "The Gated Globe."

CHAPTER 6

The Way Forward

The greatest thing in the world is not so much where we are,
but in what direction we are moving.

Oliver Wendell Holmes, 1870s

This book focuses largely on the relationship between managerial practices and the continued migration of human work activities to information technologies all functioning within a globalizing business environment. The fundamental premise has been that there is now enough connectivity among workers, managers, customers, regulators, and others brought about by the extensive use of all manner of information technologies and business cultures that how one works and manages is fundamentally altering. These developments are resulting in the evolution in the *style* in the way managers work, a way characterized by work environments structured into systems and processes, and highly reliant on significant amounts of information and appreciation of contexts. These realities, in turn, cause, indeed require, that the actions of individuals be heavily influenced by the use of large data sets, fact finding before decision-making, and the growing use of modeling and

The Essential Manager: How to Thrive in the Global Information Jungle, First Edition.
James W. Cortada.
© 2015 the IEEE Computer Society. Published 2015 by John Wiley & Sons, Inc.

simulation beyond the capabilities of laptop spreadsheet software. While the basic laws of economics and principles of business management have not changed, and probably will not in the foreseeable future, the tasks that are done and the strategies crafted and implemented by managers continue to evolve. The existence of IT in all enterprises and most government agencies in most countries today is so pervasive that it is now a necessity for management at all levels to acquire and to apply a deep understanding of how this technology evolves and affects their work and careers in order to leverage business outcomes. This is not a call to become technically savvy; rather it is a warning that to avoid appreciating the implications of using IT or how it diffuses in a market, firm, and industry puts one's work in danger of failing to be productive, let alone effective.

The successful manager and executive will increasingly be individuals who I think of as being *connected managers*. A connected manager knows a great deal about three bodies of knowledge and applies insights gained from them in their routine work:

First, this new breed of managers understands deeply what is happening in their operating environment. Specifically they focus on understanding the way people use information technologies, effective management practices, what is going on in their industry, and more broadly, about the world at large.

Second, connected managers are engaged in each of these dimensions. This occurs particularly in their applications to important decisions as part of the decision-making process, and look for ways to use those insights to generate new sources of revenue, profits, or results.

Third, they work in both the private and public sectors and are visible working around the world. To not act as a connected manager invites failed careers and decay of whole companies and governments. The upside and downside of this conclusion have been in open evidence for over three decades and so cannot be ignored.

The futurists got it right, technology has changed a lot of things, but they have remarkably missed predicting correctly the speed with which change is coming, the consequences so far, and the implications of such changes to management. But it does not matter, because much of their future has already arrived. The challenge now is how to make sure we continue to stay current with its implications and to shape it to our needs, not to allow it to dictate our destiny. The first step in that direction is to become aware of the critical features of the evolving workplace—the primary objective of this book. This final chapter is prescriptive. It is intended to answer a blunt question, "So what do you want me to do about it?" Put in more polite language, what behavioral attributes of management are required for them to thrive in the environment we have described? Some advice is familiar; a reassurance that not all things change, such as the requirement to have a business plan resulting in generating profits. Others may seem different, such as becoming a lifelong student of the economics and technological implications of new forms of IT, and how to use social media for profitable ventures in all industries.

Some readers of this book may argue that much of what has been reported on in earlier chapters is familiar—Good! Because that means they are already tuned in and understand—but they are the exception. However, the future will be filled with newly minted managers just learning their craft, just as the world is today filled more with managers young in their careers as line management or recently anointed executives. This book is for them. The advice holds true also for highly experienced managers, business school professors, and industry trainers who need to understand what to teach tomorrow's managers and executives both types of whom will work in existing enterprises and government agencies, or will be entrepreneurs starting up new businesses.

A BRIEF SUMMARY OF THIS BOOK'S KEY ADVICE

Before engaging in a discussion that pulls together the messages and lessons from all previous chapters, a brief summary of what one should consider doing is in order. Table 6.1 very briefly summarizes the lessons

Table 6.1 Key "Takeaways" by chapter

Chapter 1

Managers need to rely on data and analytical methods

Managers need skills that help them thrive in agile environments. These include project management, management of IT, process management, how to develop and wield authority and influence, teamwork

Chapter 2

Managers need to understand that there is a set of global best practices and that products and services are now delivered to global customers

Managers need to track emerging technological trends in IT and in their industry-specific technologies

Managers need to include technological considerations into decision-making

Chapter 3

Managers need to understand and participate in their industry(ies), not just in their companies

Managers need to understand political, economic, and social risks

Managers need to incorporate their broader issues into their daily work and strategies

Chapter 4

Managers need to become perpetual students

Managers need to pay attention to changing technologies

Managers need deep skills in teaming, collaborating, and networking

Managers need to understand and be sensitive to cross-cultural behaviors

Managers need to develop personal leadership styles for the new environment

Chapter 5

Managers need to maintain a good sense of how their customers, firm, and industry fit into the global economy

Managers need to acquire a "nuts-and-bolts" understanding of how regulatory and business practices vary around the world

Managers need to nurture a broad set of connections that transcend their home countries

by chapter to consider embracing and executing. This short list can also be used as a quick reference to where in this book to get more details. It is quite generalized on purpose. If you understand the need for executing on these recommendations, you will figure out the specific tasks that need to be done within your own working environment. The messages are intended to be as much a statement of one's personal intentions at work than a cookbook of managerial recipes. Individual circumstances are too varied and change too quickly to be too prescriptive. To use an American expression, managers will need to "connect the dots" about their work, a form of innovation and creativity that is as essential as inventing the next great product.

In this chapter, the key messages that are discussed can also be summarized in a short list of actions useful for staying focused on the fast moving changes underway. They cluster around three communities in the life of a manager. The communities are, first, made up of employees and fellow managers; second, customers; and third, a complex world of national economies, regulators, governments, and competitors. They interact with each other more intensely today than even 20 years ago, thanks to rapid communications, use of IT (e.g., new social media tools, evolving Internet functions, and staid e-mail), and a widespread awareness of this environment on the part of all participants. Keeping that complex ecosystem in mind in which a manager lives, here is the short list, and probably by no means a complete one:

- Consider what customers and competitors are doing worldwide
- Define diversity in broader ways than ever before
- Understand regulations affecting your industry and firm
- Understand how IT is evolving
- Understand how IT helps and hurts your organization and industry
- Gather information for decision-making and for understanding your world from a variety of sources
- Consider that customer expectations come from a growing variety of sources.

A GLOBAL SOCIETY AND ITS IMPLICATIONS FOR MANAGEMENT

Many aspects of human activities are rapidly leading to a relatively integrated global society, and one of those dimensions involves business. That is not news. What is news is that the integration is extending very tightly to more people and countries, and that it expands beyond businesses and economies to social and cultural dimensions too. Communities, regions, and nations will still count as distinctive entities.

That reality will remain as critical organizations and social infrastructures at the same time something new is developing, both simultaneously. It is evolving into some sort of political or economic social order bigger than nations, but with formal structures, like governments and other institutions and, of course, local culture. Examples of this trend underway are increasing in number. The World Trade Organization (WTO) is expanding its authority and power to tell nations what rules they must adhere to for international trade. When a national economy gets into trouble, both the International Monetary Fund (IMF) and the World Bank (WB) wield their power of the purse to force governments to reform, as occurred in the 1990s when Asian economies ran into financial trouble in exchange for monetary assistance. In Europe, the European Union (EU) is slowly assuming more responsibility for dictating the course of banking and monetary events in Europe, even at the expense of national governments grudgingly surrendering some of their sovereign power in over two dozen nations, so far. The Europeans are doing this, first, through their regulatory authority, then by applying increasingly heavy doses of fiscal central banking powers. The EU uses its abilities to promote technological innovation and job creation, and most recently through the reluctant granting of additional authority by the national governments to the EU to mandate treasury reforms in such financially troubled states as Greece, Italy, Spain, and Portugal. About the only international organization that is not increasing its authority over whole societies is the United Nations (UN), but that circumstance could always change. The point is that global institutions are expanding their sway at the same time that the private sector is increasing the number of global firms linked to smaller enterprises in massive globalized supply and value chains.

Thus, the emergence of some global, flat, or integrated society now underway is not some intellectual abstraction to be trivialized or to be ignored by senior management. It is to be respected, admired, seized upon, feared, and worked with as the playing field for business and public administration grows in scope and complexity. This new world is being shaped by various local cultures and laws, all the while emerging as well over an additional billion people—customers and employees—move soon into the middle class. Such developments scream for several actions on the part of individual managers and their enterprises of all sizes.

First, recognize that competitors and customers come from all over the world by design and by surprise. You do not get to vote on whether that happens; they own the power to pull most firms into a global whirlpool. If a product or a service you sell is portable in some way, then you have no choice but to think about your business in a global way. This is part of the message delivered in our discussion about the global enterprise. Understand globally where customers, competitors, and suppliers can come from and seek them out. The phenomenon of an expanding pool of customers, competitors, and suppliers appears in all industries; there are no known exceptions except, it appears, the one every commentator on globalization uses: barbers. Even that one is false, as any business traveler will tell you, because they have gotten haircuts wherever they travel when they needed to have their hair trimmed, and this practice applies to both men and women. Both genders travel more today than ever in history, itself a useful set of data to pay attention to, if you want to know where your potential customers are.[1]

Second, globalization means managers and their employees increasingly have to take diversity to a new level, no longer just to include women, ethnic minorities, or older citizens in the workforce. It now means having staff from various countries and cultures, speaking multiple languages, and management with working experiences in various nations. Expect that requirement to increase both as a success factor for a firm and as a personal career enhancer. This requirement has long been around, often given only casual recognition, but now must become a very serious issue. It begins with the simple international conference call with a half dozen people from four to six countries trying to understand each others' English accent, extends to a deep understanding of how to sell American goods in India, small electronics from Japan and South Korea in Sub-Saharan Africa, to bridging cultural and historical tensions among the Japanese with the Chinese and Koreans, or the Germans with the French, or the Brazilians with Asians and Africans. A connecting bridge already in wide use is the English language and its variants. Very large enterprises often standardize their corporate communications on it, but over 15% of the world speaks Chinese, while Spanish and Arabic are each used by hundreds of millions of people. English is a minority language on the Internet, Chinese is more widely used, but not in business communications, where English still dominates, if losing market share in business circles. So, more than installing great telephony, having diverse language skills has to become a corporate imperative.[2]

Third, as regulatory practices harmonize around the world, and simultaneously capital's availability does too, as a result of regulatory actions and integrated economies, management teams will have to deal with these twin issues—regulations and capital acquisition—on a global basis. No longer will they be able to specialize in American or European regulatory practices; they already have to pay attention too to Chinese, Japanese, Korean, and Latin American practices. Amazon. com can sell Nazi literature in the United States, but not in France. Google makes it possible for Americans and Europeans to search out whatever information they want in the Internet, but runs afoul of Chinese regulators perfectly prepared to shut this firm out of a market of over one billion people, of whom more use the Internet than live in either North America or in Europe. While regulators and bankers are increasingly adopting familiar practices around the world, they have not yet achieved that result; it is still a process under development. That reality, which guarantees diversity of practices, is one we need to be aware of, while at the same time, it insures many incremental changes will occur on an almost weekly basis for decades to come. Management has to figure out how to deal with that low level, incremental, constant, yet important aspect of their work and markets.

There are some questions one can ask to assess their personal preparedness:

- To what extent do I understand how my firm (or part of the enterprise) engages in the global economy?
- Do I understand the global competitive forces influencing my success and if I think I do, what is my documented and implemented strategy for dealing with these?
- What should I do to identify opportunities and threats to my business? In other words, do my SWOT analyses routinely account for global conditions?
- What is my strategy for staying current on relevant international events?
- To what extent have I prepared my staffs and organizations to function globally?

If you are a manager in a small company that has no direct dealings with the world at large, you too must understand. Take, for example, a small credit card processing company somewhere in the middle of the United

States that takes credit card transactions made at a local store or restaurant and routes them to the appropriate home bank of the credit card owner and that employs a dozen people. Let us even assume that the "home bank" is also a local firm. Everything that this small credit card processor does today—sell its services, process the transactions—can be taken over very quickly by a similar operation in China for a smaller cost to all involved. About the only two things preventing this from happening (so far) are American regulations not yet permitting such activities by foreign banks and the lack of will or knowledge on the part of Chinese retail bankers that there is an active market for such services in the middle of the United States. But that all could change if, for example, a major credit card company required merchants to process their transactions through an exchange of its own choosing, which is a more likely possibility and if a national credit card company, then it would reasonably be expected to consider services drawn out of India, Brazil, and Russia. The example of the local company is drawn from a real one, the same with the national credit card provider, and service organizations in India and Brazil. Nobody is immune from globalization's opportunities and problems.[3]

In this instance, management either has to maintain such a low profile that draws no attention from larger competitors or has to make their services so specialized such that others outside the United States cannot replicate these. To do that requires understanding alternative service models that are local, national, and international; what national credit card companies are doing about card processing; and the regulatory constraints in place. Should regulatory changes be in the offing, this little company would have to work with its local American legislators and its industry trade association to lobby to block the proposed changes or to modify them into some advantageous form.

INFORMATION, INFORMATION TECHNOLOGIES, AND THE WORK OF MANAGEMENT

The acquisition, analysis, reliance upon, and protection of information are today major daily tasks of managers. The evidence is obvious and compelling, from typing one's own e-mails to hunching over spreadsheets, from reading critically important papers to relying on formal analyses of situations and opportunities—facts—before making decisions.

Connected managers normally are techno-junkies as well, even though they may not recognize that fact. They use cell phones, laptops, computers, webinars, texting, video conferencing, conference calls, social media, and digital sensors. Many have Bluetooth phones seemingly attached permanently to one ear. They spend several trillion dollars each year on information handling and computerized data gathering and use computer-based applications. Every manager in an office is a knowledge worker and every supervisor driving around in a truck with a wireless laptop on the front seat is too.

Most react to technology either by acquiring a new IT device, such as new generations of smart phones, or by accepting a new tool mandated by their employer, such as a new software budgeting application. If a senior manager, they push for continued evolution of preexisting uses of IT in their enterprise. This is an iterative process at work as people change their tools. As a consequence people at all levels and roles in a firm increase their dependence on technology to go about their ever-larger repertoire of activities. Some of these changes occur slowly, or are unchanging, such as how an organization interacts with technology to develop and control budgets or does strategic planning. But things can come in highly innovative, dramatic fashion, as occurred with the arrival of the current generation of cell phones that include "apps," making this device an emerging standard platform for accessing computer-based uses of information. Social media's arrival and spread into the work of organizations quickly took it from being a teenager's crucial social lifeline to making it the weapon of choice to knock down governments across the Middle East in 2011–2012, and now for the delivery of business services all over the world. What is a manager to make of these events?

First, it makes sense to understand the evolution of these new tools and uses, particularly with respect to social media software and hardware, and sensors that collect information, such as video and electrical impulses tracking movement of people and things. This means more than simply reading *Wired* magazine or *CIO*. This is about keeping current on the patterns of adoption of IT within one's industry, which can readily be done by staying current with what others are doing, and reading the trade literature of the industry. This is not about understanding the features of a new release of Microsoft's operating system or Apple's latest generation of iPads, but more about their potential use. Do the same for neighboring industries that could be potential rivals, are technologically ahead, or have already experienced what you are about to go through. Movie executives are learning from the music industry what happened when iTunes became available, for example. Their borrowing from other industries makes sense to apply in all others too.

Second, take into account the fundamental strategic consideration of how technologies help and hurt industries in how your business is structured and what it does. Getting this wrong can be lethal. IBM in the late 1980s experienced considerable difficulty in riding the wave of distributed processing as work began shifting from mainframe computers—its dominant suit—to PCs, although its management was aware of what was happening. They had difficulty transforming the business model to accommodate that change as entrenched forces slowed down the process. Kodak, the world's most distinguished photography company, invented the first digital camera and conducted pioneering research on digital photography, but could not abandon the highly profitable film business even 30 years after it began exploring digital photography. Its inability to transform resulted in its stock value collapsing and, as this chapter was being written in 2013, industry watchers were speculating whether this century-old firm was about to shut down. So, becoming a student of how companies migrate from one base of technology—and its business organization—to a new one remains perhaps the single most important challenge facing senior executives in all industries. At the moment, there seem to be no exceptions, because technologies are so infused in these, even in low users of computing such as agriculture and teaching. HP is playing a catch-up game today to get into the services and software business that its major rivals began entering a few years earlier. The point is that smart people can miss timings, so pay attention to the early signs of change and begin to experiment with new ways of doing business.

Pick your customers carefully too. That might seem surprising, since the conventional mantra is to get more customers. But as the world's economy grows and becomes more integrated (in other words, more accessible), there are plenty of buyers. The larger problem is to get them to spend. In nations with weak social safety nets, such as with little or no pensions, citizens save a great deal of money, as occurs all over Asia, including China where the economy needs its growing middle class to spend more and save less. In countries that are wealthy, but have high unemployment and extensive personal and national debts, customers are saving money and reducing debts, as is happening in North America and in Europe in reaction to the Great Recession. Corporations are sitting on trillions of dollars, reluctant to spend these sums, because of their concerns over the economic well-being of national markets and the uncertainties of international economies, or because of tax laws that motivate them to park funds in other countries, so often they simply plow these back into stock buyback programs. The greater issue is how to get these various and numerous constituencies to loosen up their purse strings and buy goods. Operational challenges are enormous too: pervasive quarter-to-quarter profit performance required by stock markets, personal careers tied to expanding and shrinking products and business models, shifting sources of profits, and, of course, the ongoing often excessive fixation of senior management in many countries (but not all) on expanding "shareholder value" of stocks at the expense of investing in new capabilities and products, and development of new skills within an enterprise.

Third, become students of the business models and both positive and negative experiences of other enterprises then experiment with yours. That is crucial to one's success in a world where circumstances and best practices are so fluid. It is no surprise then, when surveyed, senior executives who self-identify themselves as connected are overwhelmingly cognizant of changes around them, and even more ominously, of their doubts about their personal and institutional abilities to navigate successfully through turbulent conditions. Such doubts are the result of prior experiences indicating this is realistically a difficult challenge for all. Market intelligence operations are essential, as always, but so too is the need to create a network of other routinely consulted sources of information that comes from outside the enterprise. These include membership and participation in peer management communities and clubs, listening to industry watchers, relying on consultants who are expert in various technologies and strategies, and paying attention to professors knowledgeable about relevant topics. In short, one's personal experience is hardly adequate to the task at hand. Spending as much as 20–25% of one's working time for the rest of their career learning, probing, asking questions, and understanding the economics and operational characteristics of various technologies and their use has to be a new way of working. The other 75–80% of one's time can then be devoted to the effective execution of traditional managerial responsibilities, but which also call for experimenting with new structures, markets, and ways of doing things. Becoming an expert on change, churn, and innovation in a structured way—and not by accident—must be a new normal approach to gaining relevant knowledge and experience.

Fourth, always remember that it is information that is most important, not information technologies. Things must come in proper order, however. A laptop or a new use of computing to reach customers is not necessarily the right first order. The core activity of management continues to be the collection, use, and decision-making that emerge from knowledge to generate profitable revenue for the corporation, and added value for the customers. Gaining information, not information technologies, is the more central priority. It is fine to be enamored with a new tool, but that attraction must be grounded in practical considerations of what information provides a manager and his or her customer, because it is information that so affects actions in the market place and when and what transactions occur, not as much the device software.

There are some questions one can ask themselves to help stay focused on the right managerial priorities:

- How effective am I in keeping up with how technologies affect business models and uses of computers and telecommunications?
- Do I have an organized way to learn about the effects of all manner of technologies on my industry and firm? If no, why not?
- How varied are my sources of input, and are they broad enough to be effective in what I do at work?
- How do I know when I am successful in the use of technologies in general, and specifically, information technologies?

Perhaps ironically, the way one approaches information and other technologies is about as close to reflecting managerial practices proven effective for nearly a century as one can find. Managing technology is largely about understanding what it can do for your organization and what outcomes (results) can be for customers, employees, and the organization as a whole. When an innovation comes along that holds out the possibility of lowering operating costs or, even better, doing something new that can hold customers and grow revenue, that is all the better. Costs get measured against quantifiable opportunities and decisions to use something (or not) then are made. These decisions are influenced by such other considerations as the capability of this organization, or a consultancy, to do the actual installation and operation of the technology, and the timing relative to what the market is expecting or, too, can absorb. ATMs came along when there were enough customers familiar with credit cards and had checking accounts; businesses acquired PCs when it became clear that centralized data centers could not provide the kind of individualized computing demanded by end users; online purchasing appeared when software made shopping transactions reasonably secure and after enough customers had already become familiar with online searches and had already acquired PCs and dial-up connections to the Net.

ORGANIZATIONAL LEVEL: STRATEGY AND DEPLOYMENT

Just as ICT made possible "new economy" business models in ICT industries, driven by various ever-evolving technologies, so too did that pattern of technological adoption spread to other industries, such as outsourcing and cloud computing. But, realize that we are swirling in a massive pool of organizational changes that have been underway for over two decades and are not yet fully completed. These changes can be presented as "old economy" business models versus "new economy" business models. Most readers probably work in "new economy" business organizations. But perspective is essential in understanding the mega-trends affecting the daily work of management, trends in organizational structure that, while profoundly influenced by the injection of computing and communications into their work, are not limited to those influences, as I have argued in this book.

In the "old economy," employees could expect to spend their entire careers within one firm, with steady rises in income normally driven by promotions and seniority for managers, in particular, and for non-managerial employees as a result of union-negotiated contracts. Employees often enjoyed defined-benefit pensions that included medical coverage while working or retired in the United States and in other countries through government-provided pensions and medical services. Stocks did not provide the primary source of wealth creation, although it was always there for the most senior executives through stock options. Product strategies involved the development and patenting of innovations in products, processes, and technologies. These were deployed into markets through vertically integrated enterprises, which then spread around the world to wherever appropriate demand existed for these offerings. One grew their business organically, that is to say, by relying on internal capabilities, hiring and training employees, expanding into new markets and products that were related to the core products and capabilities of the enterprise. Philips of the Netherlands, Toyota of Japan, General Motors, GE and Kodak of the United States were examples of that "old economy" style of organizing and working.

By the end of the twentieth century much of that had changed, but not completely, because "new economy" realities essentially displaced much of the older model. Managers and their employees no longer enjoyed secure employment; they could be let go, or their part of the organization sold off to another firm rather quickly without much compunction about the consequences for workers, increasingly so even in European economies that are militant in protecting job security for labor. Inter-firm mobility of employees became more the norm and lifelong work at one firm was now the exception. Wealth was created more through stock options for executive and non-executive employees. Unions declined worldwide in the size of their membership and in their influence on wages and benefits. Employees were personally expected to take more care of their own financial needs for retirement as defined-benefit pensions declined sharply, beginning in the United States then spreading to other advanced economies. In the United States, employees were expected to shoulder more of the cost of medical insurance, while in Europe, these services were under fiscal siege as governments struggled with massive sovereign debts and the unaffordability of social programs. Management had to raise capital for new projects outside their enterprises through venture capital, IPOs, stock manipulations, and corporate stock buybacks to drive up their values. In the old economy world, stock values were more stable and dividends were of greater relevance. Today, dividends are often not paid; value comes from increased price of stocks.

Instead of developing products through internal capabilities, such as at one's own development labs and research centers, managers now learned how to cross-license technologies and products, leading to more vertical specializations of work, products, and services. Of course, outsourcing routine tasks had become widespread as management looked at the work of the enterprise as supply chains, while increasingly more complex work was also outsourced, such as product development, manufacture, distribution, marketing, and customer product support. Learning how to manage these ever-evolving, more complex value chains became essential, as did the ability to outsource work and still keep all the work elements synchronized. Industry and technical standards proved essential to that process, and for the ability of firms to deploy technologies and technologically intensive products into global markets that customers could embrace. These were the new sources of strategies, all far different than old economy forms.

How managers now approached new markets changed as well, usually entering more specialized ones. Selling specialized goods and services to others who in turn integrated these into their own offerings is more normal. If one needed new capabilities, skills, and technologies, managers hired people already trained in these, disposing of employees who now had less relevant skills and bought patents. As this book was being written, there was a worldwide foot race on to acquire patent rights to all manner of technologies and sciences by the largest enterprises that should have done this earlier, instead of appropriating new developments without permission (as often was the case with communications technologies and electronic book rights' copyrights), or in basic scientific knowledge (as occurred frequently with medical developments and pharmaceutical companies).

All of these developments from "Old" to "New" economic and business models should make it quite evident that there are new core skills now required of any manager. And facing them all is the prospect of self-organizing organizations that self-learn, then transform, often forming new alliances and structures at the first and second line level of management. That development alone is putting a new shine on the term "New" business models. So what are managers to do?

First, they must be able and willing to learn how to learn, that is to say, how to keep up—connected—with changes underway, a point made repeatedly in this book. That activity requires the curious intellect, the practice of being interested in many topics outside their immediate areas of responsibilities and work, asking "Why" frequently, and expanding one's routine sources of information. In particular, learning how to manage large supply and value chains will increasingly prove essential to the success of a manager's career. Embedded in that body of knowledge is a deeper understanding of systems thinking, process management, new technologies, and applications (such as the use of crowd sourcing, analytics, and simulation tools).

Second, coordinate/collaborate across a much broader spectrum of associates and business partners as that task is increasingly paramount, and being prepared and capable of shifting employment from one spot in a value chain to another as warranted by circumstances. That last requirement is increasingly evident for managers under the age of 45 (as of 2013) and sadly in your author's opinion in harboring less loyalty to their employer. We live in an age where such mobility is constant and global.

Third, develop new ways of managing existing enterprises, including government agencies. Much of what older managers learned in school about how organizations are structured and run are being challenged by the new realities they face. It appears that business schools have not always quite kept up with the development of new organizational models, although many management consulting firms have clearly done so, building entire consultancies around the issue. So there is a knowledge gap that will need to be filled by a new generation of managers willing to be creative and to take personal career risks, which actually becomes easier to do as loyalty to one's employer declines and job mobility increases.

It is unclear at this time how large enterprises, in particular, will fair in the decades to come in such an environment, if indeed they will survive with a particular brand intact, or if these will evolve, devolve, or transform into new enterprises with no connections to earlier ones. Transforming large enterprises is very difficult to do. Many senior executives do not have the skills to build new enterprises out of the carcasses of the ones they grew up with. Existing clusters of employees will resist changes that threaten their positions. So far, we see long-lived corporations sometimes dying off, with parts of their enterprises and inventory being absorbed by others, and rebranded, as occurred with PanAm airlines and AT&T, the American telephone monopoly, and today literally thousands of small- to mid-sized IT firms as whole segments of that part of the global economy consolidates. Sometimes an enterprise is bought by another, as happened when IBM acquired the consulting arm of PricewaterhouseCoopers Consulting (PwC), and by mergers, as occurred when Compaq was folded into HP. Such restructurings increased in volume and speed of implementation, beginning the mid-1990s, although such activities had been going on for well over a century in both stable and emerging industries. Unclear is how these patterns of volatility will change as new players come into various markets, such as Chinese banks into Western economies, new Asian consumer electronics firms, and other science- and technology-based enterprises from Latin America and Eastern Europe.

There are some questions managers can ask to help guide how they are informed and what they should do:

- To what extent do I understand what—and who's—value chains I participate in and my contribution to those chains?
- Am I just a link in other's chains, or am I the creator and owner of value/supply chains? Really?
- To what extent do I understand the business management changes underway in my industry?
- How do I instill a learning and collaborative culture in my firm and how do I know that these twin features are alive and productive in my organization?

So far, we have taken an internal view of the role of management within an organization, on the supply side of things. But, remain very aware of an equally important constituency in the economy—customers—for they too are evolving their behavior.

THE NEW MILITANCY OF IMPATIENT POWERFUL CUSTOMERS

Since the arrival of online information search tools accessible over telephone lines using PCs in the mid-1980s, it seems every business writer has argued the case that customers were becoming more powerful in the sell-buy equation as they learned more about who offered the best price for the greatest value. The improved accessibility of the Internet, beginning in the mid-1990s, led to a massive increase in easily obtainable information about goods and services, which consumers proved eager and able to use all over the world with a speed of adoption that exceeded use of any earlier form of printed or electronic sources of data in all of human history. With well over three billion people now accessing the Internet, not to mention other sources of information about goods and services, such as catalogs and books, it is no wonder that observers of the business scene continue to declare that customers are putting their suppliers into situations in which they have to provide more value for less cost. E-commerce is back in fashion as a focus in the Corporate World too.

Put in more business terms, after nearly a century of rapidly expanding levels of profits and revenues, customers have finally been able to implement collectively a potentially long-term process of constraining traditionally high levels of profitability in many industries. Goods and services sold at a premium price even just one decade ago are now distributed as commodities, from complex consumer electronics and clothing, to management consulting and programming sophisticated IT applications. With so many years of experience with PCs and online (and now mobile) search tools, it is no wonder customers can compare prices and features to make their selections and obtain recommendations from consumer sites and from their friends and family, even while walking around a store. As vendors are able to deliver their wares and services to most parts of the world, the market has gone global, leading to the new competitors and providers mentioned throughout this book. Managers will need to learn to thrive in a world of thinner profits.

This previous paragraph could have been written in 2000 and it would have been true then, just with fewer users of the Internet at the time. However, since 2000, a new class of software tools has come into wide use among consumers and corporate buyers: social media applications, such as Facebook, LinkedIn, and literally millions of other virtual communities, and even physical tools such as iPads and mobile phones with "apps." These tools made it possible for crowdsourcing, the gathering of many like-minded people around an issue, quickly and massively. When Netflix wanted to raise prices and Bank of America its fees in 2011, within days so many of their customers protested, or dropped services, that both firms reversed course on price increases. Bank of America reportedly lost several billion dollars of deposits as customers closed their checking accounts. Use of social media tools does not lend itself to control by managers, as they are open, fast, leaderless, collaborative, and transparent. Twitter can take down a vendor as fast as it took down governments in the Middle East.

This phenomenon leads to another important implication for management. When consumers learn something in one sphere of their lives, they apply it to other aspects too with the result that customer expectations can come from many new sources. It is an old problem gone viral, even militant. In the old days—say before about 2005—a frequent business traveler might have experienced rapid check in for a rental automobile, provided by a wholly owned subsidiary of an automotive manufacturing company, such as Ford Motors, but then 15 minutes later arrive at their four or five star hotel only to have to wait in line for 20–30 minutes to check in. The wait time at the hotel was essentially no different than at any other hotel at a busy time; they were all slow. But now the customer, having just gone through a 2-minute registration for a rental car, now expected their hotel to be just as quick; 30 minutes that used to be the norm was now intolerable. Management at a hotel now had to worry about what other industries were doing and had to meet those new levels of customer expectations, in this case that level of service provided by the automotive rental industry. That phenomenon spilled over into all manner of business transactions, spurred on by the rapid and massive exchange of experiences and knowledge made possible by social media tools.

The case gets even more complicated. Add in national diversity into the picture. A wealthy Korean or Chinese traveler new to the West comes to the same hotel and has to stand in line behind a half dozen Europeans and Americans also waiting to check in. It is quite possible that the Asians will conclude that they are being snubbed because they are Asian. As wealthy travelers, they would expect prompt personal service as they receive routinely in high-end Asian hotels as they walked into the lobby. The Western hotel clerk is not slitting them, merely being democratic in registering people on a first come, first served basis. As the hotel increasingly caters to wealthy Asians, often first-generation wealthy, they will need to alter their check-in process, while keeping the delighted rental customers happy too.[4]

So what is the poor manager to do? The problem is clearly too big to delegate to sales and marketing; the whole firm must engage on the issue of how best to work with customers and to attract their business.

First, stop viewing customers as all the same, and challenge long established ways of servicing them, even how you learn about their needs. Management must account for the rapidity and diversity of information gained by their connected customers, their attitudes, and keep up with them. If their customers use social media tools, then vendors have to be seen in that space, engaging with customers there. If customers are learning about service levels from other industries, management needs to do the same. If they have Asian customers learn *in Asia* how they expect services to be rendered. Managers have to learn and then take action at the same speed as their customers.

Second, become expert in the use of social media tools. Some of the best lessons for business are coming from the political arena, an excellent case of why managers need to understand far more than business issues. Militancy, or the lack of patience for slow change on the part of customers, is coming from widely divergent sources. Perhaps the most important of these new sources is the political arena using social media. One of the lessons of the Arab Spring of 2011 that caused the overthrow of governments in many countries in the Middle East, and most notably in social media savvy Egypt, was the use of Facebook, Twitter, and other social media tools to rally protestors and to keep them energized. Literally within days, governments could be toppled as citizens demanded changes, access to jobs and education, and were prepared to risk life and limb to get these. In calmer societies, officials were not immune from the same process at work. Mothers concerned about tainted milk and other citizens irritated with police cover ups of various crimes forced Chinese officials to investigate, arrest, and otherwise mitigate concerns expressed by their citizens— all of this in supposedly an authoritarian society. In the United States, use of such tools facilitated the election of Senator Barrack Obama in 2008 as president, to riots over economic conditions in London in 2011, and to the global sit-ins and protests of citizens complaining about corporate greed, particularly of bankers and stock traders, which took place later that same year. Thousands of protests over various issues are routinely occurring all over the world organized together in days, even hours, by using such tools. Those same people are your customers. If a marketing executive was never interested in politics and the sociology of crowdsourcing and social media before, he or she had better be now.

Third, respond faster to changes in the marketplace than ever before. What these various observations make quite clear is that the economic, social, and political interests of customers are being displayed and exercised by them more aggressively than in living memory. It means their values and interests are expressed quicker. Companies will have to respond faster than in the past to satisfy their interests. If customers want environmentally "green" products, so it shall be; if they want lower prices they will get these, or some vendor will be instantly marginalized. Being able to understand this new form of quick militancy and to convert that insight into products and services that customers want will be a core skill that managers and their companies will need to develop quickly. Politicians are learning that lesson, consumer goods companies (B2C) are close behind them on the learning curve, while business-to-business firms (B2B) will be the next to experience that militancy and its impatience. That is where analytics, social media, and sensors all come into play as essential tools for management to get forewarned and insights.

There are some questions managers should ask and answer:

- How well do my firm and I understand the effects of social media and open sources of information that my customers use?
- Have I implemented marketing, advertising, and service strategies that rely upon and take advantage of emerging social media tools and behaviors? How do I measure results? Do I even measure results?
- To what extent is this new "voice of the customer" integrated into the development of my products, offerings, services, and pricing?
- How prepared are we to modify our business strategies to account for both the new militancy and new populations of customers? Are we doing that?

At the moment (2015), scores of surveys conducted by various organizations and academics are demonstrating that most organizations and the vast majority of managers are failing to keep up with their customer's use of social media. They simply are still relying on such tools to "push" information out to consumers at a time when the latter want more dialogue with their suppliers. It is a worldwide problem evident in all industries, including in retail, for example, one of the earliest to understand the significance of these new technologies. The wonderful exceptions reported about are just that, exceptions. LEGO engages with customers in the development of new toys; Ford Motor Company works with its customers on how to improve its automobiles; TD Bank focuses on getting to problems and solving them rapidly; Apple to build brand loyalty, the list is long. What this means is that a manager accepts his or her lack of effective knowledge of social media that there are already examples of how to leverage these tools both for use with consumers and also for the internal operations of their firms. Take these kinds of positive examples and modify them to fit your customers and your corporate capabilities.

RETURN ON INFORMATION—A NEW IDEA FOR A NEW TIME?

If we know nothing else about management, it is that they learn what they need to in order to be successful individually and as enterprises. Managers also take great pains to measure progress and results, quantifiably if possible, in much that is done by their employees and the firm at large. As awareness of the importance of information as a body of knowledge and assets to be managed has increased over the past half century, along with various ways of measuring the effects and value of data, then information. Although it is only now that serious attempts are being taken to do this with the same kind of discipline as one measures money, accounting, and finance. One of the most recent developments has been the attempt to quantify—some use the term monetize—the value of data. Using the old notion of ROI—Return on Investment—applied to information, as ROI, represents an early example of that, which is now endorsed by such enterprises as Vertica (an HP company), IBM, AOL, Comcast, Verizon, Blue Cross Blue Shield, Zynga, and Google, among others. They share the belief that information's value can be measured, moving from cost-cutting metrics to measures of value. They seek to identify the volume of data one has, number of users of specific types and bodies of data, the effects of analytics applied to data, and how soon data can be used after it is created (known as latency measures).

Google, in particular, has been promoting use of this new form of ROI as a means of selling its search services and, in the process, developed techniques and approaches to promote new ROI analyses. IBM's approach emphasizes the integration of information linked to management—governance—of information to increase trust in the accuracy of data that managers and employees have in large bodies of information, and to understand better the cost of collecting, analyzing, and using vast pools of data. The hunt is also extending to measuring the effectiveness of data and of its quality, a pursuit still in its infancy. The challenges involved are extensive. For example, various estimates of the nature of data suggest that as much as 80% is unstructured, such as Word documents and PDF files, unlike structured records such as numbers collected in accounting, or in process performance metrics, and instances of events (e.g., number of cars that pass through a red light at a particular street intersection).

Structured data has been measured for decades; unstructured data is a new frontier for management, and establishing its value even more unexplored territory.

The urgency of new ROI metrics for management is intensifying as awareness increases of how much time workers spend with information. Surveys now can tell us how many hours a day employees in different professions spend on e-mail, in creating documents, analyzing information, doing online searches, editing, reviewing, preparing Powerpoint presentations, and populating by hand spreadsheets, to mention a few tasks. When such surveys announce that a minimum of 20% of a worker's time is spent just on the tasks listed in this paragraph, productivity alarm bells go off in the minds of managers. Just doing searches over the Internet more efficiently can provide a new ROI. Google proposes a formula and is as follows:

> Number of workers × average annual salary (or 2080 hours worked) × hours saved per worker using a more efficient search tool = in money total productivity (or savings) per year.[5]

It is a simple formula. Another in use calls for the following:

> Data volume × depth of analysis × number of users divided by latency.

Both have their drawbacks; however, each is an indicator of management's continuous search for measures of performance.

Possible wiser uses of information are quite broad. Aside from just reducing the cost of using existing data, or the acquisition of new information (structured or unstructured), are some other real possibilities. These include increasing the speed to market with new products and services, improved responsiveness for information requested by customers, business partners, and coworkers, improved ability to analyze and share data and information, and to improve one's personal knowledge and skills. One can reasonably predict that by the time this book you are reading is out of print that these and other measures of the role, cost, and value of information will be in wider more effective use than today. That development suggests several implications and actions for managers.

First, managers should begin finding out what others are doing to measure the results of information usage. New metrics have always been developed in an *ad hoc* way relevant to an individual manager or group of employees to provide insight into the work they do; then, these are subsequently shared across an enterprise, industry, or economy. It should be a curiosity sustained for the rest of one's working career as the greatest innovations lie ahead of us, yet to be developed.

Second, experiment within your own domain, incrementally at first, then more substantively, encouraging colleagues to do similarly in their departments and divisions. But share results with others in your enterprise so as to learn from each other how to improve work and how to measure information. Follow the good practices learned from process management and reengineering of using such ROIs and other measures as tools all employees can use to gain insight to improve their work, not as a means of pressuring employees to produce more with less. Let the insights such tools generate suggest to all the next steps to be undertaken which improve productivity.

Third, measures are themselves information, so manage that asset as a corporate competitive weapon used as a central element in discussions about what to do, and in informing decisions to be made. Push those measures from simply capturing information on the use of explicit data (e.g., number of times something happened or how long it took to do) and move toward outcomes-based measures (e.g., increased sales as a result of). That is an iterative call for new behavior that only embeds itself in an enterprise if it is woven into the culture of the corporation. Business schools alone cannot train enough managers fast enough to do this. Since the majority of current management has long been out of school, they need to encourage, indeed insist, on this change in their own work, just as they had to do in the 1980s and 1990s when they compelled their enterprises to organize activities into disciplined processes and value chains.

Are measures of information a new task for managers? Are "returns on information" a new wave? The answer is, surprisingly, no. Managers have paid lip service to the role and measure of information (usually data) for a long time and have used metrics of activities and numbers for decades, always enhanced by constant innovations in computers and software to facilitate that process. New metrics, often called analytics, and even such specific techniques as ROIs, continue an historic process long in evidence of managers trying to understand what they are doing in measurable ways. What is new is the breadth of possible analytics and topics to measure.

There are some questions one can ask to inform how best to proceed:

- Are you prepared to adopt new measures of success that go beyond the more traditional accounting, financial, sales, product, and marketing indicators?
- How good are your internal capabilities to measure, let alone manage, information as a corporate asset?
- How effective is the ability of the enterprise to learn and embrace innovative uses of information and the management practices required to sustain these?
- What role does information play in generating your revenues?

WHAT PERSONAL SKILLS AND KNOWLEDGE DOES A MANAGER NEED?

There is an emerging profile of the successful manager, but that will become even more tangible in the years to come. This profile is shaped by the issues discussed in this book, ranging from a systems and process view of work activities to the influences of a vastly larger information and business/economic ecosystem all connected by a continuing evolving communications and social infrastructures that bring to the stage more Customers, Competitors, Countries, and Conditions. More than an alliteration, these four "Cs" are tightly woven together, need to be taken into account simultaneously, and are intensely active at speeds not seen even at the start of this new century.

This new manager is knowledgeable about a great many of the fundamentals of business, normally is armed with an MBA, but also quite possibly instead with an advanced degree in engineering, economics, or in some field of science. Even start-up entrepreneurs are well educated in the formal subjects of business and technology. This profile exists in North America, large swaths of Latin America, East Asia, slowly is increasingly so in the Indian Subcontinent, and across Europe from Ireland to Russia. Those managers working in the Middle East are largely trained outside the region with the notable exception of Israel, which has strong educational programs within the country. As one moves up the corporate ladder, you will encounter managers and executives that speak English, travel extensively, and attended one of roughly 150 universities around the world. In short, they are a virtual community with shared values, practices, and experiences.

This profile has been emerging since the 1980s with two patterns of expansion now more in play. First, the number of managers fitting this profile in any advanced or emerging economy is quite high and, second, the number of countries in which they work has moved from roughly less than 50 to more than 125.

Increasingly, these managers, and those that will later enter the ranks of management, will need in addition to the aforementioned skills described, other work habits and knowledge. Let us summarize what has been cataloged so far in this book: process management, systems management, IT management, a proclivity and the habit of using all manner of analytics, not just traditional accounting, sales, and process statistics. They will learn to learn as part of the way they work, relying on all manner of content and sources: books, articles, blogs, Internet content providers, industry seminars, business school programs and seminars, conversations with colleagues inside and outside their firms, attendance at industry conferences, travel experience in various countries, and tours of duty in other countries, companies, and industries. Their knowledge of explicit facts will come and go as some rapidly become out-of-date, replaced with new data and insights. A great deal of it will be collected and be presented to them by automated means, even by computers that *learn* (yes, learn, perform cognitive activities) from data they collect to make recommendations to managers, as is now just beginning to occur with doctors, law enforcement, national intelligence agencies, and the military. Tacit knowledge, largely based on prior experiences, will be challenged by the increasing flood of predigested data presented to executives based on a far larger array of data inputs than one could even have conceived as being more than an aspiration of at the start of the twenty-first century.

At the core of this new world is the ability to adapt to their changing environment in a more organized proactive way than in the past. In addition to the skills one will need or in keeping up with trends, there are others, because just applying data analytics alone will not do the trick. Managers will also to think more creatively, which more knowledge, data, and personal networking can help with. They should experiment with different options, many of which can be modeled, some using relatively easy-to-use simulation software before investing in pilot programs. They should also engage with new types of organizations as they build their value chains and update supply chains too.

Tomorrow's manager, therefore, will be a quicker learner than today's and will spend more time doing that than her father's generation. As careers transform, jobs will move from company to company and even into new industries, so a manager will also need to be a student of their business/social environment, which is why knowing two or more languages and having lived in different countries will be helpful, but not always necessary. They will subconsciously develop processes and habits for learning, for thinking in terms of systems and processes, and will maintain formal processes for their organizations to insure all are engaged in similar practices. They will insist on diversity of educational and social backgrounds of their colleagues and employees, not just more people with alternative genders and sexual orientations, or religious heritages. Although we increasingly see management working in a secular environment where the power of scientific thinking dominates, local beliefs in religion, manners, and social customs will remain, popping up in conference calls, meetings with customers, business partners, and at conferences as a normal way of life. Learning to become sensitive to this broader view of diversity will prove essential. As a parent, I would recommend that a manager expose their children to this form of diversity, which will be normal for the next generation to live with in their daily work as employees and management.

We have discussed throughout this book the implications for management and made recommendations for what individuals and their enterprises should do. There are several additional ones to recommend, not discussed adequately enough.

First, work with local universities to train future business professionals and others that might enter business or public administration in the skills and bodies of knowledge discussed in this chapter. Do not forget that students need training in how to appreciate and the ability to work with analytics, large and diverse bodies of data. They need to think in terms of systems, processes, and information ecosystems, along with the now obvious requirements of being familiar with multiple industries, cultures, teaming, and ability to collaborate.

Second, improve personal communications skills. More than making a good Powerpoint presentation are other forms of communications that are essential: the ability to write a well argued and to the point memo and e-mail; public speaking presentations that focus on the needs of the audience that can be presented in different cultures and countries; interpersonal communications with individuals one-on-one, whether in sales, in a conference room filled with people from another culture and country, or with the senior executive of your firm. The diversity of ideas and people on the one hand and the changing content of information management uses on the other also calls for more managers at more levels of an organization to take the initiative to communicate about needed changes. The operative idea is initiative, normally called leadership, but specifically the courage and expectation that part of their job is to speak up quickly, thoughtfully, and knowledgeably more often than in prior years as their organizations continue to flatten or self-organize as networks of activities. That is why additional attention to building communications skills is more crucial today than in prior decades. It is the age-old problem of, "If you had only twenty minutes to spend with Gandhi, Lincoln, or the Pope, what would you say to them and how would you do that?"

Third, wrap products and services of companies and government agencies with an increasing amount of information. A product will need more than instructions on how to assemble or use them; they will become the centers of communities in which customers and vendors discuss its use via social media. Today, if you acquire a cell phone from Motorola, for example, while it is a fine device, the user's handbook can be 135 pages long; tomorrow it will have to be less than 10 pages long, and the device will be more intuitive and "smart" in how it deals with its owner. Information will surround the device as it learns how best to work with its owner, or Motorola will simply be displaced in the market by an Asian consumer electronics rival, or some company just formed that nobody ever heard of before. So, learn what kind of information to envelop a service or product; it is more than analytics to figure out what works and who is buying it. Customers will insist that it be "smart."

SOME FINAL THOUGHTS

A great deal has changed in business management practices in the past 15 years. Global recessions, wars in the Middle East, the financial crisis in the European Union, demise of iconic companies, resurgence of information technology manufacturing and services firms, expanding online retailing, and declining communications costs, and a highly energized mass of billions of customers are just a few. iPhones, iPods, iPads, and a plethora of tablets and smart phones came into their own, while social media and its effects thundered into our lives faster than any other technology-induced development since the arrival of the personal computer in the late 1970s. With respect to social media, we are just in the early stages of its deployment as a collection of management tools. Much uncertainty remains in our lives that cut across business models, economic dynamics, and political churn. These unsettled times are becoming more intimately globalized. For an American business executive, what goes on in Vietnam or Malaysia really matters; for a Chinese senior official, events in Brussels are important too. The resurgence of Russian Cold War–styled foreign affairs and the troublesome behavior of Iran threaten everyone's automobile's gas tank, and family heating budgets in dozens of countries. The difficulty experienced by public officials in Europe in developing stabile financial regimes is economically and politically dangerous, as are the currency manipulation practices of some Asian nations. Regulators of the banking systems around the world are trying to stabilize banks and coordinate—harmonize—the rules of the financial game but face enormous difficulty in doing so too.

Meanwhile, new business models continue to emerge. Those who argue that innovation in IT is over are just wrong as the opportunities for massive gains in revenue still emerge, as we saw with Apple and Google in recent years, and more recently with Facebook, even Bitcoin. The world's standard of living is, in general, rising even while wealth continues to concentrate into fewer hands, bringing to markets many new customers who are literate, have jobs, are young, want material possessions, and seek out new experiences. These are all circumstances that bode well for existing and new companies, and for whole nations that continue to enter the increasingly integrated global economy. Barring some unforeseen climatic or medical disaster, or a global war, the next several decades will lead to new businesses becoming iconic and wealthy, some old ones will grow massively too, while the die off of many will continue.

In short, the fundamental challenge before all managers at all levels of any enterprise is to stay on top of changes occurring in a highly connected world and having the skills and the courage to take advantage of them. This is complicated because there are players from more countries with varying cultures and education participating in this game. Learning, acting, and collaborating in a far wider range of activities and markets now define the emerging world of all management teams. We have not seen this level of expanded complexity since the first decade following the end of World War II in 1945.

The long prosperity the world experienced between the end of that war and the various economic and political crises of the early 1970s has much to teach management. One should begin to understand the challenges in front of them by learning more about how an earlier generation prospered in that period and lived through a subsequent 40 years of economic and political turbulence. As with today's circumstance, earlier managers faced radically new uses of technologies, most notably computers and telecommunications and later the Internet, of course; massive expansion in large enterprises operating in scores of countries; entry of nearly two billion people into industrialized modern economies; greater linkage globally of politics, foreign affairs, wars, social media, information transfers, education, travel, and prosperity.

Capitalism is still on the ascent. Management is becoming a more disciplined profession. The global economy is integrating and expanding. The world's population is increasing. Welcome to the Connected World of the twenty-first century.

NOTES

1 A useful source is the World Bank's data, "Air Transport, Customers Carried," published each year with trends over several years, available at http://data.worldbank.org/indicator/IS.AIR.PSGR (last accessed December 20, 2013).
2 Travel Student, "Global Trends in Foreign Language Demand and Proficiency," October 1, 2013, available at http://studenttravelplanningguide.com/printguide/global-trends-in-foreign-language-demand-and-proficiency/ (last accessed November 7, 2013).
3 Client confidentiality prevents mentioning the names of the affected firms.
4 As a frequent business traveler, I have witnessed both situations—the Hertz rental car customer at a major U.S. hotel chain and Asian tourists and business travelers upset by how they are treated in European and American hotels. I, by no means wealthy, am treated like royalty upon stepping into a high-end Asian hotel. These two classes of incidents became quite visible starting in about 2005, and with wealthy Asian tourists (probably traveling outside their country for the first time) around 2010–2011.
5 Google, "Return on Information: Adding to Your ROI with Google Enterprise Search," (2009), available at Google.com (last accessed November 3, 2011).

For Further Reading

This book has argued that managers will need to stay current on a wider number of issues for the rest of their careers as they become more directly connected to a larger volume of activities and topics. These are some useful sources to begin that process of staying connected to the issues management faces today. Also consult sources cited in the endnotes to each chapter for additional materials. This list relies on books because that remains the most useful format for delivering the level of detail managers should explore if they are to be serious about learning new ways of doing their work.

About the new management style, books and articles appear all the time about aspects of the changing role of management. So evolution of the profession has to be kept up within piecemeal fashion. For collaboration, begin with Andrew McAfee's, *Enterprise 2.0: New Collaborative Tools for Your Organization's Toughest Challenges* (Boston, MA: Harvard Business School Press, 2009) and also pay attention to his articles. The issue of how people are working in a connected world gets more than one chapter in what clearly is now one of the best books on the evolution and use of the Internet today, by Lee Rainie and Barry Wellman, *Networked: The New Social Operating System* (Cambridge, MA: MIT Press, 2012). Another useful book directly applicable to our issues is by Danna Greenberg, Kate McKone-Sweet, and H. James Wilson, *The New Entrepreneurial Leader: Developing Leaders Who Shape and Social and Economic Opportunity* (San Francisco, CA: Berrett-Koehler, 2011). Not to be overlooked too is Robert D. Austin, Richard L. Nolan and Shannon O'Donnell, *Harder Than I Thought: Adventures of a Twenty-First Century Leader* (Boston, MA: Harvard Business School Press, 2012).

The Essential Manager: How to Thrive in the Global Information Jungle, First Edition.
James W. Cortada.
© 2015 the IEEE Computer Society. Published 2015 by John Wiley & Sons, Inc.

Next, the issue of analytics needs to be understood and for that there is a growing body of useful publications. One of these is by Carl Hoffman, Eric Lesser, and Tim Ringo, *Calculating Success: How the New Workplace Analytics Will Revitalize Your Organization* (Boston, MA: Harvard Business School Press, 2012). The fact-based style of modern management is well described in Thomas D. Davenport and Jeanne G. Harris, *Competing on Analytics: The New Science of Winning* (Boston, MA: Harvard Business School Press, 2007) and by Ian Ayers, *Super Crunchers: Why Thinking-by-Numbers Is the New Way to Be Smart* (New York: Bantam Books, 2007)—both are now the standard sources on this topic. For modeling practices for management, see Stephen Baker, *The Numerati* (New York: Houghton Mifflin, 2008). About modeling, see Alexander Osterwalder and Yves Pigneur, *Business Model Generation: A Handbook for Visionaries, Games Changers and Challengers* (Hoboken, NJ: Wiley, 2010). On using data to predict future activities, consult Eric Siegel, *Predictive Analytics: The Power to Predict Who Will Click, Buy, Lie, or Die* (Hoboken, NJ: John Wiley & Sons, 2013). Two well-grounded students of information have written an assessable book about information of particular relevance to management, Viktor Mayer-Schönberger and Kenneth Cukier, *Big Data: A Revolution That Will Transform How We Live, Work, and Think* (Boston, MA: Eamon Dolan/Houghton Mifflin Harcourt, 2013). And for an antidote for too much enthusiasm for computing, enjoy Evgeny Morozov, *To Solve Everything Click Here: The Folly of Technological Solutionism* (New York: Public Affairs, 2013).

How management looks at the role of information and its supportive digital plumbing is increasingly essential to understand. For an introduction to the issues across all aspects of management and business practices, see James W. Cortada, *Information and the Modern Corporation* (Cambridge, MA: MIT Press, 2011). More of a guide to how to leverage information is Donald Hislop, *Knowledge Management in Organizations* (New York: Oxford University Press, 2009). See also Sean Muffitt and Mike Dover, *Wiki Brands: Reinventing Your Company in a Customer-Driven Marketplace* (New York: McGraw-Hill, 2011). If you can obtain it, see an article by Steven Rosenbush and Michael Totty, "How Big Data Is Changing the Whole Equation for Business," March 8, 2013, *The Wall Street Journal*, http://wsj.com (last accessed March 10, 2013). I also like to keep up with those organizations that sell information to management so for that issue a useful introduction is

Miklos Sarvary, *Gurus and Oracles: The Marketing of Information* (Cambridge, MA: MIT Press, 2012). Practical and fascinating, see Peter Lucas, Joe Ballay, and Mickey McGManus, *Trillions: Thriving in the Emerging Information Ecology* (Hoboken, NJ: John Wiley & Sons, 2012). But, do not overlook Alice E. Marwick, *Status Update: Celebrity, Publicity, and Branding in the Social Media Age* (New Haven, CT: Yale University Press, 2013).

There is no substitute for subscribing to the print and electronic publications produced by your industry's national and international associations to keep up with the role of all manner of technologies in your industry and in those other ones relevant to your work. These provide monthly and sometimes weekly updates on trends in the industry, and routinely about IT. Closely related to these publications are the reports of management and IT consulting firms, which routinely publish the results of surveys and interviews, in addition to their points of view. All the key consultancies do this and make their materials available online through their web sites. These include, for example, IBM, McKinsey, Deloitte, and Accenture, but also IT industry watchers such as IDG, Gartner, and Forrester. A trip to their web sites will familiarize you with the kinds of reports they provide. Additionally, academics and consultants publish books that are industry specific; I suggest that about two to three times a year you go to an online bookstore, such as Amazon. com or Barnesandnoble.com and search for books about your industry. You will be surprised at how many are published and also how many on the role of IT in them. But for background on technology in general relevant to management, look at the fascinating study by Kevin Kelly, *What Technology Wants* (New York: Viking, 2010), which argues that technologies of all types make up a new neural system in organizations and societies. On how managers make decisions on the use of IT, see James W. Cortada, *How Societies Embrace Information Technology: Lessons for Management and the Rest of Us* (New York: John Wiley & Sons and IEEE Computer Society, 2009).

The literature on how organizations are changing is now vast and growing. I would recommend reading the *Harvard Business Review* on a regular basis for useful commentary on this topic. Because the topic is so tied to strategy, new thinkers on the topic are essential to consult, such as Michael A. Casumano, who has long commented on the interactions between strategy, industry, and technology. For a recent study by him, see *Staying Power: Six Enduring Principles for Managing*

Strategy and Innovation in an Uncertain World (New York: Oxford University Press, 2010). Just as tactical, based on a large collection of cases, see Suzanne Berger and the MIT Industrial Performance Center, *How We Compete: What Companies Around the World Are Doing to Make It in Today's Global Economy* (New York: Doubleday, 2005). A book about strategy and how one technology affects it is by Michael Saylor, *The Mobile Wave: How Mobile Intelligence Will Change Everything* (Philadelphia, PA: Vanguard Press, 2012). A very hands-on, prescriptive guide to strategy is by Rita Gunther McGrath, *The End of Competitive Advantage: How to Keep Your Strategy Moving As Fast As Your Business* (Boston, MA: Harvard Business Review Press, 2013); her earlier books are also good tactical guides to strategy, making her one of the leading experts today on the subject worth understanding.

Much useful material on how the global economy is appearing, written by distinguished economists, in nontechnical language. Begin with Dani Rodrik, *Lone Economics Many Recipes: Globalization, Institutions, and Economic Growth* (Princeton, NJ: Princeton University Press, 2007), which provides a balanced account of globalization and local economic patterns of behavior. Then move on to Nobel Prize winner Michael Spence's *The Next Convergence: The Future of Economic Growth in a Multispeed World* (New York: Farrar, Straus and Giroux, 2011) a really great read. To understand the global side of IT and economics, see two studies, the first by Peter F. Cowhey and Jonathan D. Aronson, *Transforming Global Information and Communications Markets* (Cambridge, MA: MIT Press, 2012) and a very short, but highly informed book, by Erik Brynjolfsson and Andrew McAfee, *Race Against the Machine: How the Digital Revolution Is Accelerating Innovation, Driving Productivity, and Irreversibly Transforming Employment and the Economy* (Lexington, MA: Digital Frontier Press, 2011). Two recent publications explore issues of privacy and security which will consume a considerable amount of a manager's attention in the years to come: Cole Stryker, *Hacking the Future: Privacy, Identity and Anonymity on the Web* (New York: Overlook Press, 2013) and Terence Craig and a short volume by Mary E. Ludloff, *Privacy and Big Data: The Players, Regulators and Stakeholders* (Sebastopol, CA: O'Reilly Media, 2013).

Finally, because I strongly believe management should help business schools and universities in general teach the skills and attitudes that managers will need, several books can inform on what is taught today and the issues faced by leaders in higher education. With a chapter on globalization's issues, see Srikant Datar, David A. Garvin, and Patrick G. Cullen, *Rethinking the MBA: Business Education at a Crossroads* (Boston, MA: Harvard Business Review Press, 2010). Helpful in identifying the soft skills managers need, see Henry Mintzberg, *Managers Not MBAs: A Hard Look At the Soft Practice of Managing and Management Development* (San Francisco, CA: Berrett-Koeler, 2005). As a reminder of the importance of change management skills, consult Danna Greenberg, Kate McKone-Sweet, and H. James Wilson, *The New Entrepreneurial Leader: Developing Leaders Who Shape Social and Economic Opportunity* (San Francisco, CA: Barrett-Koeler, 2011).

Index

Note: Page numbers in *italics* refer to Figures; those in **bold** to Tables.

The Age of Turbulence, 170
agility
    forms of, 28
    IT standardization for, 57
    need for, 5
    personal and institutional, 27
American Medical Association (AMA), 94
American telephone monopoly, 216
analytics
    big data, 33
    definition, 16
    tools of management, 149, 221–2,
        224, 226
autonomous vehicles
    advantage, 70
    onboard computing, 69
    robotic cars or driverless vehicles, 69
    software glitches, 70

benchmarking, 31
best practices, 6, 26, 53–4, 80
Big Data, 11, 33, 65, 72, 73
biotech-informatics-information technology
    bioengineering, 71
    consequences, 72
    genomics, 71
    IBM's Watson computer, 72
    medical informatics, 72
    medications, personalised, 71
    pharmacogenomics, 71
    protocols, 72

recombinant gene technologies, 71
business process reengineering, 107
business-to-business (B2B) enterprises,
    41, 67, 168, 194, 221

capitalism, 64–5, 145, 153, 168–70, 194, 230
cloud computing
    Amazon.com, 67
    definition, 66
    developments, 67
    glass house computing, 67
    internally run cloud computers, 67
    intranets, 68
    manager's responsibility, 68
    out-and-out cloud computing, 67
Cold War
    acts of violence, 169–70
    GPS, development, 43
    integrated technologies, 12
    long-term political events, 35
    strategy for national security, 188
communities, life of manager
    customers, 204
    employees and fellow managers, 204
    governments, and competitors, 204
    national economies, regulators, 204
communities of practice, 85
connected manager
    being engaged, 201
    operating environment, understanding
        of, 201

The Essential Manager: How to Thrive in the Global Information Jungle, First Edition.
James W. Cortada.
© 2015 the IEEE Computer Society. Published 2015 by John Wiley & Sons, Inc.

in private and public sectors, 201
consumer goods companies (B2C), 221
continuous improvement *(kaizen),* 13
corporate culture, 41, 43, 54, 56–7,
     149, 154
crowd sourcing, 215
Customer Relationship Management
     (CRM), 107
customers
   "apps," 218
   attracting customers
      B2C and B2B, 221
      expectations, 218–19
      expertise, social media tools, 220
      response to changes, marketplace,
         220–221
   e-commerce, 218
   expectations, customer, 218–19
   profits, thinner, 218
   sell-buy equation, 217
   social media applications, 218
   social media, usage survey, 221
   software tools, 218

economic and business realities
   business administration schools,
      role of, 195
   business in Africa, 188–9
   business processes, 171
   capitalism, expanded market, 169–70
   capital, labor and profits, 171
   connected economy *see* globalized
      connected economy
   corporate strategy planning, 192
   cultural and legal differences, 168
   demographics, 189, 192
   "free economies," 169
   "gated globe," 193
   global economic activities, monitoring
      of, 192
   global GDP history and projects,
      189–90, *190*
   global warming, 191
   industry associations, 190
   international markets and supply
      chains, 168

IT, use by governments *see* IT for
      national economic development
   language barriers, 189
   management teams, 194
   natural disasters, 191–2
   prices, rise and fall, 187
   public agencies, 171
   supply chains, 171, 196
   technological race, India and China, 188
   world's economy, 168
economy, global *see also* globalized
      connected economy
   competition, 176–7, 181, 183
   developed areas, 21
   functioning of, 180
   growth of, 172
   integrated, 5, 229–30, 230
   internationalized, 91
   working of, 180
electronic commerce, 107
Enterprise IT, 26
Enterprise Resource Planning (ERP), 32
Enterprise Resource Process systems, 107
enterprises (large), transformation
   activities and deployment, 135
   collaborative activities, 135
   components, 134
   features of corporations, sample, **136**
   leveraging, 134
   manufacturing, advanced, 137
   small-and medium-sized firms, 137
   transformative process, 135
European Union (EU)
   banking and monetary events,
      Europe, 205
   environmental protection practices,
      Europe, 61
   financial crisis, 228
   functions, 59–60
   global trade, 176
   influence on crops and animals, 90
   international industry-wide
      conversation, 93
   regulations, 89
   technological innovation and job
      creation, 205

European Union (EU) (*cont'd*)
  transnational initiatives, 183
  treasury reforms, 205
execution *(hoshin kanri),* 13

financial and accounting functions
  availability of employees, 144
  capitalism, 145
  CFO, 143–4
  in companies, 143
  governance structure, 143
financial engineering, 49
Five Forces Models (Porter)
  demographics, 96
  political circumstances, 96
  regulations, 96
  shifts in technology, 96
  trade barriers, 96

"gated globe," 193
glass house computing, 67
globalized connected economy
  censorship and authoritarian public
    administration, 178
  consumer goods, United State, 176, **177**
  creative destruction, 178
  economic ecosystem, advanced
    economy, (2001–2006), **179**
  economic evolution, process of
    (Schumpeter), 173
  global transactions, 177
  goods and services movement, 173
  institutional innovations, 178
  international trade, 172
  new products, customer accepted, 176
  productivity, 172
  property rights, laws, 178
  tariff level, average, 173–4, *174*
  U.S. freight-volume growth, 174–5, *175*
  U.S. manufacturing productivity, 173, *173*
  World's financial institutions, 177
  world trade growth, 173–4, *174*
globally integrated enterprise (GIE), 99,
    127–8, 131, 137
Global Peter Drucker Forum, 10, 156
global recession, 56, 89, 170, 184, 228

global society and management
  actions by managers and enterprises
    competitors and customers,
      recognition, 205
    diverse language skills, 206
    English language, use of, 206
    familiar practices, 207
    globalization, diversified, 206
    international conference, 206
    regulations and capital acquisition, 207
  emergence of, 205
  personal preparedness of managers
    alternative service models,
      understanding of, 208
    globalization's opportunities and
      problems, 208
global warming, 191
Google eyeglasses, 68–9
governmental regulations, variations, 100
Great Recession, 8, 33, 35, 48, 55, 77,
    101, 118, 211

healthcare enrollment system, U.S., 9
human relations (HR)
  job training, 142
  leadership skills, lack of, 142
  management, 138
  modern manager, 140–141
  overcoming barriers, collaboration, 141–2
  reengineering and global supply
    chains, 140
  skilled employees, 141
  workforce management, 139

IEEE Computer Society, 114, 115
Industrial Revolution
  First, 56, 137
  Second, 132
industry(ies)
  attention to, 63
  behavior of
    common buyers and suppliers, 92
    competitive intent, 92
    technical platforms, 92
  familiarity, 64
  globalization, 63

industry-wide associations, 59
limitations, 62
market capitalism, 64
national economic reporting schema, 62
national or international level, 61
risks, working within
    capabilities, gaps in, 99
    cost and value advantages,
        achieving, 99–100
    globalization, 100
    social and peer influences, 60–61
    technical standards, 61
technology, adoption of, 59
"Toyota Way," 63, 64
industry(ies) and technology *see also*
        technologies, effect on industries
associations, 92–3
definition, 91
dumping, 90
examples, 87
financial subsidies and taxation,
        government, 90
firms by name, 87–8
free trade movement, 90
globalized regulatory practices
        (harmonizing), 91
identification, 88
Kodak's experience, 88–9
managers, influence, 94
membership in associations, 93
middle and lower management, role of, 91
NAFTA, 90
non-technological factors, 89
publications, industry-specific, 92–3
regulatory practice, effects, 89
rivals, collaborating with, 92
WTO and EU, 90
industry-centric education/experience,
        114, 116–17
Information, importance of
Google, formula for ROI, 223
implications and actions, managers
    analytics, 224
    experiment within own domain, 224
    information as corporate
        competitive weapon, 224

information usage, measuring
    results, 223
    returns on information, 224
integration of information, 222
Return on Investment (ROI), 221
ROI metrics for management, 223
uses of information, 223
value of data, 221
Word documents and PDF files, 222
Information technology (IT)
"apps," significance, 50
computing and telecommunications,
        merging of, 43
corporate cultures, 43, 56
Dot-com companies, 48
financial engineering, 49
financial sector, 56–7
firms, open standards and organizing
        parts, 50
global recession, 56
GPS, 42
innovation, 43, 54–5
installations, software and hardware, 45
"intelligent" robots, 42
Internet, 50
knowledge management (KM), 54–5
mobile communications, 50
multi-firm value nets, 45
in 1950s, first computer for
        commercial work, 41
in 1970s
    accounting automation, 42
    online, 42
    production management, 42
in 1980s, PCs, 42
in 1990s
    Internet, 42
    Web, 42
operating costs, lowered, 49
outsourcing to multiple nations, 49
path dependency, notion of, 44
"plug-and-play" business modules, 57–8
process reengineering, 55
productivity of operations, improved, 49
Shift Industry report of 2013 (Deloitte), 49
social media, 50

Information technology (IT) (*cont'd*)
  standardization, IT systems and tools,
    57–8
  suggestions for management, 58
  tacit knowledge, use of, 54–5
  workforce issues, 56
International Electrotechnical
    Commission (IEC), 61
International Monetary Fund (IMF), 205
International Organization for
    Standardization (ISO), 61
International Telecommunication Union
    (ITU), 61
international trade, expansion, 101–2
intranets, 68
IT and work of management
  connected managers
    "apps," 209
    Bluetooth phones, 209
    business model, positive and
      negative experiences, 211
    business structure technologies
      support, 210
    buyback programs, stocking, 211
    customers, selection, 210
    information, importance, 212
    IT devices, 209
    Kodak and HP, 210
    market intelligence operations, 211
    new tools and applications, 209–10
    peer management communities, 211
    social media, spread of, 209
    software budgeting application, 209
    technology, knowledge in, 209
  installation and operation of
    technology, 212–13
  managerial priorities, 212
IT-dependent strategies
  barrier of entry to rivals
    American Airlines' (AA) travel
      reservation system, 109
    massive data warehouses of
      information, 109
    ordering books online, 109
  creating processes
    customers interaction, networking
      and e-mail, 108

global identity, 108
    wireless phone services, Amazon.
      com, 108–9
  cross-selling
    Amazon.com, 108
    Harrah Entertainment, 108
  evolutionary strategies
    computer-based games, 110
    digital gaming device, 110
  globalized industries, 111
  networking, 110–111
  preexisting IT capabilities
    Spain's, Zara chain, 108
    Wal-Mart's global telecommunications
      network linking, 108
  rival penetration, established IT-based
    strategy
    online banking, 109
    social networking software, 110
IT effect on industrial strategies
  behavior, patterns
    culture, multiple social and
      industry-specific, 112
    financial data and money
      movement, 111
    goods and capital, process change, 111
    physical realities, effect of, 112
  changes and transformations,
    companies, 104
  components, new style of
    management, 103
  deconstruction, misbelief of, 103
  entering the domain of another, 105
  globalization through computers, 106
  innovator's dilemma, 103–4
  Kodak as example, 104
  McGrath, research views, 112–13
  recognition and collaboration, 105
  401(k) retirement savings plan, United
    States, 105
  software firms/industry, 106
  strategic value of IT, 102
  strategies *see* IT-dependent strategies
IT for national economic development
  business managers, 180–181
  economic development strategies, 185,
    185–6

funding installations, Internet access, 183
global economy, 183–4
integrated IT, 181
Internet usage/users, 181, *182*
management, 182
national economic strategies,
    IT-influenced, 181
using IT, outside government, 182

knowledge management (KM), 42, 54–5, 60

management
  definition, 76
  globalized economy, influence of, 76
  global supply chains, 80
  historical perspective
    Big Data, 11
    core skills, development, 11
    corporate management, 11
    creative class or global business
        leaders, 11
    creative confidence, 10
    definition, 5
    "evidence based" managerial
        practices, 9–10
    "mandarin class" of managers, 10
    MBA programs, 10
    professionalization of management, 9
    systems and processes, 11
  interdependencies, 76
  international firms, power of, 76–7
  internationalization, work and
      practices, 78–9
  managerial conclusions, 79
  organizations, in future
    CEOs, ranking problems, **160**
    CIOs, 159
    curricula, organizational
        management, 158
    information, growth in, 158
    IT, 159
    language, 160
    personal brand, 158
    personal leadership, 161
    skills, 160
    supply chains, 162
  qualitative changes, 33–4

self-organizing learning, 79
social behavior and public
    administration, 80
technological innovations, 78
trade, expansion of, 78
Management (Drucker), 9
manager(s) *see also* personal skills and
    knowledge
  awareness of workplace, 202
  communications, 146
  communities, life of, 204
  computing, use of
    acquiring employees, 46–7
    globalization, 48
    open systems and social media, 47
    software tools, 47
  connected *see* connected manager
  innovation and creativity, 204
  IT tools, 146
  key "takeaways" by chapter, **203**
  knowledge and skills, 145–6
  list, guidance to managers, 204
  migratory habit *see* migratory habits,
      manager
  networking, 148
  personal brand, 22
  role of
    awareness, issues and changes, 5
    core skills and practices, 6
  social networking, 147
  strategy and values, 21
  updates for
    computing and business strategy, 41
    corporate culture and IT, 41
    industry standards and IT, 41
    technology change and
        consequences, 41
  worker-manager relations, 19
managerial practices, new style
  agility and innovation, need for, 5
  benchmarking, 31
  case studies and instances, 30
  commoditization, notion of, 31
  communication, enhanced through IT, 26
  core skills and best practices, 6
  Customer Resource Management
      (CRM) packages, 32

managerial practices, new style (*cont'd*)
  data collection, automation, 23
  data measurement, 24
  Enterprise IT, 26
  Enterprise Resource Planning (ERP), 32
  fishbone diagrams, 24
  IT, extensive use, 24–6
  leadership and collaboration, 30
  managerial responsibilities, 5
  mergers and acquisitions, 27
market capitalism, 64, 65
medical informatics, 72
migratory habits, manager
  career paths, 20
  employee health plans, 22
  loyalty to the firm, 19
  migratory practices, research on, 21
  outsourcing and layoffs, 19–20
  qualification and additional skills, 20–21
  relationships with employers, 19
multi-firm value nets, 45

natural disasters, 191–2
Network Centric Operations (NCO), 12
Network Centric Warfare (NCW), 12
North American Free Trade Agreement
  (NAFTA), 90, 176
numeric data and simulations
  adjectives, use of, 16
  analytical software and data storage,
    16–17
  analytics, 16
  decisions based on numerical data, 16
  managerial concerns
    context and culture, 17
    diversity of workers, 18
    regional cultures, 17
    simulation tools, knowledge on, 17
  software packages, 15
  spreadsheet software, 15

"one size fits all" strategy, 99
on-the-job training, 28, 132, 142
opportunities and threats
  best practices, borrowing, 53–4
  customer influences, 51–2

customization of products and
  services, 51
data security and privacy issues, 53
entertainment, options, 51
healthcare, 9, 52
insurance reimbursement culture, US, 52
user-created content, 51
organization(s)
  business students and managers, 157
  CEOs, 155
  finance and accounts, role of *see*
    financial and accounting functions
  global ecosystems, 160
  HR in transformation of corporations
    see human relations (HR)
  internal memo, 124–5
  leadership, 152–3
  management implications *see also*
    management
    CEOs, ranking problems, **160**
    CIOs, 159
    curricula, organizational
      management, 158
    information, growth in, 158
    IT, 159
    language, 160
    personal brand, 158
    personal leadership, 161
    skills, 160
    supply chains, 162
  new manager, 145–8
  people management, HR, 154
  profit and value migrations *see* profit
    and value
  "Rules of the Road" for management
    (Greenwald), 155–6, **156**
  strategy, 153
  structure and form
    emerging enterprise, 130–131
    GIE, 127–8
    global markets, 131–2
    globalwide operational initiatives, **132**
    growing influence, new business
      models, 126
    IBM's globalized processes, **133–4**
    IT, 129

partnerships, 131
process management and
    transformation techniques, 129
revenues and profits, 127
supply chains, 128
technical standards and systems, 131
transforming large enterprises *see*
    enterprises (large), transformation
Organization for Economic Cooperation
    and Development (OECD), 88, 93,
    181, 190
out-and-out cloud computing, 67
outsourcing
    firms in another country, 16
    interdependencies, 76
    low costs of labor, 49, 138
    partnerships, 131
    stagnant economic performance, 20

personal brand, 22, 34, 158 *see also*
    manager(s)
personal skills and knowledge
    advanced degrees and MBA, 225
    business/social environment, 227
    challenges, 229–30
    communications skills, 227–8
    content and sources, 226
    easy-to-use simulation software, 226–7
    educational and social backgrounds,
        employees, 227
    four "Cs," 225
    information on products and services,
        228
    IT management, 226
    process management, 226
    profile, 226
    secular environment and scientific
        thinking, 227
    systems management, 226
    tacit knowledge, 226
    training, future business professionals, 227
"plug-and-play" business modules, 31, 57–8
poor process design, 99–100
Powerpoint slides, use of, 24, 69, 223, 227
process reengineering, 13, 55
profit and value

customers, 148
emerging behaviors, managers, 149
financial industries, 151
modern profitable business, 150
reinventing, 151–2

quantum computing
    in biotechnology, 73
    definition, 73
    in military, 73
    practical application, 73
    quantum theory, 73

401(k) retirement savings plan, United
    States, 105
Return on Investment (ROI)
    Google on, 222–3
    metrics for management, 223
    notion of, 221
risk mitigation responses, 101
robotics, personal
    definition, 74
    industrial robotics, applications, 74
    job, loss of, 75
    telepresence robots, 74

simulation tools, 215
skilled labor, inadequate supply, 101
social media tools
    collaboration through, 32
    customers, active online role, 47
    customers, interaction with, 47, 50
    election of Senator Obama, 220
    experiences and knowledge, exchange
        of, 219
    expertise in, 220
    innovations, product and service, 1
    managers, use of, 146, 218
    messaging systems, 102
    riots over economic conditions,
        London, 220
strategy and deployment, organizational level
    manager's role
        adopting to changes, 215
        capable of shifting employment, 216
        developing new ways of managing, 216

strategy and deployment, organizational
   level (*cont'd*)
   help guide, 217
   management, enterprises and
      government agencies, 216
   mergers and acquisitions, 216–17
   new economy
      business models, 213
      cross-license technologies and
         products, 214
      insecure employment, 214
      outsourcing routine tasks and
         complex work, 214–15
      personal care of finance, 214
      wealth creation, 214
   old economy
      business models, 213
      capabilities of employees, 214
      defined-benefit pensions, 213
      product strategies, 213–14
   patent rights to technologies, 215
supply chain(s)
   concept of, 128
   desegregation, 63
   extension, 107
   globalization, 55, 63, 80, 140, 184
   HR practices, 138
   model, 24–5, 25
   practices, management, 128
   product, 192
   transforming, effect of, 134
   transnational, 76
   work of enterprise, 214
systems and processes
   continuous improvement *(kaizen),* 13
   corporate education centers, 14
   execution *(hoshin kanri),* 13
   international view, 12
   managers
      decision-making, 14
      knowledge and practices, 14
      learning, 14
      tacit knowledge, 14–15
   Network Centric Operations (NCO), 12
   Network Centric Warfare (NCW), 12
   operations research, 12

process reengineering, 13
process terms, usage, 14
programmers and systems analysts, 13
quality movement, 13
Taylorism in management thinking, 13
Total Quality Movement, 14

tacit knowledge, use of, 15, 21, 54–5,
   154, 226
talent war, 99
teaming
   education on, 6
   paradigm, 29
   role and importance, 26
   skills for managers, 160, 163, 169,
      203, 227
technologies, effect on industries
   behavior in industry-centric world
      'arenas,' connecting customers and
         solutions (McGrath), **113**
      characteristics, *97*
      distinctive capabilities, 98
      Five Forces Models (Porter), 95
      globalization, effect of, 98
      industry collaboration, *96*
      management considerations within
         industry, **98**
      market opportunities, 98
      McGahan industry trajectories, **95**
      McGrath's views, 98–9
      vertical and horizontal axis, 96
   behavior of industries
      common buyers and suppliers, 92
      competitive intent, 92
      technical platforms, 92
   craft unions, 85
   guilds, 85
   IT, effect *see* IT effect on industrial
      strategies
   managers, implications and role
      association-based training of
         managers, 114
      attention, international political
         and economic issues, 118
      business schools and professional
         associations, 115

communities of practice,
    development of, 117
computerized simulations of
    decisions, 114
credentialing, 114
decisions about tasks, 113
fuzzy behavior, decision
    making, 114
industry-centric experience, 115–16
IT knowledge, 119
language, power of, 117
marketing, industry-specialized
    model, 115
MBA and management programs, 117
risks *see* industry(ies)
skills, certifying, 114
transformation of activities,
    examples, 116

transnational business activities, 113
Total Quality Movement, 14

United Nations (UN), 59, 94, 205

The Wealth of Nations, 172
wearable computing
    devices, 68
    Google eyeglasses, 68–9
World Bank (WB), 94, 205
World Trade Organization (WTO)
    conventions and training sessions, 59
    establishment of, 160
    global trading agreements, 90, 176
    international industry-wide
        conversation, 93
    rules, international trade, 178, 205
    transnational initiatives, 183